"In a day when experience has bec
force in our thinking, we must recap
importance of the mind. Dr. Morelan.... ....
issues in profound, yet understandable ways, so that
this book is essential reading for every Christian
who takes his or her faith seriously."

CLYDE COOK
president, Biola University

"I thank God for J.P. Moreland. His brilliant insights
and passion for truth never fail to inspire and
motivate me. I know I'll be quoting this book
a lot in the years to come."

LEE STROBEL
teaching pastor, Willow Creek Community Church and
author of God's Outrageous Claims

"In today's climate of increasing secularism, Christians
must stop retreating from the arena of ideas and heed
the call of this book to retake the ground the church
has ceded to the University.
More than a call for action, this book provides the
historical, Biblical and philosophical groundwork for
Christians to actually begin reclaiming their secular
world. For many, this will be a whole new paradigm
of how to be a Christian in our world. If only 10%
of today's evangelical Christian leaders study this book
and take it to heart, the church will once again
transform the world!"

EDWARD KANG, J.D., M.DIV.
pastor, Berkland Baptist Church—Berkeley,
and campus minister at U.C. Berkeley with A.B.S.K.

LOVE
YOUR GOD
WITH
ALL YOUR
MIND

LOVE YOUR GOD WITH ALL YOUR MIND

THE ROLE OF REASON IN THE LIFE OF THE SOUL

J.P. Moreland

DALLAS WILLARD, GENERAL EDITOR

NAVPRESS
BRINGING TRUTH TO LIFE
NavPress Publishing Group
P.O. Box 35001, Colorado Springs, Colorado 80935

OUR GUARANTEE TO YOU

We believe so strongly in the message of our books that
we are making this quality guarantee to you. If for any
reason you are disappointed with the content of this book,
return the title page to us with your name and address
and we will refund to you the list price of the book. To
help us serve you better, please briefly describe why you
were disappointed. Mail your refund request to: NavPress,
P.O. Box 35002, Colorado Springs, CO 80935.

The Navigators is an international Christian organization. Our mission is to reach, disciple, and equip
people to know Christ and to make Him known through successive generations. We envision multitudes
of diverse people in the United States and every other nation who have a passionate love for Christ, live
a lifestyle of sharing Christ's love, and multiply spiritual laborers among those without Christ.

NavPress is the publishing ministry of The Navigators. NavPress publications help believers learn biblical truth and apply what they learn to their lives and ministries. Our mission is to stimulate spiritual
formation among our readers.

Library of Congress Catalog Card Number: 97-2300
ISBN 57683-016-0

Cover photo illustration: Mark Romine/Super Stock
General editor: Dallas Willard
Senior editor: Steve Webb

Some of the anecdotal illustrations in this book are true to life and are included with the permission of
the persons involved. All other illustrations are composites of real situations, and any resemblance to
people living or dead is coincidental.

Unless otherwise identified, all Scripture quotations in this publication are taken from the *HOLY
BIBLE: NEW INTERNATIONAL VERSION* ® (NIV®). Copyright © 1973, 1978, 1984 by International
Bible Society. Used by permission of Zondervan Publishing House. All rights reserved. Other versions
used include: the *New American Standard Bible* (NASB), © The Lockman Foundation 1960, 1962, 1963,
1968, 1971, 1972, 1973, 1975, 1977; and the *King James Version* (KJV).

Moreland, James Porter, 1948-
    Love your God with all your mind : the role of reason in the life of the
soul / J.P. Moreland.
    p.   cm.
    Includes bibliographical references.
    ISBN 1-57683-016-0 (paper)
    1. Faith and reason—Christianity. 2. United States—Intellectual life—20th
century. 3. Apologetics—20th century. 4. Christianity and culture. \#011
5. Evangelicalism. I. Title.
BT50.M62   1997
230'.01—dc21   97-2300
                                             CIP

Printed in the United States of America

4 5 6 7 8 9 10 11 12 13 14 15 16 / 00

FOR A FREE CATALOG OF
NAVPRESS BOOKS & BIBLE STUDIES,
CALL 1-800-366-7788 (USA)
or 1-416-499-4615 (CANADA)

Contents

x

Acknowledgments

There are several people who played an important role in helping this book to see the light of day. First, I wish to thank my friend and research assistant, Glenn Cudzilo, to whom this book is dedicated. Glenn gave me helpful feedback on a very rough draft of the manuscript.

Second, the President of Biola University, Clyde Cook, the provost. Sherwood Lingenfelter and dean of Talbot School of Theology, Dennis Dirks, have helped create a stimulating place to teach and study, and they gave me a sabbatical to work on the project. I am grateful to them for their confidence in me and in this book.

Third, my faculty colleagues at Talbot—including Alan Gomes, Mike Wilkins, Clint Arnold, Walt Russell, Klaus Issler, Doug Geivett, Scott Rae, Paul Cox, and John Mark Reynolds at the Torrey Institute, Biola University, are a team of which I feel honored to be a part. They live what this book is all about. Also, my graduate students in the Talbot M.A. in philosophy and ethics are partly responsible for my own life of study. Their questions in class are so sophisticated that I am frequently sent back to my study to find answers that satisfy them. God bless them for pushing me as they do.

I cannot adequately express my indebtedness to my mentor and friend, Dallas Willard. For some time now, he has been my most important role model for combining a rigorous intellectual life with a vital spiritual devotion to Jesus and His Kingdom. I also want to thank my friend and editor, Steve Webb. His encouragement and excellent editorial suggestions have made this book much better than it would have been without his help. Thanks as well to the whole NavPress team who've worked so hard at excellence in the publishing experience.

Finally, my precious wife, Hope, and my lovely daughters, Ashley and Allison, are simply what make my life possible. I have never met anyone with as gracious and tender a spirit as my wife's, and I love her for who she is. My prayer is that this book will contribute to restoration of the church's intellectual life because it is the church that is the pillar and support of the truth.

J.P. Moreland
March 1997

General Introduction

B Y   D A L L A S   W I L L A R D

The Spiritual Formation Line presents discipleship to Jesus Christ as the greatest opportunity individual human beings have in life and the only hope corporate mankind has of solving its insurmountable problems.

It affirms the unity of the present-day Christian with those who walked beside Jesus during His incarnation. To be His disciple then was to be with Him, to learn to be like Him. It was to be His student or apprentice in kingdom living. His disciples heard what He said and observed what He did, and then, under His direction, they simply began to say and do the same things. They did so imperfectly but progressively. As He taught: "Everyone who is fully trained will be like his teacher" (Luke 6:40).

Today it is the same, except now it is the resurrected Lord who walks throughout the world. He invites us to place our confidence in Him. Those who rely on Him believe that He knows how to live and will pour His life into us as we "take *His* yoke . . . and learn from *Him*, for *He is* gentle and humble in heart" (Matthew 11:29, emphasis added). To take His yoke means joining Him in His work, making our work His work. To trust Him is to understand that total immersion in what He is doing with our life is the best thing that could ever happen to us.

To "learn from Him" in this total-life immersion is *how* we "seek first His kingdom and His righteousness" (Matthew 6:33). The outcome is that we increasingly are able to do all things, speaking or acting, as if Christ were doing them (Colossians 3:17). As apprentices of Christ we are not learning how to do some special religious activity, but how to live every moment of our lives from the

11

reality of God's kingdom. I am learning how to live my actual life as Jesus would if He were me.

If I am a plumber, clerk, bank manager, homemaker, elected offi-cial, senior citizen, or migrant worker, I am in "full-time" Christian service no less than someone who earns his or her living in a specif-ically religious role. Jesus stands beside me and teaches me in all I do to live in God's world. He shows me how, in every circumstance, to reside in His word and thus be a genuine apprentice of His—His dis-ciple indeed. This enables me to find the reality of God's world everywhere I may be, and thereby to escape from enslavement to sin and evil (John 8:31-32). We become able to do what we know to be good and right, even when it is humanly impossible. Our lives and words become constant testimony of the reality of God.

A plumber facing a difficult plumbing job must know how to integrate it into the kingdom of God as much as someone attempt-ing to win another to Christ or preparing a lesson for a congregation. Until we are clear on this, we will have missed Jesus' connection between life and God and will automatically exclude most of our everyday lives from the domain of faith and discipleship. Jesus lived most of His life on earth as a blue-collar worker, someone we might describe today as an "independent contractor." In His vocation He practiced everything He later taught about life in the kingdom.

The "words" of Jesus that I primarily reside in are those recorded in the New Testament Gospels. In His presence, I learn the goodness of His instructions and how to carry them out. It is not a matter of meriting life from above, but of receiving that life con-cretely in my circumstances. Grace, we must learn, is opposed to *earning*, not to *effort*.

For example, I move away from using derogatory language against others, calling them twits, jerks, or idiots (Matthew 5:22), and increasingly mesh with the respect and endearment for persons that naturally flows from God's way. This in turn transforms all of my dealings with others into tenderness and makes the usual cold-ness and brutality of human relations, which lays a natural foundation for abuse and murder, simply unthinkable.

Of course, the "learning of Him" is meant to occur in the con-text of His people. They are the ones He commissioned to make disciples, surround them in the reality of the triune name, and teach to do "everything I have commanded you" (Matthew 28:20). But the disciples we make are His disciples, never ours. We are His apprentices along with them. If we are a little farther along the way, we can only echo the apostle Paul: "Follow my example, as I follow the example of Christ" (1 Corinthians 11:1).

It is a primary task of Christian ministry today, and of those who write for this line of books, to reestablish Christ as living teacher in the midst of His people. He has been removed by various historical developments: assigned the role of *mere* sacrifice for sin or social prophet and martyr. But where there is no teacher there can be no students or disciples.

If we cannot be His students, we have no way to learn to exist always and everywhere within the riches and power of His Word. We can only flounder along as if we were on our own so far as the actual details of our lives are concerned. That is where multitudes of well-meaning believers find themselves today. But it is not the intent of Him who says, "Come to me . . . and you will find rest for your souls" (Matthew 11:28-29).

Each book in this line is designed to contribute to this renewed vision of Christian spiritual formation and to illuminate what apprenticeship to Jesus Christ means within all the specific dimensions of human existence. The mission of these books is to form the whole person so that the nature of Christ becomes the natural expression of our souls, bodies, and spirits throughout our daily lives.

The Christian and the Well Formed Mind

BY DAVID HAZARD

In too many churches, a questing mind can be a plague to its owner. The thinking woman or man seldom gets much support today—and more often than not meets with resistance and suspicion. This is true, not only for those inclined to dig more deeply for a more reasoned, better-founded faith, but for the Christian who is laboring out in the world to resolve debates and value-clashes in fields like social justice, medical research, education, law, and finance.

And so, the Christian who must use his or her mind, because they are driven by the joy of using it, can exist in an odd, ambivalent relationship with his brothers and sisters in Christ. This should not be.

Why have we lost, or neglected, the ability to *discipline the mind* for Christ?

In part, it may be that we have confused the need for a childlike faith (that is, an attitude of profound trust in God, and a faithful love for Him) with childish thinking. The apostle Paul, for one, had no confusion on this point. Reading any one of his epistles will show you that. And even Peter—the everyday workman, the fisherman—was no intellectual slouch, judging by his writings. What we have, everywhere in scripture, are profoundly intelligent teachings poured out from minds that are also inspired and centered in a love for God.

Step one generation away from the New Testament writers to meet the men who were discipled by the apostles and you find treatises, apologies, and circular letters of stunning intelligence from those intensely devoted Church fathers.

Faith and a disciplined mental life were not natural enemies then. A well-formed mind held a place of honor. And it was believed that the Christian mind could be the best mind.

There are many reasons why Christians today neglect, even resist, the building of vigorously intelligent minds—lack of training and misunderstanding. Reaction against today's anti-God (and anti-human) philosophies, and against dead rationalism. But a flabby mind is no badge of spiritual honor. And today's deadly philosophies are not the result of human intelligence and thinking, but rather, thinking that is unyoked from the true knowledge that comes from above, from God.

We need to admit the mind into Christian fellowship again. We need the mind disciplined in Christ, enlightened by faith, passionate for God and His creation, to be let loose in the world.

J. P. Moreland writes herein about the disciplining of the mind. He writes to the woman and man of faith, the student and the professional, to the everyday workman like Peter and the church-builder/theologian like Paul. Because the world we live in is full of influences that would shape the way we think—and consequently how we act and live—we need more rigorous discipline to be Christians and thinking people, not less. Moreland brilliantly tells us how to take our mental skills "captive to Christ".

For that reason, NavPress is pleased to offer *Love Your God with All Your Mind* in its Spiritual Formation line.

PART ONE

WHY THE MIND MATTERS IN CHRISTIANITY

X

How We Lost the Christian Mind and Why We Must Recover It

X

*We live in what may be the most anti-intellectual period
in the history of Western civilization. . . . We must have
passion—indeed hearts on fire for the things of God.
But that passion must resist with intensity the
anti-intellectual spirit of the world.*

R. C. SPROUL[1]

K

*We are having a revival of feelings
but not of the knowledge of God. The church today
is more guided by feelings than by convictions.
We value enthusiasm more than informed commitment.*

1980 GALLUP POLL ON RELIGION

K

*The God of the Jews was to exist in the Word
and through the Word, an unprecedented conception
requiring the highest order of abstract thinking.*

NEIL POSTMAN[2]

I HAD JUST RETURNED FROM THE MAILBOX AND OPENED A LETTER FROM A woman who had attended a series of lectures I had recently given at her church. One never knows what a letter from a parishioner will say, so it was with a certain ambivalence that I opened the envelope. Here is what I read:

> My life has changed drastically during the past few weeks since you have been teaching and encouraging us to think. I used to be deathly afraid of witnessing and terribly fearful that someone might ask me something about my faith. Whenever I got into any kind of discussion, I was rather defensive and nervous. Well, I have been reading, rather, plowing through some of your lecture notes at church. As I absorb the information and logically understand the foundations for my faith, a calm is resting in my soul. I have been a believer for a long time and the Lord has done marvelous, specific things in my life. But now I understand why I believe, and this has brought me both peace and a non-defensive boldness to witness to others. Please don't stop encouraging people to risk thinking objectively and arriving at conclusions based on logic and fact. My life will never be the same because of this encouragement.

My heart was at once deeply grateful and profoundly saddened. I was grateful to think that God could use someone like me to help one of His children. I was saddened to be reminded of how unusual it is for Christian people to be taught how to think carefully and deeply about what they believe and why they believe it. Not long ago, the newspaper featured a leading politician's statement about the Christian political right in which he charged that the Christian right was populated by dumb, uninformed people who are easily led by rhetoric. While I would dispute the complete accuracy of this charge, nevertheless, we Christians must ask ourselves why, if there is not a grain of truth in it, someone would think to make this accusation of us in the first place. Judged by the Scriptures, church history, and common sense, it is clear that something has gone desperately wrong with our modern understanding of the value of reason and intellectual development for individual discipleship and corporate church life.

As we approach the twenty-first century, it doesn't take a rocket scientist to recognize that our entire culture is in trouble. We are staring down the barrel of a loaded gun, and we can no longer afford to act like it's loaded with blanks. Recently, the guidance counselor at a local public high school near my home confessed to a parents' group that the teenagers that have attended the school during the last ten years are the most dysfunctional, illiterate group he has witnessed in close to forty years at the same school. Our society has replaced heroes with celebrities, the quest for a well-informed character with the search for a flat stomach, substance and depth with image and personality. In the political process, the makeup man is more important than the speech writer, and we approach the voting booth, not on the basis of a well-developed philosophy of what the state should be, but with a heart full of images, emotions, and slogans all packed into thirty-second sound bites. The mind-numbing, irrational tripe that fills TV talk shows is digested by millions of bored, lonely Americans hungry for that sort of stuff. What is going on here? What has happened to us?

There are no simple answers to these questions, and I don't pretend to offer a full analysis as a solution to this quandary. But I do think the place to start looking for an answer is to remind ourselves of something Jesus Christ said long ago. In His inaugural address, Jesus was concerned to spell out how His community of followers were to understand themselves. With characteristic insight, He asserted that "You are the salt of the earth. But if the salt loses its saltiness, how can it be made salty again?" (Matthew 5:13).

One job of the church is to be salty to the world in which it finds itself, so if that world grows saltless, we should look first to the church herself to glean what we can about her contribution to the situation. In the rest of this chapter, I will demonstrate that a major cause of our current cultural crisis consists of a worldview shift from a Judeo-Christian understanding of reality to a post-Christian one. Moreover, this shift itself expresses a growing anti-intellectualism in the church resulting in the marginalization of Christianity in society — its lack of saltiness, if you will — and the emergence of the most secular culture the world has ever seen. That secular culture is now simply playing out the implications of ideas that have come to be widely accepted in a social context in which the church is no longer a major participant in the war of ideas.[3] In the rest of this book, then, I'll try to demonstrate how the church must overcome the neglect of this critical area of the development of the Christian mind, perhaps the most integral component of the believers sanctification. The role of intellectual development is primary in evangelical Christianity, but you might not know that from a cursory look at the church today. In spite of this, if we are to be formed in Christ (Galatians 4:19), we must realize the work of God in our minds and pay attention to what a Christlike mind might look like. As our Savior has said, "Love the Lord your God with all your heart and with all your soul and with all your mind" (Matthew 22:37). To do this, we cannot neglect the soulful development of a Christian mind.

THE LOSS OF THE CHRISTIAN MIND IN AMERICAN CHRISTIANITY

Two major developments emerged in the late nineteenth century that contributed to the loss of the Christian mind in America. The legacy of the Pilgrims and Puritans waned, and two new movements emerged from which the evangelical church has never fully recovered. Let's take a brief look at these two movements, and then we'll examine the deeper problems that have resulted.

Historical Overview

1. The emergence of anti-intellectualism. While generalizations can be misleading, it is safe to say that from the arrival of the Pilgrims to the middle of the nineteenth century, American believers prized the intellectual life for its contribution to the Christian journey. The Puritans were highly educated people (the literacy rate for men in early Massachusetts and Connecticut was between 89 and 95 percent)[4] who founded colleges, taught their children to read and write before the age of six, and studied art, science, philosophy, and other fields as a way of loving God with the mind. Scholars like Jonathan Edwards were activists who sought to be scholarly and well informed in a variety of disciplines. The minister was an intellectual, as well as spiritual authority in the community.[5] As Puritan Cotton Mather proclaimed, "Ignorance is the Mother not of Devotion but of HERESY."[6]

In the middle 1800s, however, things began to change dramatically, though the seeds for the change had already been planted in the popularized, rhetorically powerful, and emotionally directed preaching of George Whitefield in the First Great Awakening in the United States from the 1730s to the 1750s. During the middle 1800s, three awakenings broke out in the United States: the Second Great Awakening (1800-1820), the revivals of Charles Finney (1824-1837), and the Layman's Prayer Revival (1856-1858). Much good came from these movements. But their overall effect was to overemphasize immediate personal conversion to Christ instead of a studied period of reflection and conviction; emotional, simple, popular preaching instead of intellectually careful and doctrinally precise sermons; and personal feelings and relationship to Christ instead of a deep grasp of the nature of Christian teaching and ideas. Sadly, as historian George Marsden notes, "anti-intellectualism was a feature of American revivalism."[7]

Obviously, there is nothing wrong with the emphasis of these movements on personal conversion. What was a problem, however, was the intellectually shallow, theologically illiterate form of Christianity that came to be part of the populist Christian religion that emerged. One tragic result of this was what happened in the so-called Burned Over District in the state of New York. Thousands of people were "converted" to Christ by revivalist preaching, but they had no real intellectual grasp of Christian teaching. As a result, two of the three major American cults began in the Burned Over District among the unstable, untaught "converts": Mormonism (1830) and the Jehovah's Witnesses (1884). Christian Science arose in 1866 but was not connected with this area.

2. Evangelical withdrawal began. Sadly, the emerging anti-intellectualism in the church created a lack of readiness for the widespread intellectual assault on Christianity that reached full force in the late 1800s. This attack was part of the war of ideas raging at that time and was launched from three major areas. First, certain *philosophical ideas* from Europe, especially the views of David Hume (1711-1776) and Immanuel Kant (1724-1804), altered people's understanding of religion. Hume claimed that the traditional arguments for God's existence (for example, the world is an effect that needs a personal cause) were quite weak. He also said that since we cannot experience God with the five senses, the claim that God exists cannot be taken as an item of knowledge. In a different way, Kant asserted that human knowledge is limited to what can be experienced with the five senses, and since God cannot be so experienced, we cannot know He exists. The ideas of Hume and Kant had a major impact on culture as they spread across Europe and into America.[8]

For one thing, confidence was shaken in arguments for the existence of God and the rationality of the Christian faith. Additionally, fewer and fewer people regarded the Bible as a body of divinely revealed, true propositions about various topics that requires a devoted intellect to grasp and study systematically. Instead, the Bible increasingly was sought solely as a practical guide for ethical guidance and spiritual growth.

Second, *German higher criticism* of the Bible called its historical reliability into question. The Mosaic authorship of the Pentateuch was challenged and the search for the historical Jesus was launched. Believers grew suspicious of the importance of historical study in understanding the Bible and in defending its truthfulness. An increased emphasis was placed on the Holy Spirit in understanding the Bible as opposed to serious historical and grammatical study. Third, *Darwinian evolution* emerged and "made the world safe for atheists," as one contemporary Darwinian atheist has put it. Evolution challenged the early chapters of Genesis for some and the very existence of God for others.[9]

Instead of responding to these attacks with a vigorous intellectual counterpunch, many believers grew suspicious of intellectual issues altogether. To be sure, Christians must rely on the Holy Spirit in their intellectual pursuits, but this does not mean they should expend no mental sweat of their own in defending the faith.

Around the turn of the nineteenth century, fundamentalists withdrew from the broader intellectual culture and from the war with liberals that emerged in most mainline denominations at the time. Fundamentalists started their own Bible institutes and concentrated their efforts on lay-oriented Bible and prophecy conferences. This withdrawal from the broader, intellectual culture and public discourse contributed to the isolation of the church, the marginalization of Christian ideas from the public arena, and the shallowness and trivialization of Christian living, thought, and activism. In short, the culture became saltless.

More specifically, we now live in an evangelical community so deeply committed to a certain way of seeing the Christian faith that this perspective is now imbedded within us at a subconscious level.

This conceptualization of the Christian life is seldom brought to conscious awareness for debate and discussion. And our modern understanding of Christian practice underlies everything else we do, from the way we select a minister to the types of books we sell in our bookstores. It informs the way we raise our children to think about Christianity; it determines how we give money to the cause of Christ; and it shapes our vision, priorities, and goals for both local and parachurch ministry. If our lives and ministries are expressions of what we actually believe, and if what we believe is off center and yet so pervasive that it is seldom even brought to conscious discussion, much less debated, then this explains why our impact on the world is so paltry compared to our numbers. I cannot overemphasize the fact that this modern understanding of Christianity is neither biblical nor consistent with the bulk of church history.

What, exactly, is this modern understanding of Christianity?

Anti-intellectualism's Impact on the Church

I believe it is critical that the evangelical church overcome these characteristics and move toward a clearer, more biblical understanding of the Christian mind and how Christ Himself wants to shape our thinking. The rest of this book will attempt to provide countermeasures to these unbiblical problems so that our spirituality is informed by an appropriate biblical view of the mind and how Jesus Himself wishes to transform the mind by renewing it (in fact, we'll look at Romans 12:1-2 in some depth later). Five characteristics capture the essence of the impact of anti-intellectualism on today's evangelicalism. Read carefully and see how these may have impacted your own ideas.

1. A misunderstanding of faith's relationship to reason. First, while few would actually put it in these terms, faith is now understood as a blind act of will, a decision to believe something that is either independent of reason or that is a simple choice to believe while ignoring the paltry lack of evidence for what is believed. By contrast with this modern misunderstanding, biblically, *faith is a power or skill to act in accordance with the nature of the kingdom of God*, a trust in what we have reason to believe is true. Understood in this way, we see that faith is built on reason. We should have good reasons for thinking that Christianity is true before we dedicate ourselves completely to it. We should have solid evidence that our understanding of a biblical passage is correct before we go on to apply it. And so on.

If this is correct, then sermons should target people's thinking as much as their wills and feelings. Sunday school should be more effective in training believers how to think carefully about their faith. Training in apologetics should be a regular part of discipleship. Apologetics is a New Testament ministry of helping people overcome intellectual obstacles that block them from coming to or growing in the faith by giving reasons for why one should believe Christianity is true and by responding to objections raised against it. Local church after local church should be raising up and training a group of people who serve as apologists for the entire congregation.

Unfortunately, our contemporary understanding of these important concepts treats faith and reason as polar opposites. Let me give you two illustrations from my own ministry.

A few years ago I conducted a series of evangelistic messages for a church in New York. The series was in a high school gym, and both believers and unbelievers attended each night. The first evening I gave arguments for the existence of God from science and philosophy. Before closing in prayer, I entertained several questions from the audience. One woman (who was a Christian) complained about my talk, charging that if I "proved" the existence of God, I would leave no room for faith. I responded by saying that if she were right, then we should pray that currently available evidence for God would evaporate and be refuted so there would be even more room for faith! Obviously, her view of faith utterly detached itself from reason.

The second illustration comes from repeatedly hearing small group Bible studies go straight to the question, What does this passage mean to me? while bypassing the prior question, What does the passage say and why do I think my interpretation is correct?[10] We allow one another to get away with applying an understanding of a passage that is based on vague feelings or first impressions and not on the hard work of reading commentaries and using study tools such as concordances, Bible dictionaries, and the like. Why? Because a careful exercise of reason is not important in understanding what the Bible says for many of us. Besides, it takes work!

For many, religion is identified with subjective feelings, sincere motives, personal piety, and blind faith. As the song puts it, "You ask me how I know He lives, He lives within my heart." In other words, we test the truth of our religion not by a careful application of our God-given faculties of thought, or even by biblical mandates (see, for example, 2 Corinthians 10:5), but rather by our private experiences. For the most part, theoretical reason is just not part of our local church life any longer. We often hear it said in church that we don't want a discussion to get too theological, we want to keep it practical, as though good practice did not require careful thought to direct it. We sing, "In my *heart*, Lord, be glorified," but when was the last time you heard someone sing, "In my *intellectual life*, Lord, be glorified"? Unfortunately, this misunderstanding of the relationship between faith and reason has led to an even more sinister trend among modern evangelicals.

2. The separation of the secular and the sacred. There has emerged a secular/sacred separation in our understanding of the Christian life with the result that Christian teaching and practice are privatized and placed in a separate compartment from the public or so-called secular activities of life. The withdrawal of the corporate body of Christ from the public sphere of ideas is mirrored by our understanding of what is required to produce an individual disciple. Religion has become personal, private, and too often, simply a matter of "how I feel about things." By contrast, the culture encourages me to invoke my intellect in my secular, public life. By way of example, I'm always encouraged to use my intellect in how I approach my vocation, select a house, or learn to use a computer. But within the sphere of my private, spiritual life of faith, it is my heart, and my heart alone, that operates. The life of the mind is thus separated, broken off, and compartmentalized as a function of the "secular" life instead of more naturally being integrated with the spiritual. As a result, Sunday school classes, discipleship materials, and sermons too often address the heart and not the head, or focus on personal growth and piety and not on cultivating an intellectual love for God in my vocation.

When was the last time your church had Sunday school classes that were divided up by vocations—classes for thinking Christianly as a lawyer, businessman, health care professional, educator, and so forth? Parachurch ministries have produced excellent tools for training the private, "spiritual" lives of converts. But where are the tools that take ten or fifteen different university majors and spell out issues and resources for integrating ideas in those majors with Christian theology? We have organizations for businessmen that emphasize personal testimonies, devotional reading, and the like. But where do these organizations train businessmen to develop a Christian understanding of economic theory, capitalism, business ethics, or moral issues in the employer/employee relationship?

Our children can attend virtually any university and major in any subject they wish. But in a four-year course of study they will almost never interact with a Christian thinker in their field or with Christian ideas relevant to their course content. Why? No doubt, many reasons could be given. But clearly, one reason is that the cream rises to the top. If there are few Christian intellectuals who write college textbooks from a Christian perspective, it must be because our evangelical culture is simply not producing such people because we do not value the intellectual life. After all, the purpose of college for many is to get a job, and course work is considered secular, not sacred. What is important for our children is that they stay pure in college and, perhaps, witness, have a quiet time, and pray regularly. Obviously, these are important. But for a disciple, the purpose of college is not just to get a job. Rather, it is to discover a vocation, to identify a field of study in and through which I can serve Christ as my Lord. And one way to serve Him in this way is to learn to think in a Christian manner about my major. A person's Christianity doesn't begin at a dorm Bible study, when class is over; it permeates all of one's life, including how one thinks about the ideas in one's college major.

The church must train high school students for the intellectual life they will encounter at college. As theologian Carl Henry put it, "Training the mind is an essential responsibility of the home, the church, and the school. Unless evangelicals prod young people to disciplined thinking, they waste—even undermine one of Christianity's most precious resources."[11] But if faith and reason are polar opposites, and if discipleship is private and sacred but college studies are public and secular, then training the intellect will not be valued as a part of teenage mentoring. That is why our discipleship materials often leave Christian young people vulnerable to atheistic college professors with an ax to grind. For such professors, shredding an intellectually unprepared undergraduate's faith is like shooting fish in a barrel.

We have seen that the church was attacked intellectually in the latter half of the nineteenth century and was not adequately prepared to respond to this attack in kind. Instead, with notable exceptions, the church withdrew from the world of ideas and the intellectual life and was thereby marginalized. As former president of the United Nations General Assembly, Charles Malik has said, "I must be frank with you: the greatest danger confronting American evangelical Christianity is the danger of anti-intellectualism. The mind in its greatest and deepest reaches is not cared for enough."[12] This withdrawal and marginalization of the church has had devastating consequences for our attempt to produce vibrant, confident disciples and to penetrate our culture with a Christian worldview and the gospel of Christ. These consequences are most evident in three more areas.

3. Weakened world missions. One critical consequence of our first two anti-intellectual trends is the combined effect of weakening world missions. I once attended a meeting of missionaries from around the world, at which a national Christian leader from Central America stood up and passionately exhorted North American mission agencies to stop sending evangelists to his country because their efforts were producing Marxists bent on overthrowing the government. You could have heard a pin drop in that meeting, and confusion was written on everyone's face. This leader went on to explain that the leading "Christian" thinkers in his country held to liberation theology, a form of Marxism draped in religious garb. Evangelical missionaries would lead people to Christ, but the liberals were attracting the thinking leaders among the converts and training them in Marxist ideology, which these liberals identified as the true center of biblical theology. The leader pleaded with North Americans to send more theologians and Bible teachers and to help set up more seminaries and training centers in his country because the need for intellectual leadership was great. (And you wondered where the Sandinistas came from!)

For some time, theological liberals have understood that whoever controls the thinking leadership of the church in a culture will eventually control the church itself. Recently, I met a man from Fiji who was won to Christ by an evangelical missionary and who, subsequent to conversion, wanted to come to the United States for seminary training. Unfortunately, there was no money for this sort of "intellectual" development in the evangelical missions strategy there, but theological liberals gave him a scholarship to study at a liberal seminary in Texas. By the time I met him, he had given up his faith and was going back to Fiji with an extremely secular view of Christianity. His mission: to pastor a church! If evangelicals placed more value on the mind, we would give more to developing intellectual leadership around the world. Happily, some good things are now being done in this area, but we need to intensify our efforts in this regard, and this will happen only if we evangelicals come to value more fully Christ's admonitions to be good stewards of the intellectual life. Unfortunately, there remain two more deadly trends that have infected the church because of anti-intellectualism.

4. Anti-intellectualism has spawned an irrelevant gospel. Today, we share the gospel primarily *as a means of addressing felt needs.* We give testimonies of changed lives and say to people that if they want to become better parents or overcome depression or loneliness, then Christ is the answer for them. As true as this may be, such an approach to evangelism is inadequate for two reasons. First, it does not reach people who may be out of touch with their feelings. Consequently, if men in our culture are in general less in touch with their feelings than women, this approach will not reach men effectively. Second, it invites the response, "Sorry, but I don't have a need." Have you ever wondered why no one responded to the apostle Paul in this manner? If you look at his evangelistic approach in Acts 17–20, the answer becomes obvious. He based his preaching on the fact that the gospel is true and reasonable to believe. He reasoned with and tried to persuade people intelligently to accept Christ.

Now, if the gospel is true and reasonable to believe, then it is obvious that every person has a need for Christ's forgiveness and power, whether or not that person "feels" that need. The only response to the Pauline evangelistic approach is either to accept Christ or deny the truth of the gospel. The person approached is not let off the hook simply because he is out of touch with his feelings or doesn't recognize the "felt need." The fact that many respond to our evangelistic efforts by denying a need for Christ should tip us off to an important fact. If truth and reasonableness are not uppermost in our presentation of the gospel to a pagan culture already predisposed to regarding religion as a set of private feelings, then we'll consistently hear this response: "Well, that's fine for you if having those feelings helps you." Religion is now viewed by many as a placebo or emotional crutch precisely because that is how we often pitch the gospel to unbelievers.

I wish I could stop here. But again, there's another trend in evangelicalism that we must place at the feet of anti-intellectualism.

5. A loss of boldness in confronting the idea structures in our

culture with effective Christian witness. Now this is a mouthful, but anti-intellectualism has drained the church of its boldness in witnessing and speaking out about important issues in the places where ideas are generated. And for those who do have such courage, anti-intellectualism has created a context in which we Christians often come off as shallow, defensive, and reactionary, instead of thoughtful, confident, and articulate.

One evening a couple came to our home for dinner. During the meal the husband said almost nothing (except "Pass the chicken!"). Despite repeated attempts to engage him, the conversation took place primarily among the two wives and me. However, as dessert was being served, the topic of conversation turned to motorboats, and from that point on we could hardly get a word in edgewise. Why? Boats were the man's hobby. He owned two of them, knew how to build one from scratch, and truly was an expert on the subject. He had courage to speak up because he knew what he was talking about; he did not need to be defensive when someone differed with his viewpoint because he was confident about his knowledge.

I have trained people to share their faith for over twenty-six years. I can tell you from experience that when people learn what they believe and why, they become bold in their witness and attractive in the way they engage others in debate or dialogue. While pastoring a church in Baltimore, I once taught a twelve-week class on Christian apologetics. The course cost fifty dollars to take, required two textbooks, and had several homework assignments, including two papers. When the sixth week ended, a man named Bob came up to me after class and, with tears running down his cheeks, expressed his gratitude for the high academic standards and requirements in the class. I asked him why he was grateful about this. I will never forget his response. He told me he had worked at the same place for ten years but had never shared his faith with anyone because he was afraid someone would ask him a question, he would not know the answer, and his inadequate preparation would embarrass him and the Christian faith. But at his workplace the week before this particular class, he had shared his faith with three workers because for the first time he felt he had some answers, and his boldness was strengthened by that conviction. Being a Christian is no different from caring about boats in this regard. There is nothing magic about being confident, articulate, and bold in either area. Knowing what you're talking about may be hard work, but it clearly pays off.

Anti-intellectualism has not merely impacted the lives of believers within the bosom of Christ. It has had serious repercussions in the culture at large. As anti-intellectualism has softened our impact for Christ, so too has it contributed to the secularization of the culture. If the salt loses its saltiness, the meat will be impacted. In the aftermath of the Scopes trial in 1925, conservative Christianity was largely dismissed as an embarrassment among intellectual and cultural movers and shakers.[13] As a result, we now live in one of the most secular cultures in history.

THE EMERGENCE OF A SECULAR CULTURE IN WHICH THE CHURCH IS CALLED TO LIVE AND MINISTER

Culture Is Secular

Modern American culture is largely secular in this sense: most people have little or no understanding of a Christian way of seeing the world, nor is a Christian worldview an important participant in the way we as a society frame and debate issues in the public square. Three of the major centers of influence in our culture—the university, the media, and the government—are largely devoid of serious religious discussion. In fact, it is not unfair to say that university, media, and governmental leaders are often illiterate about how Christians see the world and why. This is evident, for example, in those rare cases when the major television news media try to feature a Christian perspective on abortion, the state, or anything else. Usually, Christians watching the program feel misrepresented and misunderstood. More often than not, however, Christian perspectives are simply ignored and not covered at all.

If a Martian were watching television before coming to earth, he would get the idea that Americans are irreligious. Secularists tolerate religion as long as it remains a privatized perspective relative to a subgroup in society and as long as Christians don't assert that their views are objectively true and defend them articulately. R. C. Sproul, John Gerstner, and Arthur Lindsley have accurately captured this secular attitude toward Christianity:

> The church is safe from vicious persecution at the hands of the secularist, as educated people have finished with stake-burning circuses and torture racks. No martyr's blood is shed in the sec-

ular west. So long as the church knows her place and remains quietly at peace on her modern reservation. Let the babes pray and sing and read their Bibles, continuing steadfastly in their intellectual retardation; the church's extinction will not come by sword or pillory, but by the quiet death of irrelevance. But let the church step off the reservation, let her penetrate once more the culture of the day and the . . . face of secularism will change from a benign smile to a savage snarl.[14]

Secularism Is Primarily a View About Knowledge

The primary characteristic of modern secularism is its view of the nature and limits of knowledge. It is critical to understand this because if knowledge gives one power — we give surgeons and not carpenters the right to cut us open precisely because surgeons have the relevant knowledge not possessed by carpenters — then those with the cultural say-so about who does and doesn't have knowledge will be in a position to marginalize and silence groups judged to have mere belief and private opinion.

For many secularists, knowledge is obtained solely by means of the senses and science. Something is true and reasonable to believe to the degree that it can be tested by the five senses — it can be seen, heard, touched, tasted, or felt. Seeing is believing. Likewise, knowledge is identical to *scientific* knowledge. If you can prove something scientifically, then it is culturally permissible or even obligatory to believe it. Science is the measure of all things, and when a scientist speaks about something, he or she speaks *ex cathedra*. For example, if theological arguments imply homosexuality is in some sense a choice over which one is responsible, and science makes a "claim" to the contrary, which one will win in public debate? We often hear it said that "if your religious beliefs work for you, that's great, but don't impose them on others." However, no one would say that a scientist is imposing anything on anyone when he says that water is H_2O or that $2 + 2 = 4$. Nor would these claims be viewed as private opinions whose sole value was their usefulness for those who believe them. Why? Because only science supposedly deals with facts, truth, and reason, but religion and ethics allegedly deal with private, subjective opinions.

I have no bone to pick with legitimate science. Indeed, it has been argued repeatedly that science was born in Christian Europe precisely because Christian theology helped provide worldview justification for its assumptions.[15] *What I do reject is the idea that science and science alone can claim to give us knowledge*. This assertion — known as scientism — is patently false and, in fact, not even a claim of science, but rather, a philosophical view about science. Nevertheless, once this view of knowledge was widely embraced in the culture, the immediate effect was to marginalize and privatize religion by relegating it to the back of the intellectual bus.[16] To verify this, one need only compare the number of times scientists, as opposed to pastors or theologians, are called upon as experts on the evening news.

If knowledge and reason are identical with what can be tested scientifically or with scientific theories that a majority of scientists believes to be correct, then religion and ethics will no longer be viewed as true, rational domains of discourse because, supposedly, religious or ethical claims are not scientifically testable. This line of thought has led to several trends in society whose combined influence is to hinder ideal human flourishing as God intended it to be. It is similar to the sort of cultural milieu that spawned Stalinism in the Soviet Union and Nazism in pre–World War II Germany, with all of their attendant evils and tragic loss of human life and dignity. As G. K. Chesterton once bemoaned, once people stop believing in God, the problem is not that they will believe nothing; rather, the problem is that they will believe anything. This is just what we are seeing happen in our secular culture bereft of the presence of an engaged, articulate evangelical community.

Secular Views of Knowledge Are Responsible for Unfortunate Social Trends

Scientism is responsible for a number of unfortunate contemporary trends in society.

1. In our scientifically oriented culture, traditional understandings of morality and related notions are considered passe. The primary trend in ethical thinking today is toward *moral* and *religious relativism*. As I have already said, if ethics and religion are not scientifically testable, then many today will think they are mere "expressions of belief" that are true only for those who believe them. Science claims to deal only with fact; religion and ethics supposedly deal with feelings and privatized values. Therefore, religion and ethics are considered merely subjective notions in modern society.

Another modern trend is a change in what we mean by the *good life*. From Old Testament times and ancient Greece until this century, the good life was widely understood to mean a life of intellectual and moral virtue. The good life is the life of ideal human functioning according to the nature that God Himself gave to us. According to this view, prior to creation God had in mind an ideal blueprint of human nature from which He created each and every human being. Happiness (Greek: *eudaimonia*) was understood as a life of virtue, and the successful person was one who knew how to live life well according to what we are by nature due to the creative design of God. When the Declaration of Independence says we are endowed by our Creator with certain inalienable rights, among them the right to pursue happiness, it is referring to virtue and character.[17] So understood, happiness involves suffering, endurance, and patience because these are important means to becoming a good person who lives the good life.

Freedom was traditionally understood as the power to do what one ought to do. For example, some people are not free to play the piano or to say no to lust because they have not undergone the training necessary to ingrain the relevant skillful habits. Moreover, since community is possible only if people accept as true a shared vision of the good life, it is easy to see why a sense of community and public virtue could be sustained given this understanding of the good life, happiness, and freedom.

Traditionally, *tolerance* of other viewpoints meant that even though I think those viewpoints are dead wrong and will argue against them fervently, nevertheless, I will defend your right to argue your own case. Just as importantly, I will treat you with respect as an image bearer of God, even though your views are abhorrent to me. Finally, while *individual rights* are important, they do not exhaust the moral life because virtue and duty are more central than rights to the moral life properly conceived.

2. The traditional view is neither scientifically testable nor easily compatible with evolution. Unfortunately, this traditional understanding of the good life, freedom, community, and tolerance is not scientifically testable. Moreover, Darwin's theory of evolution caused many to lose their belief in the *existence* of natures, human or otherwise. As Harvard zoologist Ernst Mayr has said:

The concepts of unchanging essences and of complete disconti-
nuities between every eidos (type) and all others make genuine
evolutionary thinking impossible. I agree with those who claim
that the essentialist philosophies of Aristotle and Plato are
incompatible with evolutionary thinking.[18]

This belief has, in turn, led evolutionary thinkers like David Hull to
make the following observation:

The implications of moving species from the metaphysical
category that can appropriately be characterized in terms of
"natures" to a category for which such characterizations are
inappropriate are extensive and fundamental. If species evolve
in anything like the way that Darwin thought they did, then
they cannot possibly have the sort of natures that traditional
philosophers claimed they did. If species in general lack
natures, then so does *Homo sapiens* as a biological species. If
Homo sapiens lacks a nature, then no reference to biology can
be made to support one's claims about "human nature."
Perhaps all people are "persons," share the same "person-
hood," etc., but such claims must be explicated and defended
with no reference to biology. Because so many moral, ethical,
and political theories depend on some notion or other of
human nature, Darwin's theory brought into question all these
theories. The implications are not entailments. One can
always dissociate *"Homo sapiens"* from *"human being,"* but
the result is a much less plausible position.[19]

Note Hull's comment that if a person or group dissociates the species-spe-
cific designation "Homo sapiens" from the designation "human being,"
with all of its attendant moral and theological implications (a "being"
might presuppose a creator), then that person or group has a "less plausible position." Why? Why should that which we see, hear, feel, taste, or
touch (or observe through scientific method) have sway over any cultural
debate, since Hull's entire conclusion rests on the giant "if"—"if species
evolve in anything like the way Darwin thought they did . . ."? Yet, as
we'll see in the next section, we have allowed secular thinkers to frame
the debate, and the Christian voice has been muffled at best.

3. Secular ideas have replaced the traditional view. What Mayr and Hull are saying is that if naturalistic evolution is the story of how we came to be, then there is no human nature answering to a divine blueprint and no good life that expresses that nature. There are only accidentally formed individual human beings who are free to create whatever version of happiness they wish. According to the modern view, the good life is the satisfaction of any pleasure or desire that someone freely and autonomously chooses for himself or herself. The successful person is the individual who has a life of pleasure and can obtain enough consumer goods to satisfy his or her desires. Freedom is the right to do what I want, not the power to do what I by nature ought to. Community gives way to individualism with the result that narcissism—an inordinate sense of self-love and self-centered involvement—is an accurate description of many people's lives. If I am free to create my own moral universe and version of the good life, and there is no right or wrong answer to what I should create, then morality—indeed, everything—ultimately exists to make me happy. When a person considers abortion or physician-assisted suicide, the person's individual rights are all that matter. Questions about virtue or one's duty to the broader community simply do not arise.

Tolerance has come to mean that no one is right and no one is wrong and, indeed, the very act of stating that someone else's views are immoral or incorrect is now taken to be intolerant (of course, from this same point of view, it is all right to be intolerant of those who hold to objectively true moral or religious positions). Once the existence of knowable truth in religion and ethics is denied, authority (the right to be believed and obeyed) gives way to power (the ability to force compliance), reason gives way to rhetoric, the speech writer is replaced by the makeup man, and spirited but civil debate in the culture wars is replaced by politically correct special-interest groups who have nothing left but political coercion to enforce their views on others. While the Christian faith clearly teaches that believers are to be involved as good citizens in the state, nevertheless, it is obvious why so many secularists are addicted to politics today because political power is a surrogate for a Higher Power. As Friedrich Nietzsche said, once God died in Western culture—that is, once the concept of God no longer informed the major idea-generating centers of society turned secular—there would be turmoil and horrible secular wars unchecked by traditional morality because the state would come to be a surrogate god for many.

Finally, individual rights have come to dominate our public discussion of moral issues. The public square—those aspects of society where all citizens must interface regardless of personal views; for example, public schools, and government—has become naked: religious, moral, and political debate therein is no longer informed by a clear, robust vision of the moral life shared by most citizens and taken to be true and rational. Once objective duty, goodness, and virtue were abandoned under the guise of scientism and secularism, the only moral map that could replace objective morality is what Daniel Callahan has called minimalistic ethics—anything whatever is morally permissible provided only that you do not harm someone else.[20]

Individual rights are important, and, for the Christian, they are grounded in the image of God and not in the state. In other words, the Christian believes that human rights are derived from the image of God in us; they do not ultimately come from the state. But there are more fundamental questions of virtue and duty that are relevant to the overall development of a moral outlook. For example, the abortion debate should not be framed primarily as a debate about the right to life versus the right to choice. Basically, it should be discussed in terms of this question: What does a woman or a community committed to moral virtue and duty do when faced with the question of abortion? The tenor of the debate changes drastically when issues of virtue and duty to others is brought to the foreground and rights are relegated to a secondary position in the moral context.

Until Christians can do a better job of seeing these issues and articulating them in terms of objective duty and virtue, the Jack Kevorkians will continue to win the "debate" (if that is what we should call the media rhetoric that surrounds the framing of moral dilemmas), precisely because the Kevorkians are on the side of individual rights. If the only morally relevant question to ask a patient is whether or not he freely and competently chooses physician-assisted suicide, then we are left with no moral categories in which to introduce more basic questions of duty and virtue. And this is where our secular society is at present, given its commitment to scientism that emerged in no small measure because a marginalized and inarticulate church withdrew into privatized religion as she welcomed the Trojan horse of anti-intellectualism within her walls.

WHAT SHOULD I DO TO LIVE FOR CHRIST
IN THIS HOUR OF CRISIS?

If you are like I am, your heart may be saddened by what you have read in this chapter. As disciples of Jesus Christ, we must ask how we can become the kind of people we need to be to bring honor to Christ, to help turn the culture toward Him, and to be lights in the midst of darkness for our families, friends, churches, and communities. There is no simple answer to this question, but one thing is crystal clear. We must rededicate ourselves to being deeply spiritual people of whom it can truly be said that "Christ is formed in you" (Galatians 4:19). And, given the times in which we live, we must also obey Jesus' admonition to be as wise as serpents and as innocent as doves (Matthew 10:16, KJV). Surrounded by a fragmented culture, how do we become deeply spiritual people who are wise and savvy, yet innocent and pure? How do we raise children, develop good marriages, serve as role models at work, and make an attractive impact on our communities?

More than ever before, we need what the Old Testament calls wisdom. In later chapters we'll talk more about the biblical view of wisdom, but for now I want to make something very clear: The spiritually mature person is a wise person. And a wise person has the savvy and skill necessary to lead an exemplary life and to address the issues of the day in a responsible, attractive way that brings honor to God. As we will see throughout this book, wisdom is the fruit of a life of study and a developed mind. Wisdom is the application of knowledge gained from studying both God's written Word and His revealed truth in creation. *If we are going to be wise, spiritual people prepared to meet the crises of our age, we must be a studying, learning community that values the life of the mind.* The rest of this book develops the case for why this is so and presents resources for making it a reality in your own sojourn and in the life of your church. Clearly, to become spiritually formed in Christ, a person of wisdom, requires that we follow Christ's teaching in this critical area—and it was He who taught us to love the Lord our God with all our minds.

SUMMARY

In closing, I want to repeat that I am neither adequate for, nor do I have space to conduct, a full analysis of what has happened to the culture and the church. Obviously, more is going on here than a changed perspective of the intellectual life. But we as Christians must face the main fact of this chapter, to wit: Due to certain forces in the 1800s, conservative American Christianity responded to intellectual attack by withdrawing from public discourse and developing an anti-intellectual view of the Christian faith. This response created both a marginalized church with a softened impact for Christ and a secular culture.

English professor Carolyn Kane wrote an article in *Newsweek* about the loss of thinking in American culture generally. After putting her finger squarely on the problem, Kane identified her solution in front of both God and the *Newsweek* readership: "But how can we revive interest in the art of thinking? The best place to start would be in homes and churches of our land."[21] It is striking that she did not appeal to government, or for more money for public schools or better college facilities. Instead, she identified the church as the key factor. Perhaps Kane has a better grasp of the importance of the intellectual life in the Christian faith than many of us do. Perhaps she has read enough Scripture to know that the church was meant to be and has often been the instrument of reason in society. In the next chapter, we will see what Scripture tells us about the role of reason in the Christian life.

Sketching a Biblical Portrait of the Life of the Mind

X

The scandal of the evangelical mind is that there is not much of an evangelical mind. . . . Despite dynamic success at a popular level, modern American evangelicals have failed notably in sustaining serious intellectual life. They have nourished millions of believers in the simple verities of the gospel but have largely abandoned the universities, the arts, and other realms of "high" culture. . . . The historical situation is . . . curious. Modern evangelicals are the spiritual descendants of leaders and movements distinguished by probing, creative, fruitful attention to the mind.

MARK NOLL[1]

K

Unreasonable and absurd ways of life . . . are truly an offense to God.

WILLIAM LAW[2]

K

Your great learning is driving you mad.

FESTUS TO THE APOSTLE PAUL, ACTS 26:24, (NASB)

I N GRADUATE SCHOOL, ONE OF MY PROFESSORS WAS A RADICAL SKEPTIC and relativist who went out of his way to debunk anything that had to do with Christianity. The professor was a well-known scholar whose ideas influenced hundreds of thousands of people since he regularly contributed a guest editorial to a widely read newspaper. One year after my graduation I learned that this professor had been raised in an evangelical home and church and, in fact, had been the leader of his high school youth group. Because he was bright, he developed certain intellectual doubts as a teen. When he approached the elders and pastors of his church, they failed to answer his questions. Unfortunately, they also gave him the message that faith does not require answering intellectual queries and that his problem was really spiritual and not intellectual. Needless to say, this approach did not help him in his Christian journey.

Contrast this story with Saint Augustine's (A.D. 354-430) description of his own conversion. Prior to his conversion, Augustine was a member of a religious cult called Manichaeanism. Being bright, Augustine had intellectual doubts about Manichaeanism, but no fellow members of the sect could answer his questions. Instead, they kept telling him to wait for the arrival of Faustus, a leading Manichaean teacher. But when Faustus came, Augustine was bitterly disappointed to find out that he relied on rhetorical skills and eloquence of speech to persuade people of the Manichaean point of view, yet his answers were shallow and poorly reasoned. Eventually, Augustine abandoned Manichaeanism. Thankfully, over the next few years, Augustine came across two Christian leaders—Ambrose and Pontitianus—who intelligently discussed with him different issues concerning the faith. This profoundly influenced Augustine and helped him on his way toward conversion.[3]

What is the difference in these two stories? Ambrose and Pontitianus exhibited a more *biblical* appreciation of the role that reason plays in Christian life and ministry than did the leaders in my professor's church. Now don't get me wrong on this, those elders were right about the Christian's desire to be like God and to live a deep and fruitful Christian life. And no doubt the leaders in my professor's church had these desires.

Unfortunately, sincerity is not enough for powerful Christian ministry. We must also have an accurate biblical understanding of what we are to be about. In this chapter, I want to show that the importance of reason and a Christian intellectual life is clearly taught in Scripture. My purpose is not to proof-text my claims by merely tacking a few verses onto my thesis here and there. Rather, my passion is to paint a picture, to sketch out a vision of what the Christian way is like and to illustrate how important a life of study and thought is to flourishing in that way. This chapter weaves together strands of evidence into a tapestry to show that Augustine and his friends had it right: *According to the Bible, developing a Christian mind is part of the very essence of discipleship unto the Lord Jesus.*

Since I will be saying a lot about reason in this chapter, it is important from the start to clarify what I mean by it. Obviously, I do not mean by the term something that is opposed to faith or revelation. By "reason" I mean all our faculties relevant to gaining knowledge and justifying our beliefs about different things. We all possess a number of different human faculties. For example, through my *senses* I know there is a computer before me and it is colored gray. Through my *memory* I know I had coffee this morning. Through my *logical abilities* I know that if a tree is taller than a car and a car is taller than a dog, then a tree is taller than a dog. Through my *moral faculty* I know kindness is a virtue and torturing babies is wrong. By reason, I simply mean the faculties, in isolation or in combination, I use to gain knowledge and justify my beliefs.

In this chapter, I want to show that the careful cultivation of reason should be a high value for the Christian community. To do this, we will look at biblical teaching about reason and the Christian mind. Let us begin in earnest, then, and see what the Bible says about the importance of the intellect.

A BIBLICAL SKETCH OF THE VALUE OF REASON

The Nature of the God of the Bible

Our Lord is a God of reason as well as of revelation. The Bible teaches, for example, that among God's attributes is omniscience: God is perfect in knowledge and, in fact, knows everything both actual and possible (1 Samuel 23:11-13, Job 37:16, 1 John 3:20). The Son of God became incarnate as the Logos (Greek: "the word"), which some take to represent and emphasize this reasoned, omniscient aspect of God's character, that is, the divine reason or wisdom that is made manifest and understandable in the God-man Jesus Christ.

There are other examples of God's nature that demonstrate a biblical harmony with reason. For example, God exhibits wise intelligence in choosing the best goals and the best means of accomplishing them. So wise is He that Scripture calls Him "the only wise God" (Romans 16:27). He is the God of truth who cannot lie (Titus 1:2) and who is completely reliable (Romans 3:4, Hebrews 6:18). His very word is true (John 17:17), and His church—*not the university*—is the pillar and support of the truth (1 Timothy 3:15). He invites His creatures to come and reason together with Him (Isaiah 1:18) by bringing a legally reasoned case against His actions to which He will respond (Ecclesiastes 6:10; Jeremiah 12:1, 20:12).

What a contrast the God of the Bible is with the god of Islam, who is so transcendent that his ways are inscrutable (beyond understanding)! How different He is from the irrational, fickle, finite deities of the Greek pantheon or other polytheistic religions! These mythological "gods" exhibit the folly of human emotion and the danger of ignoring revelation. The God of the Bible requires teachers who diligently study His Word and handle it accurately (compare 2 Timothy 2:15 and 1 Timothy 4:15-16). He demands of His evangelists that they give rational justification to questioners who ask them why they believe as they do (1 Peter 3:15). On one occasion His chief apostle, Paul, emphasized that his gospel preaching was by way of "words of truth and rationality" (Acts 26:25, NASB) when Festus charged that his great learning was driving him mad (Acts 26:24, NASB). No anti-intellectualism here! By contrast, the monistic religions of the East promote gurus who offer koans, paradoxes like the sound of one hand clapping, upon which to meditate in order to free the devotee from dependence on reason and enable him to escape the laws of logic. The Buddhist is to leave his mind behind, but the Christian God requires transformation by way of its renewal (Romans 12:1-2).

Is it any wonder that we Christians started the first universities and have planted schools and colleges everywhere our missionaries have gone? Is it any wonder that science began in Christian Europe because of the belief that the same rational God who made the human mind also created the world so the mind would be suited to discern the world's rational structure placed there by God? God is certainly not a cultural elitist, and He does not love intellectuals more than anyone else. But it needs to be said in the same breath that ignorance is not a Christian virtue if those virtues mirror the perfection of God's own character.

How the Bible as Revelation Points Us to a Christian Mind

We have now revisited what the Scriptures say about the nature of God Himself and briefly contrasted the biblical portrait of God with other religious worldviews (Islam, Eastern pantheism, polytheism). We've seen that only the God of the Bible has a natural affinity for reason and rationality in humans (we are after all, created in His image). Now let us look at how God's revelation of Himself in the Scriptures points us further toward the importance of developing a Christian mind.

1. Revelation is truth. When the God we love chose to reveal Himself, He did so in creation itself and in more specific, special ways — most importantly, in the Scriptures and Jesus Christ. For now, I want to focus on the nature of the Bible as a revelation from God and see what implications this may have for the importance of the mind. The central biblical terms for revelation — *galah*[4] (Hebrew), *apocalupto, phaneroo* (Greek)—express the idea of revealing, disclosing, making manifest or known. When we affirm that the Bible is a revelation from God, we do not simply assert that God as a person is known in and through it. We also mean that God has revealed understandable, objectively true propositions. The Lord's Word is not only practically useful, it is also theoretically true (John 17:17). God has revealed *truth* to us and not just Himself. This truth is addressed to our minds and requires an intellectual grasp to understand and then apply.

2. How does the Holy Spirit help us understand the Bible? Because of the Bible's nature, serious study is needed to grasp what it says. Of course, the Scripture contains easily grasped portions that are fairly straightforward. But some of it is very difficult, intellectually speaking. In fact, Peter once said that some of Paul's writings were intellectually challenging, hard to understand, and easily distorted by untaught (that is, uneducated in Christian theology) and unstable people (2 Peter 3:16). Anyone who has tried to grasp the theological depths of Romans or Ephesians will say "Amen!" to that. The more a person develops the mind and the understanding of hermeneutics (the science of interpreting the Scriptures), the more he or she will be able to understand the meaning and significance of the Scriptures.

Unfortunately, many today apparently think that hard intellectual work is not needed to understand God's propositional revelation to us. Instead, they believe that the Holy Spirit will simply make known the meaning of a text if implored to do so. Tragically, this represents a misunderstanding of the Spirit's role in understanding the Scriptures. In my view, the Spirit does not help the believer understand the meaning of Scripture. Rather, He speaks to the believer's soul, convicting, comforting, opening up applications of His truth through His promptings. There are three passages typically used to justify the idea that the Spirit helps us understand the meaning of a scriptural text: 1 Corinthians 2:14-15, John 14:26, and 1 John 2:27. Let's unpack these biblical bags.

First Corinthians 2:14-15 (NASB) reads as follows:

> But a natural man does not accept the things of the Spirit of God; for they are foolishness to him, and he cannot understand them, because they are spiritually appraised. But he who is spiritual appraises all things, yet he himself is appraised by no man.

The context of the passage is a discussion of the disunity in the Corinthian church, the manner in which Paul came to them, and the spiritual state in which he discovered them. There are three keys for interpreting the verse. First, the word for "accept" is *dechomai*. The more frequently used word in Greek with a similar meaning is *lambano*, which means simply "to receive." *Dechomai* sometimes has a slightly different shade of meaning, namely, "to receive *willingly*." It is used in 2 Corinthians 8:17 to refer to Titus's acceptance of Paul's request to visit Corinth. The term has nothing to do with Titus grasping Paul's request intellectually. It expresses his willingness and openness to accept it. So in our passage, the natural man—the unbelieving person—does not receive *willingly* the things of God.

In 1 Corinthians 2:14, what are the "things of the Spirit of God" that the unbeliever does not receive willingly? The context indicates that Paul has in mind the very words and meanings of Holy Scripture. Paul is concerned to preserve the unity in the Corinthian church, and he does this by defending the divine authority of the apostles' message, including his own "words of wisdom" to mature believers. In 1 Corinthians 2:10, Paul assures his readers that the apostles' words of wisdom were revealed to them by God's Spirit. Even more, Paul says in verse 13, God's Spirit took the thoughts and ideas He had revealed to the apostles and combined them with just the right words necessary to convey these thoughts! It is these inspired words of the Scriptures that the unbeliever resists.

Second, the word for "understand" is *ginosko* in the Greek text and has the sense of "discerning as true and good" or "to know experientially by entering into." It does not mean simply to grasp something *cognitively*. It is in this experiential sense that the Bible says a man "knows" his wife in sexual intercourse. Third, the term for "appraised" is *anakrino*, which means "to spiritually appraise or sift something." It is used in Acts 17:11 of the Bereans, who tried to assess whether or not Paul's understanding of the Old Testament was good and acceptable. Note that the Bereans had to already possess an intellectual grasp of Paul's teachings before they could assess them. Combining these three insights, we see that 1 Corinthians 2:14-15 tells us that the Spirit aids the believer in being open to Scripture, in entering into it experientially, and in finding it good and acceptable. The Spirit helps us apply the significance of the text, but He does not teach us the cognitive meaning of the text. He leaves that up to us.

John 14:26 (NASB) reads this way: "But the Helper, the Holy Spirit, whom the Father will send in My name, He will teach you all things, and bring to your remembrance all that I said to you." This passage does not affirm that the Holy Spirit will teach the meaning of Scripture to believers. It promises to the apostles that the Spirit will inspire them and aid them in remembering the words of Jesus. The context makes this clear. Several verses (John 14:1,25,28-29; 16:16; 17:12-14,26) show that the disciples themselves are being spoken of and not believers in general. John 17:20 (NASB) is conclusive evidence of this: "I do not ask in behalf of these alone, but for those who believe in Me through their word." Here Jesus makes a distinction between the disciples who are present and whom He is addressing ("you" in John 14:26 and "these alone" in 17:20) and believers in general ("those who believe in Me through their word").

In 1 John 2:27 (NASB) we are told that "you have no need for anyone to teach you; but as His anointing teaches you about all things, and is true and is not a lie, and just as it has taught you, you abide in Him." Some take this to say that the Holy Spirit teaches the believer the truths of Scripture and that there is no need for a teacher—directly or in the form of commentaries—to understand the Bible. Common sense tells us this cannot be the correct way to take the passage, for two reasons. First, if we don't need a teacher, we wouldn't need John to teach us that we don't need a teacher! We would already know this by the "anointing!" Second, the disposition of the entire New Testament is that God has given His people gifted teachers who are to work diligently at their teaching (for example, Ephesians 4:11).

More specifically, John is addressing a historical situation in which Gnostic-like teachers were claiming special, secret insight into the Bible, a sort of specially illumined wisdom of which they were gatekeepers in much the same way some people today appeal to the Spirit to validate their biblical interpretations! John is saying that since the believers have been baptized (anointed) into the body of Christ by the Spirit, they have no need of some additional, special, secret knowledge only given to certain teachers. John is not making a statement about the need for teachers generally.

I don't want to belabor the point about the Spirit and biblical interpretation, but it is crucial to grasp the implications of what I am saying. When cultists come to my door, I often point out that they take passages out of context. To prove my charge I ask them to state the historical setting, main theme, and basic structure of just *one* of the sixty-six books of the Bible. It would be unfair to expect someone to do this for all the books, but if someone is in the habit of studying Scripture properly and with an eye on context, then over the years that person should have a growing ability to do this. I have never once had a cultist answer this question.

Could you do it? If the answer is no, you should ask yourself whether your approach to the Bible is adequate. I fear that our inaccurate emphasis on the Holy Spirit's role in understanding Scripture has become an easy shortcut to the hard work of building a personal library of study tools and using them. As Gallup poll after Gallup poll has shown, the result of our inaccurate emphasis on the Spirit, along with our intellectual laziness, is that modern Christians are largely illiterate about the content of their own religion and feel inadequate because of it. We need local churches dedicated to the task of training believers to think theologically and biblically. We must develop intelligent Christians; that is, Christians who have the mental training to see issues clearly, make important distinctions carefully, and weigh various factors appropriately. If we are not really planning to see this happen, then at the end of the day, what we are really saying is that a deep understanding of the Scripture, creeds, and theology of Christianity just doesn't matter that much. But as we'll see in the next section, the Scriptures themselves attest to the importance of our minds in our spiritual formation in Christ. Let's look at the most critical texts in the New Testament in this regard.

Three Important Texts

Any disciple of Jesus who is doing his or her best to raise children, nurture other believers, or grow in the Christian way needs a plan for making certain progress in these endeavors. And any plan must take into account three critical New Testament texts: Paul's most important statement of Christian dedication in Romans 12:1-2, Jesus' summary of the Old Testament in Matthew 22:37-39, and Peter's imperative for flourishing courageously in a hostile, unbelieving environment in 1 Peter 3:15.

1. Romans 12:1-2: Because of its special relevance to the topic of chapter 3, I will defer in-depth treatment of Romans 12:1-2 (NASB) to the next chapter. For our purposes here, let's simply look at the text and relate it to our overall understanding of the importance of the Christian mind and what the Scriptures are teaching us:

> I urge you therefore, brethren, by the mercies of God, to present your bodies a living and holy sacrifice, acceptable to God, *which is* your spiritual service of worship. And do not be conformed to this world, but be transformed by the renewing of your mind, that you may prove what the will of God is, that which is good and acceptable and perfect.

Now these words of Paul's are familiar to many, but the critical point of verse 2 is that we cannot "prove," that is, "make known to ourselves and to others," what God's will is, *without the renewing or transformation of our minds*. This brings the mind to the spiritual stage, front and center! We all want to know God's will, but this text is telling us we can't unless we present our bodies, including our soul and minds, to the Lord for transformation and renewal! We'll look at this in more depth in the next chapter, but for now, be aware of this important insight:

by "presenting our bodies," Paul means we must be available to do the hard work of understanding what God has said in His Word and take the time to study it in order to have our minds transformed!

2. *Matthew 22:37-39:* In Matthew 22:35-40, an expert in Mosaic Law challenged Jesus to summarize the entire Old Testament. In order to answer this question, Jesus must have studied the Old Testament thoroughly. Remember, even though He was God, He was also human, and during most of His earthly life He hid and subordinated His divine nature to His Father and lived as a genuine human being. The Scriptures tell us He grew in knowledge, learned things, and so forth. His now-famous answer to the lawyer included these words: "You shall love the Lord your God with all your heart, and with all your soul, and with all your mind" (NASB). In other words, God is worthy of being loved with every single facet of human personality, not simply with one or two aspects of our nature. Note carefully that Jesus included an intellectual love for God with the mind.

What would it look like for a church, a parent, a teen, or any individual disciple to try to nurture an intellectual love for God in himself and others? We will look more fully at this question in later chapters, but for now I want to press home that answering this question is the duty of any disciple of Jesus. We get a hint at what might be included in loving God with the mind in the context preceding Jesus' answer. In Matthew 22:23-33 (NASB) a group of Sadducees (who did not believe in the resurrection of the dead) tried to trap Jesus with an intellectual argument involving a story of a woman who had successively been married to seven brothers. Whose wife will she be in the resurrection? they asked. Jesus' options seemed to be: (1) deny the resurrection, (2) accept polygamy and adultery by affirming her marriage to all seven in heaven, or (3) unfairly and arbitrarily limit her marriage to one brother only.

It is interesting to note that Jesus did something His followers should emulate: He *intelligently* answered the Sadducees' question! First, He addressed the surface issue by denying the necessary condition for the Sadducees' argument to get off the ground; that is, He denied that there is marriage in heaven. He then went for the deeper issue about the resurrection, and His strategy is instructive. He cites what on the surface appears to be a verse inadequately related to the issue of resurrection: "'I am the God of Abraham, and the God of Isaac, and the God of Jacob'[.]

He is not the God of the dead but of the living." As a young Christian, I was puzzled by Jesus' response because I myself could have cited better verses than this one, for example, Daniel 12:2, which explicitly affirms the resurrection. Or so I thought. Jesus' genius is revealed when we recognize that He had studied Sadducean theology and knew that they did not accept the full authority of the prophets, including Daniel. He also knew that the very passage He used was one of the very defining verses for the entire Sadducean party! His argument hinged on the tense of the Hebrew verb. Jesus does not say, "I *was* the God of Abraham, etc.," but, "I *am* (continue to be) the God of Abraham, et cetera," a claim that could be true only if Abraham and others continued to exist.

For our purposes, two things are important about the narrative. First, Jesus revealed His intellectual skills in debate by: (1) showing His familiarity with His opponents' point of view; (2) appealing to common ground (a text all the disputants accepted) instead of expressing a biblical text He accepted but they rejected (Daniel 12:2); and (3) deftly using the laws of logic to dissect His opponents' argument and refute it powerfully. Second, because it forms the immediately preceding context for Matthew 22:37-39, this incident may inform at least part of what it means to love God intellectually: be prepared to stand up for God's truth and honor when they are challenged, and do so with carefully thought-out answers.

3. 1 Peter 3:15: The need to have answers to people's questions is the core of our third passage: "And do not fear their intimidation, and do not be troubled, but sanctify Christ as Lord in your hearts, always *being* ready to make a defense *[apologia]* to everyone who asks you to give an account *[logos]* for the hope that is in you, yet with gentleness and reverence" (1 Peter 3:14-15, NASB). Two key words are central to Peter's meaning: *apologia* and *logos*. The word *apologia* means "to defend something," for example, offering positive arguments for and responding to negative arguments against your position in a courtroom. It is important to recognize that this is exactly how the apostle Paul did evangelism (Acts 14:15-17; 17:2,4,17-31; 18:4; 19:8). He persuaded people to become Christians by offering rational arguments on behalf of the truth of the gospel. He even cited approvingly two pagan philosophers, Epimenides and Aratus (Acts 17:28), as part of his case for the gospel. In 1 Peter 3:15, the apostle does not suggest that we be prepared to do this, he *commands* it.

The word *logos* means "evidence or argument which provides rational justification for some belief." In his dialogue *Theaetetus*, Plato attempted to define knowledge. According to Plato, if you know something, what you know must at least be true and you must believe it. If you said you knew it was raining outside, but either it was not raining outside or you did not even believe it was, others would rightly be puzzled at your claim to knowledge. But as Plato pointed out, knowledge is more than just true beliefs. We all have many true beliefs that don't count as knowledge. If someone hits you on the head and, as a result, somehow you form the true belief that a methane molecule has four carbon atoms in it, no one would claim that you knew this to be the case, especially compared to a scientist who had spent five years studying methane. You and the scientist both have true beliefs about methane, but he has knowledge and you don't. What is the difference? Plato says the scientist has a true belief plus *logos* (evidence) and you fail to have *logos*. The scientist has good reasons that justify his true belief, you have a blind faith that just happens to be true. Applied to our passage, Peter is saying that we are to be prepared to give rational arguments and good reasons for why we believe what we believe, and this involves the mind. Peter's reference to gentleness and reverence implies that we are to argue but not be argumentative.

Have you been afraid to stand up for Christ when the opportunity presented itself? Or when you have done so, have you come off as shallow, reactionary, and defensive? If so, there is nothing magical about changing your life in this area. First, as with every other area of life, you have to study hard and gain an intellectual grasp of the issues so you can be confident and courageous. Second, you need to be sure that Jesus Christ is the Lord of your life; that is, you are to serve His name, not make one for yourself. This was Peter's counsel to fearful believers being intimidated by powerful forces outside the church.

Before we leave this passage, I cannot resist making one more observation. In Acts 4:13 we read that certain Jewish elders and rulers noted that Peter and John were uneducated and unlearned. Some have taken this to have anti-intellectual implications for Christian life and witness. However, the Jewish leaders did not mean that Peter and John were irrational or intellectually unskilled. Rather, they meant that Peter and John had not undergone formal rabbinic training. There are no implications whatever from this verse about the value of education per se. Moreover, this was said of Peter at the beginning of his ministry. When he wrote his first epistle some thirty years later, he had changed. Many liberals deny that Peter could have written 1 Peter because it is written in a highly educated, intellectual Greek style unlikely to be within the purview of a simple fisherman. However, it is more likely that Peter took his own advice (see 1 Peter 3:15) and, from the time of Acts 4:13 to the time he wrote his epistle, devoted himself to intellectual cultivation as a part of his discipleship unto the Lord Jesus. By the time the opportunity presented itself for him to address a dispersed group of Greek Christians, some of them well-educated, he was up to the task. Even if we grant that Silvanus polished Peter's style (cf 1 Peter 5:12), there were limits to the degree that a scribe could exercise such polishing, and Peter's grammar would have been better than average and certainly an improvement over the Greek linguistic skills of a typical fisherman. Moreover, the care and precision of the argument of 1 Peter reveals a carefully trained mind.

Scripture on the Value of Extrabiblical Knowledge

A picture is emerging from our glance at Holy Scripture, a portrait of the mature Christian life in which the intellectual life, the careful development of our faculty of reason, is an essential, valuable component. The spiritual journey is certainly more than loving God with our minds, but just as surely, that journey is at least a life of such intellectual devotion. As we grow in our love for God and seek to be like Him, we make it our intention to become as well-informed and knowledgeable as we can, given that our intellectual development must be balanced with devotion to growth in other aspects of our human selves.

1. The Scriptures show us the value of extrabiblical knowledge for a life of wisdom. The Bible has a lot to say about wisdom and reverence for God is where it begins (Proverbs 1:7). But such reverence alone will not bring wisdom. Wisdom results when a respectful heart is united with a disciplined mind. Knowledge is the fruit of study, and knowledge is necessary for wisdom.

Holy Scripture is the central object of study in loving God with the mind. However, it is not the only object of such study. God has revealed Himself and various truths on a number of topics outside the Bible. As Christians have known throughout our history, common sense, logic, and mathematics—along with the arts, humanities, sciences, and other areas of study—contain important truths relevant to life in general and to the development of a careful, life-related Christian worldview. According to the Bible, wisdom comes from studying ants as well as learning Scripture (Proverbs 6)!

In 1756, John Wesley delivered an address to a gathering of clergy on how to carry out the pastoral ministry with joy and skill. In his address, Wesley cataloged a number of things familiar to most contemporary believers—the cultivation of a disposition to glorify God and save souls, a knowledge of Scripture, and similar notions. However, at the very beginning of his list, Wesley focused on something seldom expressly valued by most pastoral search committees: "Ought not a Minister to have, First, a good understanding, a clear apprehension, a sound judgment, and a capacity of reasoning with some closeness?"[5] Time and again throughout the address, Wesley unpacked this remark by admonishing ministers to know what would sound truly odd and almost pagan to the average person in the pew today: logic, metaphysics, natural theology, geometry, and the ideas of important figures in the history of thought (philosophy, history, literature). For Wesley, study in these areas (especially philosophy and geometry) helped train the mind to think precisely, a habit of incredible value, he asserted, when it comes to thinking as a Christian about theological themes or scriptural texts. For Wesley, the study of extrabiblical information and the writings of unbelievers was of critical value for growth and maturity. As he put it elsewhere, "To imagine none can teach you but those who are themselves saved from sin, is a very great and dangerous mistake. Give not place to it for a moment."[6]

Wesley's remarks were not unusual in his time. A century earlier, the great Reformed pastor Richard Baxter was faced with lukewarmness in the church and unbelief outside it. In 1667 he wrote a book to meet these needs, and in it he used philosophy, logic, and general items of knowledge outside Scripture to argue for the existence of the soul and the life to come.[7] The fact that Baxter turned to philosophy and extrabiblical knowledge instead of therapy or praise hymns is worth pondering. Over a millennium earlier, Augustine summarized the view of many early church fathers when he said that "We must show our Scriptures not to be in conflict with whatever [our critics] can demonstrate about the nature of things from reliable sources."[8] Philosophy and extrabiblical knowledge were the main tools Augustine used in this task. In fact, it is safe to say that throughout much of church history, Scripture and right reason were considered twin allies to be prized and used by disciples of Jesus.

In valuing extrabiblical knowledge, our brothers and sisters in church history were merely following common sense and Scripture itself. Repeatedly, Scripture acknowledges the wisdom of cultures outside Israel; for example, Egypt (Isaiah 19:11-13), the Edomites (Jeremiah 49:7), the Phoenicians (Zechariah 9:2), and many, many others. The remarkable achievements produced by human wisdom are acknowledged in Job 28:1-11. The wisdom of Solomon is compared to that of the "men of the east" and Egypt in order to show that it surpassed that of people with a longstanding, well-deserved reputation for wisdom (1 Kings 4:29-34). Paul approvingly quotes pagan philosophers (Acts 17:28) and Jude cites the noncanonical book *The Assumption of Moses* in Jude 1:9. The book of Proverbs is filled with examples in which knowledge, even moral and spiritual knowledge, can be gained from studying things (for example, ants) in the natural world. Once Jesus taught that we should know we are to love our enemies, not on the basis of an Old Testament text, but from careful reflection on how the sun and rain behave (Matthew 5:44-45). We can and must cultivate the Christian mind, but in that tilling we must include the study of the works of extrabiblical knowledge.

2. Scripture teaches us the value of the natural moral law. Two specific aspects of scriptural teaching about extrabiblical knowledge are worthy of special note. First, Scripture repeatedly acknowledges the existence of natural moral law: true moral principles rooted in the way God made things, addressed to humans as humans (instead of to man as a believing member of the kingdom of God) and knowable by all people independently of the Bible (Job 31:13-15, Romans 1–2).[9] Among other things, what this means is that believers need not appeal to Scripture in arguing for certain ethical positions, say, in the abortion debate.

Indeed, in my own view, the church is to work for a just state, not a Christian state or theocracy.[10] We are not to place the state under Scripture. But if this is true, where is the source of moral guidance for the state to be just and to punish wrongdoers as Romans 13:1-7 teaches? The answer is the natural moral law. God has revealed enough of His moral law in the creation for the state to do its job. The church may *preach* to unbelievers what Scripture says about some topic, but when believers *argue* for their views in the public square or *defend* them against those who do not accept the Scriptures, they should use general principles of moral argument and reasoning.

This is precisely what the prophet Amos did. In chapters 1 and 2, he denounced the moral behavior of several people-groups outside of Israel, and he never once appealed to Scripture. Instead, he was content to rest his case with an appeal to self-evident moral principles in the natural law, which he assumed were known by those without Scripture. But when he turned to rebuke the people of Israel, for the first time he said that they had violated the "law of the LORD" (Amos 2:4), knowing that they had a familiarity with Holy Scripture. Amos appealed to common ground in all these cases, just as Jesus did in reasoning with the Sadducees (Matthew 22:23-33) and Paul in evangelizing the Greeks (Acts 17:16-31).

3. Scripture shows the value of being qualified to minister from a position of influence. The second aspect of scriptural teaching about extrabiblical knowledge is, Scripture shows people qualified to minister in God's name in situations that required them to have intellectual skills in extrabiblical knowledge. In Daniel 1:3-4, 2:12-13, 5:7, we see Daniel and his friends in a position to influence Nebuchadnezzar, king of Babylon, only because they showed "intelligence in every branch of wisdom." These men had studied and learned Babylonian science, geometry, and literature. And because of this, they were prepared to serve when the occasion presented itself.

I remember being in a meeting with Dr. Bill Bright, founder of Campus Crusade for Christ, shortly after Ronald Reagan had been elected president. Dr. Bright came into the meeting late because Reagan had called to ask him to confer with other evangelical leaders in order to suggest a list of qualified evangelicals to serve in his presidential cabinet. With sadness in his heart, Dr. Bright said that after numerous phone conversations with other evangelical leaders, they had concluded that there simply were not many evangelicals with the intellectual and professional excellence for such a high post. C. Everett Koop was all they could think of and, as we now know, Koop got the position of surgeon general. Had evangelicals valued the study of extrabiblical knowledge the way Daniel and his friends did, things may have turned out quite differently.

How, then, should this attitude toward extrabiblical intellectual training inform parents and youth groups when they prepare Christian teenagers to go to college and tell teens why college is important? According to various studies, increasing numbers of college freshmen, on the advice of parents, say their primary goal in going to college is to get a good job and ensure a secure financial future for themselves. This parallels a trend in the same students toward valuing a good job more than developing a meaningful philosophy of life. Given this view of a college education, it is clear why the humanities have fallen on hard times. It is equally clear why the level of our public discourse on topics central to the culture wars is so shallow, since it is precisely the humanities that train people to think carefully about these topics.

What is not so clear is why Christians, with a confidence in the providential care and provision of God, would follow the secular culture in adopting this approach to college. How different this approach is compared to the value of a college education embraced by earlier generations of Christians: A Christian goes to college to discover his vocation—the area of service to which God has called him—and to develop the skills necessary to occupy a section of the cultural, intellectual domain in a manner worthy of the kingdom of God. A believer also goes to college to gain general information and the habits of thought necessary for developing a well-structured soul suitable for a well-informed, good citizen of both earthly and heavenly kingdoms. If the public square is naked, it may be because Christians have abandoned the humanities due to a sub-biblical appreciation for extrabiblical knowledge.

We have just looked at three important arguments that show the value of extrabiblical knowledge and the baptism of such knowledge by the Scriptures themselves. So, why do Christians continue to ignore the value of the life of the mind in the face of all this evidence? Let's look briefly at five barriers to reason.

Biblical Resistance to the Intellectual Life

In spite of the multifaceted case for the centrality of a well-developed Christian mind to the Christian life, you still may be hesitant to accept its value. I will address these sources of resistance in chapter 4, but here I want to demolish five misconceptions that in one way or another wage war on the Christian mind by distorting what Scripture says on this topic.

1. The distortion of 1 Corinthians 1–2. Two frequently cited but misunderstood texts relevant to the Christian mind are 1 Corinthians 1–2 and Colossians 2:8. In 1 Corinthians 1 and 2, Paul argues against the wisdom of the world and reminds his readers that he did not visit them with persuasive words of wisdom. Some conclude from this that human reasoning and argument are futile, especially when applied to evangelism. There are several problems with this understanding of the passage. For one thing, if it is in fact an indictment against argumentation and reasoning, then it contradicts Paul's own practices in Acts and his explicit appeal to argument and evidence on behalf of the Resurrection in the very same epistle (1 Corinthians 15).

Second, this passage is more accurately seen as a condemnation of the false, prideful use of reason, not of reason itself. It is *hubris* (pride) that is in view, not *nous* (mind). God chose foolish *(moria)* things that were offensive to human pride, not to reason properly used. For example, the idea of God being crucified was so offensive that the Greek spirit would have judged it to be morally disgusting.

The passage may also be a condemnation of Greek rhetoric. Greek orators prided themselves in possessing "persuasive words of wisdom," and it was their practice to persuade a crowd of any side of an issue for the right price. They did not base their persuasion on rational considerations but on speaking ability, thus bypassing issues of substance. Paul is most likely contrasting himself with Greek rhetoricians. If so, then Paul is arguing against evangelists who spend all of their time working on their speaking techniques yet fail to address the minds of unbelievers in their gospel presentations!

Paul could also be making the claim that the content of the gospel cannot be deduced by pure reason from some set of first principles. No one could start off with an abstract concept of a first mover and deduce that a crucifixion would happen from this information alone. Thus, the gospel could never have been discovered by pure deductive reason from self-evident first principles, but had to be revealed by the biblical God who acts in history. Paul was insistent that the intellect could assess whether or not there was sufficient evidence to judge that God had so acted (1 Corinthians 15). So we cannot conclude from this passage that using reason is futile.

2. The distortion of Colossians 2:8. In this passage, Paul says, "See to it that no one takes you captive through hollow and deceptive philosophy, which depends on human tradition and the basic principles of this world rather than on Christ". Some take this to be a command to avoid secular studies, especially philosophy. However, upon closer inspection of the structure of the verse, it becomes clear that philosophy in general was not the focus. Rather, it is a certain sort of philosophy — hollow and deceptive philosophy.

In the context of Colossians, Paul was warning the church not to form and base doctrinal views according to a philosophical system hostile to orthodoxy. His remarks were a simple warning not to embrace heresy; in context, they were not meant to represent his views of philosophy as a discipline of study. In fact, one of the best ways to avoid hollow and deceptive philosophy is to study philosophy itself, so you can learn to recognize truth from error, using Scripture and right reason as a guide. *This is exactly what Paul himself did.* Colossians reveals an apostle who was entirely familiar with the type of proto-Gnostic philosophy threatening Colossian believers, who possessed a thorough knowledge of that philosophical system and an ability to point out its inadequacy. And remember, Paul himself cited pagan philosophers approvingly in Acts 17:28. Neither of these texts should dampen our enthusiasm to cultivate a Christian mind or use reason in our Christian walk.

3. The doctrine of depravity doesn't mean reason is irrelevant. Some argue that the human intellect is fallen, depraved, darkened, and blinded, and therefore human reason is irrelevant or suspect when it comes to becoming or growing as a Christian. Now, even if this point is granted in the case of evangelizing unbelievers, it doesn't follow that Christians should not use or cultivate their intellects once they have become disciples. Moreover, from the fact that reasoning alone will not bring someone to Christ, it does not follow that we should not persuade or reason with people. Preaching alone will not save people without the Spirit's work, but we still preach and work on our messages. We should do the same thing with our use of reason in evangelism.

The will is fallen and depraved too, but God still commands people to make a choice to believe. The doctrine of total depravity does not mean that the image of God is effaced, that sinners are as evil as they could possibly be, or that the intellect, emotions, and will are gone or completely useless. Rather, total depravity means that the entire person, including the intellect, has been adversely affected by the Fall and is separate from God. The sinner alone cannot extricate himself from this condition and cannot merit God's favor or commend himself to

God on the basis of his own righteousness. Further, the entire personality is corrupt but not inoperative, and every aspect of our personality has a natural inclination to run in ways contrary to God's ways. However, none of this means that reason, considered in itself, is bad.

4. Distorting the nature of faith as a matter of the heart, not the head. As we have already seen, some think faith is opposed to or should be separate from reason. This is sometimes supported by Jesus' own teaching about the importance of being like little children in order to enter the kingdom of God (Matthew 18:1-4). It is also justified by the idea that a relationship with God is a matter of the heart, not the head.

Unfortunately, the opinions just expressed do not capture the substance of biblical teaching. In Scripture, faith can be directed at different things—most frequently, at a statement or a person, especially God. To have faith in a statement means to let yourself be convinced of and, therefore, accept the statement as true. To have faith in God means to firmly rely on Him. Either way, *faith is relying on what you have reason to believe is true and trustworthy.* Faith involves the readiness to act as if something were so.

Throughout church history, theologians have expressed three different aspects of biblical faith: *notitia* (knowledge), *fiducia* (trust), and *assensus* (assent). *Notitia* refers to the data or doctrinal content of the Christian faith (see Jude 1:3). *Assensus* denotes the assent of the intellect to the truth of the content of Christian teaching. Note that each of these aspects of faith requires a careful exercise of reason, both in understanding what the teachings of Christianity are and in judging their truthfulness. In this way, reason is indispensable for the third aspect of faith—*fiducia*—which captures the personal application or trust involved in faith, an act that primarily involves the will but includes the affections and intellect too.[11]

What about being like a little child and the importance of the heart over the head in the Christian life? In the context, Jesus' teaching about becoming like a little child had nothing to do with the intellect. It was directed against being self-sufficient and arrogant. To be a child in this sense is to be humble and willing to trust in or rely on others, especially God. The opposite of the child is a proud, stiff-necked person, not an intelligent, reasonable one. Further, the distinction between the head and the heart is very misleading. In Scripture, the term *heart* has several meanings. Most of the time it simply refers to the seat or center of the entire person, the total self, including intellect, emotion, and will. Sometimes it simply refers to the emotions or affections (Romans 1:24, Philippians 1:8). However, the term *heart* often actually refers to the mind itself (Romans 1:21; 2 Corinthians 4:6, 9:7; Ephesians 1:18). Therefore, it is safe to say that when the term *heart* is used in a verse, it most likely includes or explicitly refers to our mental faculty unless the context shows otherwise. Let's not allow hollow or false teaching to distort our understanding of the critical nature of the heart and move on in our development of a Christian mind.

5. A grotesque distortion: Our response to God's way should be ignorance. Finally, I sometimes hear two claims that express the idea that it is futile to use your reason or to emphasize its importance when it comes to the Christian way: God's ways and thoughts are higher than ours (Isaiah 55:9) and knowledge puffs people up and makes them arrogant (1 Corinthians 8:1). It should be clear what is wrong with these claims. The fact that God's thoughts are higher than ours means that we will never be able to fully grasp God's motives, purposes, or providential guidance in the world. But who in his right mind ever thought that we could gain such a thing! To admit this, however, says absolutely nothing about whether or not we should try to love God and serve Him better with our minds.

Regarding the arrogance that comes from knowledge, we need to keep two things in mind. First, Paul's statement is not against knowledge per se, but against a certain attitude toward it. The proper response to his warning is *humility*, not ignorance! Second, for every knowledgeable person who is arrogant, there is an unknowledgeable person who is defensive and proud as a cover-up for his or her lack of knowledge. Arrogance is not possessed solely by people who have developed their reasoning abilities.

SUMMARY

We Christians have a desire deep within us to be like God and to bring honor to His name. But what are we to look like if we are to fulfill these desires? In this chapter, I have not tried to give a full answer to that question. But a picture has emerged from several strands of biblical evidence, and that picture clearly implies that a growing, vibrant disciple will be someone who values his intellectual life and works at developing his mind carefully.

Two of the most prominent Christian leaders of this century are an evangelist and a pastor: Billy Graham and John Stott. Both have expressed their deep commitment to reason and the intellectual life. In 1981, Billy Graham was asked if it bothered him that so many evangelicals seem to be theologically illiterate. He answered, "It bothers me terribly, as much as anything I can think of."[12] Later, as the October 22, 1996, issue of *Parade* magazine reports, Graham was asked what he would do differently if given the chance. He replied, "I would have studied more. I would have gotten my Ph. D. in anthropology."[13] In the same vein, British pastor John Stott was asked to reflect on fifty years of ministry and give advice to a new generation of Christian leaders. Upon reflection, here was his response:

> I'd want to say so many things. But my main exhortation would
> be this: Don't neglect your critical faculties. Remember that
> God is a rational God, who has made us in His own image. God
> invites and expects us to explore His double revelation, in
> nature and Scripture, with the minds He has given us, and to go
> on in the development of a Christian mind to apply His mar-
> velous revealed truth to every aspect of the modern and
> post-modern world.[14]

Graham and Stott are expressing the very heart of New Testament religion. We neglect their admonitions to our own peril. In the next chapter, we will see exactly why the mind and its cultivation are so important for spiritual growth in God's kingdom.

The Mind's Role in Spiritual Transformation

X

*God usually exerts that power in connection with
certain prior conditions of the human mind,
and it should be ours to create, so far as we can,
with the help of God, those favourable conditions
for the reception of the gospel. False ideas
are the greatest obstacles to the reception of the gospel.
We may preach with all the fervour of a reformer
and yet succeed only in winning a straggler here and there,
if we permit the whole collective thought of the nation
or of the world to be controlled by ideas which,
by the resistless force of logic, prevent Christianity
from being regarded as anything more
than a harmless delusion.*

J. GRESHAM MACHEN[1]

I HAVE A CONFESSION TO MAKE. I AM NO FIX-IT MAN. IN FACT, ONE OF MY friends said that if I were considered a handyman, then Pee-Wee Herman would be an NFL lineman! Ouch! Because of my mechanical ineptness, I usually call for help when something breaks down or needs to be installed. However, last summer I worked up the courage to put in a ceiling fan. I break out in hives when I remember my first glance at the instructions (who writes these instructions, anyway?). I had to take it step by step, and I had absolutely no idea about the overall picture of what I was doing or why each step was located where it was. I finally got it in and, for eleven months, it has worked. A few days ago I tried to put in a second fan. Interestingly, it was as though I had never done one before. I couldn't remember a thing about how to do it, and I had to take it step-by step just as I had the first time.

My father is very different. He is literally a mechanical wizard. He usually throws instructions away, and when he does look at them it is only for a moment, and then he follows his own skill and knowhow. And if he does something once, he knows how to do it from then on. It sticks with him. Why is this the case with my dad but not with me? The answer is very simple. The more you know about something, the more you're able to see when you look at it, the more you can remember about it, and the less tied you will be to following a mindless series of steps in working with what you know. My father simply knows how things work and I don't. He sees the world mechanically; I see the world as a bloomin', buzzin' confusion.

Learning to value, develop, deepen, and use your intellect in the overall process of spiritual transformation is a lot like being a fix-it man. In chapters one and two, we examined the serious problems in society and the church due to an emergence of anti-intellectualism in the body of Christ. We also learned that there are solid biblical grounds for nurturing and developing our intellectual lives. But if this were all we had, we would be like a person tied to a step-by-step set of instructions. The information of chapters one and two would not stick very well, we would have to be reminded of it regularly, and we certainly would not see the world as a growing Christian thinker. What we need is an understanding of what the mind is and how it fits into the process of human transformation and spiritual growth. And that is what I want to discuss in this chapter.

NEW TESTAMENT TRANSFORMATION AND OLD TESTAMENT WISDOM

That the mind is the crucial component in the spiritual journey cannot be accurately denied. The apostle Paul's writings are probably the most complete set of biblical instructions about what individual and corporate discipleship are and how they are to be attained. Arguably, the most important text he ever penned about spiritual transformation is Romans 12:1-2. In this wise and tender admonition, the devotional master, Paul, puts his finger on the very essence of how we grow to become like Jesus: "Do not conform any longer to the pattern of this world," he tells us, "but be transformed by the renewing of your mind." "Renewing" is *anakainosis* in the Greek, and its meaning is fairly straightforward: making something new. Later in this chapter we will appreciate how appropriate this term is for describing what happens to the mind when it incorporates new thoughts and beliefs. "Mind" is *nous* and means "the intellect, reason, or the faculty of understanding."

We are so familiar with this verse that some of its oddness or peculiarity is lost on us. But to see how truly peculiar this teaching is, think of what Paul could have said but did not. He could have said, "Be transformed by developing close feelings toward God," or "by exercising your will in obeying biblical commands," or "by intensifying your desire for the right things," or "by fellowship and worship," and so on. Obviously, all are important parts of the Christian life. Yet Paul chose to mention none of them in his most important précis of the spiritual life. Why is that? What is it about the mind that justifies Paul's elevation of it to such a position of prominence in religious life?

In the preceding verse, Paul reminds us that we should offer our bodies to God because this is the most reasonable way to express service to Him in light of His mercies toward us. Paul mentions the body and its members—our faces, hands, tongues, feet—for two reasons. First, the body is the vehicle through which we interact with the world. For example, to get groceries, it is not enough for me just to think about the grocery store. I have to move my body and go to the store! Likewise, it is not enough to think about showing love to my wife or to feel a desire inside to evangelize a friend. In both cases, I have to move my body—I smile, use my tongue to bless or communicate, and so forth.

Second, my habits dwell in my body and its members. Some people frown so much, gossip so often, or eat certain soothing foods so regularly that routines and habits get deeply woven into their bodies. In the right circumstances, their faces are habituated to frown, their tongues to talk, and their legs to walk to the refrigerator *without even thinking about it*. To change our habits and to interact differently with the world, we need to retrain our bodies to form new habits that replace the old ones.

But how do we gain the motivation, the insights, the perspective necessary to change? Anyone who has struggled with bad habits knows that you don't become transformed by just willing the old habits to go away. This is why preaching that centers too much on exhortation without instruction is ineffective. According to Paul, the key to change is the formation of a new perspective, the development of fresh insights about our lives and the world around us, the gathering of the knowledge and skill required to know what to do and how to do it. And this is where the mind comes in. Truth, knowledge, and study are powerful factors in the transformation of the self and the control of the body and its habits for a healthy life in the kingdom of God.

Paul's teaching about the centrality of the intellect for spiritual renewal was not new. The Old Testament is pregnant with this same idea in its teaching about the nature and role of wisdom in life. It summons us to think long, hard, and carefully because God has placed His stamp of reason all about us:

> Do you know the ordinances of the heavens . . .
> Who has put wisdom in the innermost being,
> Or has given understanding to the mind? (Job 38:33,36, NASB)

As James L. Crenshaw says, "Wisdom is a particular attitude toward reality, a worldview. . . . That worldview assumes . . . the one God embedded truth within all reality."[2]

The Old Testament proclaims that the same rational God who reveals Himself to the prophets also created the world as an orderly, understandable cosmos. And the Old Testament assures us that this God made our minds to be apt for gaining knowledge and understanding so as to avoid foolish living and ignorant beliefs. For those willing to pay the price of exercising their minds and studying diligently, there is knowledge and wisdom to be found in Scripture (Psalm 119); in the natural world and its operations (Isaiah 28:23-29); and in the accumulated insights embedded in the art, literature, and science of the different cultures of the world (Isaiah 19:11-13; Jeremiah 49:7; Daniel 2:12-13, 5:7).

But just as surely as the Old Testament places a value on wisdom and knowledge, it warns us that they only come to the diligent:

> Make your ear attentive to wisdom,
> Incline your heart to understanding. (Proverbs 2:2, NASB)

We are to

> seek her [wisdom] as silver,
> And search for her as for hidden treasure. (2:4, NASB)

A wise life of virtue and knowledge comes to those who, with humility of heart and reverence for God, work hard at using their minds to study, to seek understanding, to capture truth.

But what is it about our makeup that requires us to use our minds in order to change? How does intellectual growth change the soul, and what is it about a well-formed mind that makes it so valuable for gaining a new way of seeing life?

In order to answer these questions, we will first examine the nature of the soul and the mind it contains and second, investigate how the mind relates to other aspects of human personality. Here is the thesis of the chapter: *The mind is the soul's primary vehicle for making contact with God, and it plays a fundamental role in the process of human maturation and change, including spiritual transformation. In thought, the mind's structure conforms to the order of the object of thought. Since this is so, and since truth dwells in the mind, truth itself is powerful and rationality is valuable as a means of obtaining truth and avoiding error. Therefore, God desires a life of intellectual growth and study for His children.*

THE STRUCTURE OF THE SOUL

The Soul and the Body

During a family time one evening, my sixth-grade daughter, Allison, complained that if only she could see God, say, sitting in a chair, then prayer would be much easier. I pointed out that not only had she never seen God, neither had she ever seen me. She could see my body, but she could not see my I, my self, my ego, nor could she see my thoughts, feelings, and so forth. Persons, I told her, are invisible objects and, since God is too big to have a body, He is not perceivable in the same way a chair or a person's body is.[3]

That evening, I expressed to Allison the Christian understanding of human persons. Historically and biblically, Christianity has held to a dualistic notion of the human being. A human being is a unity of two distinct realities—body and soul.[4] More specifically, I *am* my soul and I *have* a body. The soul, while not by nature immortal, is nevertheless capable of entering an intermediate disembodied state upon death and, eventually, being reunited with a resurrected body. The formal name for this position is "substance dualism." The soul (which is the same thing as the self or the I) is that immaterial, invisible thing that makes me a conscious, living human being. The soul is what I am aware of when I engage in various acts of introspection in which I am aware of what is going on "inside" me. I go where my soul goes. If God took my soul and put it into your body and placed your soul into my body, we would have different bodies. If my soul leaves my body, I leave my body because I am my soul.

What Am I?
During the Los Angeles riots following the Rodney King beating, a bystander said on a TV interview how surprised she was that people were acting like animals. What was unclear was why this should surprise anyone, given that we are taught all week long in public schools that this is exactly what we are—evolved animals. Our judgments about right and wrong, virtue and vice, and appropriate or inappropriate lifestyles depend largely upon what we take a human being to be. More personally, an individual's sense of well-being is in good measure a function of his or her self-concept. Thus, a proper grasp of what we are and how we function is foundational to a well-ordered society and a life well lived.

The Bible has a rich, deep anthropology expressed in terms like "soul," "spirit," "heart," and "mind."[5] Properly understood, they convey important insights about what we are and how we function. Terms in a language have a wide field of meaning. The term "red" can mean a color, being embarrassed, or being a communist. Caution should be exercised in grasping just exactly how the term is used in a specific context. For example, "my book is red" is not saying that my book is embarrassed or communist, even though these are correct meanings for "red" in other contexts.

Likewise, the biblical terms listed above have a wide variety of meanings. Sometimes they are used as synonyms, and on other occasions they have different nuances. We should be careful not to read all of the meanings associated with, say, "heart" into a specific passage.

Having said this, I want to sketch a brief portrait of the more important meanings of the biblical terms within our purview. When applied to the human being, the term "soul" sometimes stands for the total person, including the body (Genesis 2:7, KJV; Psalm 63:1). Frequently, however, the term refers to the total immaterial self, or "I," which can survive the destruction of the body (Matthew 10:28, John 12:25). It contains desires (2 Samuel 3:21) and emotions (Psalm 119:28), and the soul is what knows (Psalm 139:14) and exercises volition (Psalm 130:6, 119:129).

Sometimes "spirit" is used as a synonym for "soul." But "spirit" also refers to that aspect of human beings through which they relate to God (Psalm 51:10, Romans 8:16, Ephesians 4:23). "Heart" refers to the center of human personality (Proverbs 4:23), in which case it is equivalent to "soul." At other times, "heart" signifies the seat of volition and desire (Exodus 35:5, Deuteronomy 8:2, Romans 2:5), of feelings (Proverbs 14:30, 23:17), and of thought and reason (Deuteronomy 29:2-4, Psalm 90:12, Isaiah 65:17). Finally, the mind is that which reasons and thinks (Romans 14:5, Philippians 4:8, Colossians 3:2).

Does all this seem a bit complicated? Let's see if we can take these biblical terms, add some careful reflection, and develop a map of what is inside the soul.

What's Inside My Soul?

The soul is a very complicated thing with an intricate internal structure that we need to understand if we are to appreciate the mind's role in spiritual transformation. In order to understand that structure, we need to grasp two important issues: *the different types of states within the soul* and the notion of a *faculty of the soul*. The soul is a substantial, unified reality that informs its body. The soul is to the body what God is to space—it is fully "present" at each point within the body. Further, the soul and body relate to each other in a cause-effect way. For example, if

I worry in my soul, my brain chemistry[6] will change; if I exercise my will to raise my arm in my soul, the arm goes up. If I experience brain damage, this can cause me to lose the ability to remember certain things in my soul. And so forth. The soul also contains various mental states within it—for example, sensations, thoughts, beliefs, desires, and acts of will. This is not as complicated as it sounds. Water can be in a cold or a hot state. Likewise, the soul can be in a feeling or thinking state.

The Five States of the Soul
The soul contains more states than the five I just mentioned, but it will be helpful to single these out and explain them more fully. A *sensation* is a state of awareness or sentience, a mode of consciousness, for example, a conscious awareness of sound, color, or pain. A visual sensation, like an experience of a tree, is a state of the soul, not a state of the eyeballs. The eyes do not see. I (my soul) see with or by means of the eyes. The eyes, and the body in general, are instruments, tools the soul uses to experience the external world. Some sensations are experiences of things outside me like a tree or table. Others are awarenesses of other states within me like pains or itches. Emotions are a subclass of sensations and, as such, forms of awareness of things. I can be aware of something angrily or lovingly or fearfully.

A *thought* is a mental content that can be expressed in an entire sentence and that only exists while it is being thought. Some thoughts logically imply other thoughts. For example, "All dogs are mammals" entails "This dog is a mammal." If the former is true, the latter must be true. Some thoughts don't entail but merely provide evidence for other thoughts. For example, certain thoughts about evidence in a court case provide evidence for the thought that a person is guilty. A *belief* is a person's view, accepted to varying degrees of strength, of how things really are. If a person has a belief (for example, that it is raining), then that belief serves as the basis for the person's tendency or readiness to act as if the thing believed were really so (for example, the person gets an umbrella). At any given time, one can have many beliefs that are not currently being contemplated. A *desire* is a certain felt inclination to do, have, or experience certain things. Desires are either conscious or such that they can be made conscious through certain activities, for example, through therapy. An *act of will* is a volition or choice, an exercise of power, an endeavoring to do a certain thing.

The Faculties of the Soul Include the Mind and Spirit

In addition to its states, at any given time the soul has a number of capacities that are not currently being actualized or utilized. To understand this, consider an acorn. The acorn has certain actual characteristics or states—a specific size, shape, or color. But it also has a number of capacities or potentialities that could become actual if certain things happen. For example, the acorn has the capacity to grow a root system or change into the shape of a tree. Likewise, the soul has capacities. I have the ability to see color, think about math, or desire ice cream even when I am asleep and not in the actual states just mentioned.

Now, capacities come in hierarchies. There are first-order capacities, second-order capacities to have these first-order capacities, and so on, until ultimate capacities are reached. For example, if I can speak English but not Russian, then I have the first-order capacity for English as well as the second-order language capacity to have this first-order capacity (which I have already developed). I also have the second-order capacity to have the capacity to speak Russian, but I lack the first-order capacity to do so. Higher-order capacities are realized by the development of lower-order capacities under them. An acorn has the ultimate capacity to draw nourishment from the soil, but this can be actualized and unfolded only by developing the lower capacity to have a root system, then developing the still lower capacities of the root system, and so on. When something has a defect (for example, a child who is colorblind), it does not lose its ultimate capacities. Rather, it lacks some lower-order capacity it needs for the ultimate capacity to be developed.

The adult human soul has literally thousands of capacities within its structure. But the soul is not just a collection of isolated, discrete, randomly related internal capacities. Rather, the various capacities within the soul fall into natural groupings called *faculties* of the soul. In order to get hold of this, think for a moment about this list of capacities: the ability to see red, see orange, hear a dog bark, hear a tune, think about math, think about God, desire lunch, desire a family. Now it should be obvious that the ability to see red is more closely related to the ability to see orange than it is to the ability to think about math. We express this insight by saying that the abilities to see red or orange are parts of the same faculty—the faculty of sight. The ability to think about math is a capacity within the thinking faculty. In general, *a faculty is a compartment of the soul that contains a natural family of related capacities.*

We are now in a position to map out the soul in more detail. All the soul's capacities to see are part of the faculty of sight. If my eyeballs are defective, then my soul's faculty of sight will be inoperative just as a driver cannot get to work in his car if the spark plugs are broken. Likewise, if my eyeballs work but my soul is inattentive—say I am daydreaming—then I won't see what is before me either. The soul also contains faculties of smell, touch, taste, and hearing. Taken together, these five are called sensory faculties of the soul. The will is a faculty of the soul that contains my abilities to choose. The emotional faculty of the soul contains my abilities to experience fear, love, and so forth.

Two additional faculties of the soul are of crucial importance. The *mind* is that faculty of the soul that contains thoughts and beliefs along with the relevant abilities to have such things. It is with my mind that I think, and my mind contains my beliefs. The *spirit* is that faculty of the soul through which the person relates to God (Psalm 51:10, Romans 8:16, Ephesians 4:23).[7] Before the new birth, the spirit is real and has certain abilities to be aware of God. But most of the capacities of the unregenerate spirit are dead and inoperative. At the new birth, God implants new capacities in the spirit. These fresh capacities need to be nourished and developed so they can grow.

Scripture tells us that we are fearfully and wonderfully made, and this insight applies to the soul as well as the body. As we have seen, the soul contains a rich set of faculties within it and each faculty contains a large number of specifically ordered abilities. As we learn more about how the soul functions, it becomes clear that the abilities present in a faculty of the soul can have an impact on other abilities within that very faculty. For example, a person can be so enslaved to eating that he or she cannot say no to ice cream if it is in the freezer. The person simply does not have the volitional ability to refrain. But the person may very well have the second-order ability to develop the ability to refrain. If the person works on this second-order ability—for example, by choosing to ask one's self regularly (especially just prior to a snack attack!) what comfort need is being met by eating ice cream and finding alternative ways to meet that need—he or she can develop the first-order ability to refrain. The various spiritual disciplines of fasting, solitude, and so on work in just this way. They allow people to develop spiritual abilities that would be unavailable to them by direct effort.

Sometimes the abilities within one faculty of the soul affect those in another faculty. If my emotional faculty is filled with feelings of racial hatred for a certain person, then I will not be able to see that person as valuable and precious, nor will I be able to think deeply about working for his or her welfare. The fact that one faculty can affect others explains why the new birth has the potential of transforming every aspect of one's personality. Just as a seed grows to maturity, so the new spiritual life implanted in the soul can grow in its capacities. When this happens, the strengthened, maturing spirit can exert an influence on other aspects of the self. Similarly, a problem in a different faculty of the soul may need therapeutic counsel before a spiritual capacity can be developed.

Further, the body can impact my various faculties and vice versa. If my eyes are defective, I will not be able to use my faculty of sight to see anything. If I am angry or anxious much of the time, I can deplete my brain chemistry and this, in turn, can contribute to depression.[8] Though we are unified selves, nevertheless, we are complicated beings in which the various faculties of the soul interact with each other and with the body in a number of different ways. The ancient Greeks and the Fathers of the church were right to believe that a virtuous, mature person is an individual with a well-ordered soul. With this in mind, let us look at why that specific faculty of the soul, the mind, is of such importance for spiritual transformation and maturity in virtue.

THE MIND'S ROLE IN TRANSFORMATION

Beliefs, Behavior, and Character

Beliefs are the rails upon which our lives run. We almost always act according to what we really believe. It doesn't matter much what we say we believe or what we want others to think we believe. When the rubber meets the road, we act out our actual beliefs most of the time. That is why behavior is such a good indicator of a person's beliefs. Let us look, then, at five aspects of belief that are critical to the shape of our minds.

1. The content of a belief. A belief's impact on behavior is a function of three of the belief's traits: its content, strength, and centrality. The *content* of a belief helps determine how important the belief is for our character and behavior. *What* we believe matters—the actual content of what we believe about God, morality, politics, life after death, and so on will shape the contours of our lives and actions. In fact, the contents of one's beliefs are so important that, according to Scripture, our eternal destiny is determined by what we believe about Jesus Christ.

Today, people are inclined to think that the sincerity and fervency of one's beliefs are more important than the content. As long as we believe something honestly and strongly, we are told, then that is all that matters. Nothing could be further from the truth. Reality is basically indifferent to how sincerely we believe something. I can believe with all my might that my car will fly me to Hawaii or that homosexuality is caused solely by the brain, but that fervency doesn't change a thing. As far as reality is concerned, what matters is not whether I like a belief or how sincere I am in believing it but whether or not the belief is true. I am responsible for what I believe and, I might add, for what I refuse to believe because the content of what I do or do not believe makes a tremendous difference to what I become and how I act.

2. The strength of a belief. There is, however, more to a belief than its content. There is also its *strength* and centrality for the person who believes it. We are all familiar with the idea of a belief having strength. If you believe something, that does not mean you are certain that it is true. Rather, it means that you are at least more than 50 percent convinced the belief is true. If it were fifty-fifty for you, you wouldn't really have the belief in question. Instead, you would still be in a process of deciding whether or not you should adopt the belief. A belief's strength is the degree to which you are convinced the belief is true. As you gain evidence and support for a belief, its strength grows for you. It may start off as plausible and later become fairly likely, quite likely, beyond reasonable doubt, or completely certain. The more certain you are of a belief, the more it becomes a part of your very soul, and the more you rely on it as a basis for action.

3. The centrality of a belief. You may be less familiar with this concept than with the previous two, but with a little reflection the idea of *centrality* is easy to grasp. The centrality of a belief is the degree of importance the belief plays in your entire set of beliefs, that is, in your worldview. The more central a belief is, the greater the impact on one's worldview were the belief given up. My belief that prunes are good for me is fairly strong (even though I don't like the belief!), but it isn't very central for me. I could give it up and not have to abandon or adjust very many other beliefs I hold. But my beliefs in absolute morality, life after death, or the Christian faith are very central for me—more central now, in fact, than just after my conversion in 1968. If I were to lose these beliefs, my entire set of beliefs would undergo a radical reshuffling—more so now than in, say, 1969. As I grow, some of my beliefs come to play a more central role in the entire way I see life.

4. How do we change beliefs? In sum, the content, strength, and centrality of a person's beliefs play a powerful role in determining the person's character and behavior. But here is an apparent paradox about one's beliefs. On the one hand, Scripture holds us responsible for our beliefs since it commands us to embrace certain beliefs and warns us of the consequences of accepting other beliefs. On the other hand, experience teaches us that we cannot choose or change our beliefs by direct effort. For example, if someone offered you $10,000 to believe right now that a pink elephant was sitting next to you, you could not really choose to believe this in spite of having a good motive to do so!

Happily, there is a way out of this paradox: we *can* change our beliefs *indirectly*. If I want to change my beliefs about something, I can embark on a course of study in which I choose to think regularly about certain things, read certain pieces of evidence and argument, and try to find problems with evidence raised against the belief in question. More generally, by choosing to undertake a course of study, meditation, and reflection, I can put myself in a position to undergo a change in the content, strength, and centrality of my beliefs. (We will look more at these truths in chapters four and five.) And if these kinds of changes in belief are what cause a change in my character and behavior, then I will be transformed by these belief changes. This is exactly why Paul tells us to be transformed by *the renewing of the mind*, because it is precisely activities of the mind that change these three aspects of belief, which, in turn, transform our character and behavior.

5. How beliefs form the plausibility structure of a culture. There is a critical corollary of this insight. I will never be able to change my life if I cannot even entertain the belief needed to bring about that change. By "entertain a belief" I mean to consider the *possibility* that the belief *might* be true. If you are hateful and mean to someone at work, you will have to change what you believe about the person before you will treat him or her differently. But if you cannot even entertain the thought that he or she is a good person worthy of kindness, you won't change.

There is a straightforward application here for evangelism. A person's plausibility structure is the set of ideas the person either is or is not willing to entertain as possibly true. For example, no one would come to a lecture defending a flat earth because this idea is just not part of our plausibility structure. We cannot even entertain the idea. Moreover, a person's plausibility structure is a function of the beliefs he or she already has. Applied to evangelism, J. Gresham Machen got it right when he said:

> God usually exerts that power in connection with certain prior conditions of the human mind, and it should be ours to create, so far as we can, with the help of God, those favourable conditions for the reception of the gospel. False ideas are the greatest obstacles to the reception of the gospel. We may preach with all the fervour of a reformer and yet succeed only in winning a straggler here and there, if we permit the whole collective thought of the nation or of the world to be controlled by ideas which, by the resistless force of logic, prevent Christianity from being regarded as anything more than a harmless delusion.[9]

If a culture reaches the point where Christian claims are not even part of its plausibility structure, fewer and fewer people will be able to entertain the possibility that they might be true. Whatever stragglers do come to faith in such a context would do so on the basis of felt needs alone, and the genuineness of such conversions would be questionable to say the least. This is why apologetics is so crucial to evangelism. It seeks to create a plausibility structure in a person's mind, "favourable conditions" as Machen puts it, so the gospel can be entertained by a person. To plant a seed in someone's mind in pre-evangelism is to present a person with an idea that will work on his or her plausibility structure to create a space in which Christianity can be entertained seriously. If this is important to evangelism, it is strategically crucial that local churches think about how they can address those aspects of the modern worldview that place Christianity outside the plausibility structures of so many.

Our modern post-Christian society is perilously close to regarding Christian claims as mere figments in the minds of the faithful. Speaking of fundamentalists after the Scopes trial in 1925, historian George Marsden observes that they could not "raise the level of discourse to a plane where any of their arguments would be taken seriously. Whatever they said would be overshadowed by the pejorative associations attached to the movement by the seemingly victorious secular establishment."[10] Tragically, as we approach the twenty-first century, our current context for proclaiming Christian truth is even worse than it was in the decades following 1925. During those decades, at least *argumentation* was considered relevant to making or accepting religious claims. But now, religious assertions are regarded as mere expressions of private belief or emotion, far below the level needed for argument itself to be considered at all relevant.

In summary, the plausibility, content, strength, and centrality of our beliefs play a key role in determining our character and behavior. And various activities of thought and study affect our beliefs and thereby impact our character and behavior. Because thoughts and beliefs are contained in the mind, intellectual development and the renewal of the mind transform our lives.

The Mind's Role in Seeing, Willing, Feeling, and Desiring

1. How three types of seeing feed our minds. The mind plays an important role in determining what a person is able to see, will, feel, and desire. If this is true, then intellectual development can pay rich dividends in the changes that result in one's other faculties. In order to focus our thoughts about this topic, let us consider the mind's role in the process of seeing. Philosophers distinguish three different kinds of seeing.

Consider an ordinary case of seeing a dog. First, there is *simple seeing:* having the dog directly present to you in your visual field and noticing the dog. You don't need to have a concept of what a dog is to see one. For example, a little child could see a dog without having a concept of what a dog is supposed to be. In fact, you don't even need to be thinking about a dog to see it. I could see a dog while looking out my window as I ponder the topic of this chapter. Even though I wouldn't be thinking about the dog, I could still see it and, later, recall from memory the dog's color. In simple seeing, a person sees merely by means of the soul's faculty of sight.

Second, there is *seeing as.* Here I see an object as being something or other. I may see the dog as a dog. I may even see the dog as a cat if the lighting is poor and I have been led to believe that only cats, but no dogs, live in the area. I can see the dog as my neighbor's favorite pet. An act of seeing as involves classifying the object of sight as an example of a mental concept, and concepts are located in the mind. Thus, an act of seeing as requires both the faculties of sight and mind working together. When I see a dog as a dog, I must have some concept of what it is to be a dog and apply this concept to the object I am seeing. I could not see a dog as a dog the first time I saw one since I wouldn't have the relevant concept yet.[11] Likewise, to see a dog as my neighbor's favorite pet, I need the concept of a neighbor, a pet, and being a favorite.

Third, there is *seeing that*. Here one judges with the mind that some perceptual belief is true. If I see *that* the dog is my neighbor's favorite pet, I judge that this belief is true of the object I am seeing. If I merely see the dog as my neighbor's favorite pet, I don't really have to think this is true. I may just be playing with different concepts in my mind. I may be thinking, *What would it be like to see this dog as my neighbor's favorite pet?* even though I don't think it really is.

2. How a developed mind helps us see. Simple seeing only involves the faculty of sight. But seeing as and seeing that involve the mind. This is why the more one knows, the more one can see. A doctor and I can look at the same skin problem (a case of simple seeing), but he observes more than I do. Why? Because his mind is filled with medical concepts and beliefs I do not have, which enable him to notice things I fail to observe. He can see the sore as a basal cell or as a squamous cell carcinoma—that is, he can look at the skin area in both ways to be in a position to look for the right things, so that he can identify it, or "see it as," a basal cell. I cannot do this because my mind lacks the relevant intellectual categories the doctor possesses. I can stare at the same sore all day long and not see what he sees.

Consider another example. Last week the evening news covered a march on Washington in favor of children's rights. A congresswoman made the following argument: "Government should honor children's rights. Therefore, just as the government should vouchsafe a child's right not to be molested, so it should do so for a child's right to government-sponsored day care."

Now, what is wrong with this argument as it stands? Do you see what I see in this piece of reasoning? It may help your seeing if I place a mental distinction in your mind: the distinction between negative and positive rights. A negative right is a right to be protected from some sort of harm. Negative rights place a duty on the government to keep others from doing something to me. A positive right is a right to have something provided for me. Positive rights place a duty on the government to force others (for instance by taxation) to do something for me. For example, if health care is a negative right, the government must see to it that I can get whatever health care I can afford by my own labor unhindered by unfair limitations based on race, creed, or gender. But if health care is a positive right, the government has a duty to raise the taxes sufficient to provide me with health care.

In the congresswoman's argument about children's rights, she fails to make this distinction. Moreover, many people believe that New Testament teaching on the state implies that it is responsible for protecting negative rights, not for providing positive ones. The issue here is not that these people (conservatives) are correct in this regard (though I think they are). The issue is that, for a long time, the distinction between negative and positive rights has been recognized, and many informed political philosophers have raised arguments against positive rights. This means that a person cannot simply assert that because the government should guard a child's negative right to be protected against abuse, it is also the government's duty to provide day care for children.

A person could read the congresswoman's statement several times and not see this issue if he or she did not have the intellectual concepts and beliefs already in mind. This example illustrates the way knowledge helps one see things unavailable to one who has not developed his or her intellect in the relevant area of study.

We often read the Bible, hear the news, listen to a sermon, or talk to friends, yet we don't get much out of it. One central reason for this may be our lack of knowledge and intellectual growth. The more you know, the more you see and hear because your mind brings more to the task of "seeing as" or "seeing that." In fact, the more you know about extrabiblical matters, the more you will see in the Bible. Why? Because you will see distinctions in the Bible or connections between Scripture and an issue in another area of life that would not be possible without the concepts and categories placed in the mind's structure by gaining the relevant knowledge in those extrabiblical areas of thought. Thus, general intellectual development can enrich life and contribute to Bible study and spiritual formation.

There is a closely related reason why intellectual development can enhance spiritual development: The mind forms habits and falls into ruts. One day at a chapel meeting, a missions professor showed a film clip of a foreign culture unfamiliar to most of us. He asked us to write down everything we noticed. He then showed the clip a second time and asked us to repeat the exercise. Everyone in the chapel meeting compared his or her first and second lists and, in every case, they were virtually identical! The professor's lesson: our minds get into ruts in which we tend to look for things we have already seen in order to validate our earlier perceptions. We seldom look at things from entirely fresh perspectives!

If we're honest with ourselves, we have to admit that we get into ruts in our thinking and develop habits of thought that can grow stale after a while. This is where renewing the mind comes in. A life of study can give us a constant source of new categories and beliefs that will lead to fresh new insights and stave off intellectual boredom. Many people become bored with the Bible precisely because their overall intellectual growth is stagnant. They cannot get new insights from Scripture because they bring the same old categories to Bible study and look to validate their old habits of thought.

3. How the mind interacts with other parts of the person. Space forbids me to develop in depth the mind's role in shaping our willing, feeling, and desiring. But it should be easy to apply our discussion of the mind's role in seeing to these other areas of human functioning. I can't choose to do something if I don't know what it is or how it works. I can't desire something if I don't believe it is good, valuable, and desirable. I can't feel tender toward someone if my thoughts and beliefs about that person run in the opposite direction.

It is true that the other faculties of the soul affect the mind too. And an overall strategy for personal growth should work on developing and integrating every facet of human personality under Christ's lordship. Still, I think the mind stands out for special emphasis because it is so neglected today by many Christians. The contemporary Christian mind is starved, and as a result we have small, impoverished souls.

The Mind, Truth, and Reality

There is another reason why the mind warrants special emphasis. Of all the soul's faculties, the mind is the one that ponders, contains, and judges truth and falsity. The mind places me in contact with the external world, and when functioning properly it conforms itself to the nature of the object of thought itself. As Richard Foster puts it:

The ingrained habits of thought that are formed *will* conform to the order of the thing being studied. *What* we study determines what kind of habits are to be formed. That is why Paul urged us to center on things that are true, honorable, just, pure, lovely and gracious.[12]

To understand this, let us consider two features of the mind: intentionality and internal structure.

1. The intentionality of the mind. Intentionality refers to the "of-ness" or "about-ness" of our mental states. We have a thought of God, a hope for a new car, a belief about the media. The mind points *beyond itself* to the objects we use our minds to contemplate. Because of intentionality, thought puts us in contact with the external world. For example, if I am in Los Angeles, I can be in direct contact with London by thinking about it. My mind is directed on London, and it makes contact with this object of thought. After all, I am not thinking about the word "London" (unless someone asks me to spell it) or something else; I am thinking about London itself.

2. The internal structure of the mind. Second, when we come to understand something, the mind develops a conceptualization of the thing so understood. If I come to understand the workings of a car, my mind will possess a conceptualization of those workings. If my understanding is accurate, the conceptualization in my mind will conform to the car itself. If my mind develops a conceptualization of morality, then there will be an order in my mind that locates the role of virtue and character in the overall moral life. If accurate, this conception of the role of virtue will conform to the nature of true morality that actually exists outside my mind.

If my conceptualizations are false, I will fail to grasp the object as it really is. But if my mind conforms to the nature of the object itself, I will not only grasp it truly but also gain a certain power that comes from a correct understanding of reality. Just as electricity was real but its power unavailable to us until Ben Franklin's discovery opened our minds to grasp the true nature of electricity, so the power of the spiritual life is real but unavailable to us if we don't understand the true nature of prayer, fasting, and so forth. This is why truth is so powerful. *It allows us to cooperate with reality, whether spiritual or physical, and tap into its power.* As we learn to think correctly about God, specific scriptural teachings, the soul, or other important aspects of a Christian worldview, we are placed in touch with God and those realities. And we thereby gain access to the power available to us to live in the kingdom of God.

SUMMARY

It may be a good idea at this point to stop and ask yourself how you are feeling and thinking about all of this. In chapter one we saw that modern Christianity has become anti-intellectual, resulting in a softened impact for Christ and has contributed to the secularization of American culture. In chapter two we wove together several strands of evidence that assure us of the biblical basis for the importance of the intellectual life and the cultivation of the mind. And in this chapter we have seen just how the mind works in affecting the transformation of our lives in the spiritual sojourn so important to all disciples of Jesus.

However, several years of teaching have led me to believe that you may still feel a certain sense of resistance to the idea that Christians should be concerned with developing intellectual lives. For many, this idea feels risky and can create a sense of a loss of control about where such a quest might lead them at the end of the day. For others, there is a sense of guilt or inadequacy about this whole topic. In the next chapter, I will identify and address certain enemies of the Christian mind, certain foes that hinder us in our spiritual journey.

HOW TO DEVELOP A MATURE CHRISTIAN MIND

X

CHAPTER FOUR

Harassing the Hobgoblins of the Christian Mind

X

The empty self is filled up with consumer goods,
calories, experiences, politicians, romantic partners,
and empathetic therapists. . . . [The empty self] experiences
a significant absence of community, tradition,
and shared meaning, . . . a lack of personal conviction
and worth, and it embodies the absences as a chronic,
undifferentiated emotional hunger.

PHILIP CUSHMAN[1]

K

Neurosis is always a substitute for legitimate suffering.

CARL JUNG[2]

K

In their uncompromising determination to proclaim truth,
Christians must avoid the intellectual flabbiness
of the larger society. They must rally against the prevailing
distrust of reason and the exaltation of the irrational.
Emotional self-indulgence and irrationalities have always
been the enemies of the gospel, and the apostles
warned their followers against them.

HERBERT SCHLOSSBERG[3]

H AVE YOU EVER INADVERTENTLY LOOKED AT THE SUN AND THEN CLOSED your eyes? What did you see? Most likely two spots. Have you ever tried to examine those spots? I did once, and was immediately presented with a difficulty. When I closed my eyes and tried to focus my attention on the spots, they would move and stay at a place in my visual field just ahead of the center of my focus. After a minute of chasing the spots around in my consciousness, I finally figured out what to do. I looked past the spots and focused my attention on a point in the background. When I did this, the spots stabilized and came into focus in the foreground of my awareness!

According to Jesus of Nazareth, our lives are very much like these spots. If we spend all of our time trying to look directly at ourselves, our lives dart around, become unstable, and get drastically out of focus. However, if we deny ourselves daily for Christ's sake (Matthew 16:24-27)—that is, if we gaze past ourselves and stare at Him with dedication and affection—as a byproduct we come into focus and stabilize in the foreground. This sort of self-denial actually requires a strong, integrated self. An immature, fragmented, narcissistic person cannot bring himself or herself to live with this sort of focus and discipline.

The intellectual life requires the same sort of self-denial and dedication to be part of a larger life of spiritual power and productivity for the kingdom of God. For Christians, the intellectual life of cultivating the mind and valuing rationality makes sense and receives its proper motivation and balance when seen as part of an overall view of what life is all about. The purpose of life is to bring honor to God, to know, love, and obey Him, to become like Him, and to live for His purposes in this world as I prepare to live in the next one. A life that is intentionally lived for this purpose will be characterized by certain attitudes and actions. For one thing, if I am to progress in this sort of life, I must regularly live for a larger whole. I must live for the kingdom of God and be involved aggressively in the war between that kingdom and the kingdom of darkness.

Further, while self-interest and personal joy are important components of Christian motivation, they are not adequate in and of themselves to carry the weight of a skillful Christian life. I must also seek to live for others. Among other things, this means that I need to discover my vocation, my overall calling in life, composed of my talents, spiritual gifts, historical circumstances, and so forth. And I should passionately seek to occupy my vocational place for the good of believers and unbelievers alike. This would be my understanding of the good life. Make no mistake about it. Such a life is not easy. It involves discipline, hard work, suffering, patience, and endurance in forming habits conducive to and characteristic of this kind of life. It requires taking a long-haul view of life and learning to defer gratification if required of me in my sojourn. And I must develop intellectual and moral virtues and habits before I can become fully skilled at living this way.

Unfortunately, the intellectual life, the life of intentional, habitual cultivation of my mind under Christ's lordship, can be valued and entered into only as a part of the overall approach to life just described, and this approach runs contrary to the conditions that define our modern lifestyles. Many people today, including many Christians, simply do not read or think deeply at all. And when believers do read, they tend to browse self-help books or other literature that is not intellectually engaging. I once wrote a piece for what is most likely the top Christian periodical of the last thirty years, and I was warned to keep my prose to about an eighth-grade level. How far we have come since the time of Joseph Butler (1692-1752) when, as one historian put it, the church could still out-think her critics. Butler was an Anglican minister at Rolls Chapel in England. His fifteen-part sermon series on ethics is regarded as one of the finest pieces of moral reasoning in the history of philosophy and has, in the words of philosopher Stephen L. Darwall, "influenced moral philosophy ever since."[4]

The mind is like a muscle. If it is not exercised regularly and strenuously, it loses some of its capacities and strength. We modern evangelicals often feel small and without influence in the public square. We must recapture our intellectual heritage if we are to present to our brothers and sisters, our children, and a post-Christian culture a version of Christianity rich and deep enough to challenge the dehumanizing structures and habits of thought of a society gone mad. To do this, we must change our reading habits; indeed, we must alter our entire approach to the life of the mind as part of Christian discipleship.

This chapter offers help doing this in two ways. First, we will look at the modern emergence of the empty self and see how it has shaped our intellectual habits or lack thereof. Second, we will identify some specific hobgoblins—mischievous little enemies—of the life of the mind and offer advice for defeating them.

The Empty Self as a Hobgoblin to the Life of the Mind

Seven Traits of the Empty Self

In modern American culture, what psychologists call the empty self has emerged in epidemic proportion. The empty self is constituted by a set of values, motives, and habits of thought, feeling, and behavior that perverts and eliminates the life of the mind and makes maturation in the way of Christ extremely difficult. There are several traits of the empty self that undermine intellectual growth and spiritual development.

1. The empty self is inordinately individualistic. A few years ago, I was sitting in an elementary school gym with other parents at a DARE graduation (a public school program designed to help children say no to drugs) for my daughter's sixth-grade class. Five sixth graders were about to read brief papers expressing their reasons for saying no to drugs. I leaned over to the couple sitting next to me and made a prediction: each paper, I said, would be a variation of the same reason for refusing to take drugs: *self-interest.* Sure enough, student after student said he or she would refuse drugs because of a desire to stay healthy, become a doctor or athlete, or do well in school. Conspicuous by its absence was one single reference to virtue or duty to community.

Not one student anathematized drug use because of the shame it would bring to family, community, or God. Individualistic reasons were the only ones given, a fact to be expected in a generation whose moral education is *exhausted* by values clarification. By contrast, when a Japanese ice skater fell during an Olympic performance a few years ago, her main concern was *not* the endorsement opportunities she had lost. She feared that shame had been brought onto her family and people. Community loomed large in the way she understood her own sense of self.

A healthy form of individualism is a good thing. Sadly, we have all known people who fail to draw appropriate boundaries and do not separate and individuate from others in a healthy way. Such people do not think or feel for themselves, they are easy to manipulate, and their well-being is far too dependent on what others think of them. A person with a healthy individualism learns to avoid these problems in order *mutually* to depend upon and relate to members of the body of Christ. This sort of individualism produces strong selves who have the power to practice self-denial to enrich the broader groups (for example, family, church) of which they are a part. But the empty self-populating American culture is a self-contained individual who defines his or her own life goals, values, and interests as though he or she were a human atom, isolated from others with little need or responsibility to live for the concerns of the broader community.[5] Self-contained individuals do their own thing and seek to create meaning by looking within their own selves. But as psychologist Martin Seligman warns, ". . . the self is a very poor site for finding meaning."[6]

2. The empty self is infantile. It is widely recognized that adolescent personality traits are staying with people longer today than in earlier generations, sometimes manifesting themselves into the early thirties. Created by a culture filled with pop psychology, schools and media that usurp parental authority, and television ads that seem to treat everyone like a teenager, the infantile part of the empty self needs instant gratification, comfort, and soothing. The infantile person is controlled by infantile cravings and constantly seeks to be filled up with and made whole by food, entertainment, and consumer goods. Such a person is preoccupied with sex, physical appearance, and body image and tends to live by feelings and experiences. For the infantile personality type, pain, endurance, hard work, and delayed gratification are anathema. Pleasure is all that matters, and it had better be immediate. Boredom is the greatest evil, amusement the greatest good.

3. The empty self is narcissistic. Narcissism is an inordinate and exclusive sense of self-infatuation in which the individual is preoccupied with his or her own self-interest and personal fulfillment.[7] Narcissists manipulate relationships with others, including God, to validate their own self-esteem and cannot sustain deep attachments or make personal commitments to something larger than their own ego. Narcissists are superficial and aloof and prefer to "play it cool" and "keep their options open." Self-denial is out of the question.

The Christian narcissist brings a Copernican revolution to the Christian faith. Historically, the Copernican revolution dethroned the earth from the center of the universe and put the sun in its place. Spiritually, the narcissist dethrones God and His purposes in history from the center of the religious life and replaces them with his or her own personal fulfillment.

The narcissist evaluates the local church, the right books to read, and the other religious practices worthy of his or her time on the basis of how they will further his or her own agenda. God becomes another tool in a narcissistic bag of tricks, along with the car, workouts at the fitness center, and so on—things that exist as mere instruments to facilitate a life defined largely independent of a biblical worldview.

Narcissists see education solely as a means to enhance their own careers. The humanities and general education that historically were part of a university curriculum to help develop people with the intellectual and moral *virtues* necessary for a life directed at the common good, just don't fit into the narcissist's plans. As Christopher Lasch notes, "[Narcissistic] students object to the introduction of requirements in general education because the work demands too much of them and seldom leads to lucrative employment."[8]

4. The empty self is passive. The couch potato is the role model for the empty self, and without question, modern Americans are becoming increasingly passive in their approach to life. We let other people do our living and thinking for us: the pastor studies the Bible for us, the news media does our political thinking for us, and we let our favorite sports team exercise, struggle, and win for us. From watching television to listening to sermons, our primary agenda is to be amused and entertained. Holidays have become vacations. Historically, a "holiday" was a "holy day," an intrinsically valuable, special, active change of pace in which, through proactive play and recreation, you refresh your soul. A "vacation" is a "vacating"—even the language is passive—in order to let someone else amuse you. The passive individual is a self in search of pleasure and consumer goods provided by others. Such an individual increasingly becomes a shriveled self with less and less ability to be proactive and take control of life.

Many factors have contributed to the emergence of passivity as an aspect of the empty self. But in my view, television is the chief culprit, and its impact begins early in life. Elementary school children watch an average of twenty-five hours of television per week, and high schoolers spend six times as many hours watching television as they invest doing homework.[9] Studies indicate that such widespread television viewing induces mental passivity, retards motivation and the ability to stick to something, negatively affects reading skills (especially those needed for higher-level mental comprehension), weakens the ability to listen and stay focused, and encourages an overall passive withdrawal from life.[10] The widespread passivity of the empty self explains the proliferation of magazines like *People*, of television shows like *Entertainment Tonight*, and of an overidentification with sports teams and figures. Passive people do not have lives of their own, so they must live vicariously through the lives of others, and celebrities become the codependent enablers of a passive lifestyle. The very idea of a Christian celebrity is an oxymoron. But for the passive, empty self, it is a spiritual life-support system.

5. The empty self is sensate. As Christopher Lasch has observed, "Modern life is . . . thoroughly mediated by electronic images."[11] Lasch goes on to point out that today, we make decisions and even judge what is and is not real on the basis of sense images. If it's on TV, it's real. Advertisements sell us things based on images, not on thoughtful content about a product. Neil Postman complains that "on television, discourse is conducted largely through visual imagery, which is to say that television gives us a conversation in images, not words."[12]

The emergence of the sensate self has produced two disastrous results. For one thing, people no longer base their decisions on a careful use of abstract reasoning in assessing the pertinent issues, nor are they as capable of doing so compared to earlier generations when thought was communicated by writing and abstract ideas, not by images.

For another thing, people are coming to believe more and more that the sense-perceptible world is all there is. In 1941, Harvard sociologist Pitirim A. Sorokin wrote a book entitled *The Crisis of Our Age*.[13] In it, Sorokin claimed that cultures come in two major types: sensate and ideational. In a sensate culture people believe only in the reality of the physical universe capable of being experienced with the five senses. A sensate culture is secular, this-worldly, and empirical. By contrast, an ideational culture embraces the sensory world but also accepts the notion that an extra-empirical, immaterial reality can be known as well—a reality consisting in God, the soul, immaterial beings, values, purposes, and various abstract objects like numbers and propositions. Sorokin claimed that a sensate culture will eventually disintegrate because it lacks the intellectual resources necessary to sustain a public and private life conducive of corporate and individual human flourishing. And this is precisely what we see happening to modern American culture. The widespread emergence of the sensate self has caused us to be shallow, small-souled people.

6. The empty self has lost the art of developing an interior life. In a fascinating study, Roy Baumeister traces the changing views of the self and of success from medieval to modern times.[14] According to Baumeister, the self used to be defined in terms of internal traits of virtue and morality, and the successful person, the person of honor and reputation, was the person with deep character. In such a view, the cultivation of an interior life through intellectual reflection and spiritual formation was of critical importance. In the last few decades, however, the self has come to be defined in terms of external factors—the ability to project a pleasurable, powerful personality and the possession of consumer goods—and the quest for celebrity status, image, pleasure, and power has become the preoccupation of a self so defined. A careful development of an inner life is simply irrelevant in such a view of the good life.

7. The empty self is hurried and busy. Finally, the empty self is a *hurried, busy* self gorged with activities and noise. As Philip Cushman observes, "The empty self is filled up with consumer goods, calories, experiences, politicians, romantic partners, and empathetic therapists. . . . [The empty self] experiences a significant absence of community, tradition, and shared meaning, . . . a lack of personal conviction and worth, and it embodies the absences as a chronic, undifferentiated emotional hunger."[15]

Because the empty self has a deep emotional emptiness and hunger, and because it has devised inadequate strategies to fill that emptiness, a frenzied pace of life emerges to keep the pain and emptiness suppressed. One must jump from one activity to another and not be exposed to quiet for very long or the emptiness will become apparent. Such a lifestyle creates a deep sense of fatigue in which passivity takes over. And fatigued people either do not have the energy to read or, when they do, choose undemanding material. Shortly after noting that our capacity to think is on the decrease today, writer Robert Banks correctly observes that, frequently, the modern individual is too rushed and distracted to "look for something to 'improve his mind,' demand an effort from him[self], or give rise to reflection, awareness or sustained thought."[16] Distraction and noise are enemies of an intellectual and spiritual life; focus and quiet are its friends.

Empty Selves Are a Danger to Society and the Church

A society filled with empty selves is a morally bankrupt, intellectually shallow society. To cite but one example: many people approach the abortion debate not on the basis of a thoughtful analysis of the relevant arguments, but from an infantile craving to seek promiscuous sexual soothing of the empty self free from any responsibility or consequences. Moreover, a church with largely empty selves is an immature, dysfunctional church. It is clear that the empty self is contrary to the nature of the mature follower of Jesus Christ.

The empty self is also the enemy of the Christian mind and its cultivation. Try to think about what a church filled with empty selves would look like in a culture. What would be the theological understanding, the reading habits, the evangelistic courage, the articulate cultural penetration of such a church? Pretty inadequate, I'm afraid. If the interior life does not really matter all that much, why spend the time reading and trying to develop an interior, intellectual, spiritually mature life? If someone is basically passive, he or she will just not make the effort to read, preferring instead to be entertained. If a person is sensate in orientation, music, magazines filled with pictures, and visual media in general will be more important than mere words on a page or abstract thoughts. If one is hurried and distracted, one will have little patience for theoretical knowledge and too short of an attention span to stay with an idea while it is being carefully developed. Instead, there will be a rush to get to the bottom line, an overemphasis on practical application and how-tos, a *Reader's Digest* approach to sermon evaluation or reading selection.

And if someone is overly individualistic, infantile, and narcissistic, what will that person read, if he or she reads at all? Such a person will read Christian self-help books that are filled with self-serving content, many slogans, simplistic moralizing, a lot of stories and pictures, and inadequate diagnosis of issues that place no demand on the reader. Books about Christian celebrities will be selected to allow the reader to live vicariously through the celebrity. What will not be read are books that equip people to engage in "destroying speculations . . . raised up against the knowledge of God" (2 Corinthians 10:5, NASB), develop a well-reasoned, theological understanding of the Christian religion, and fill their role in the broader kingdom of God for the common good and the cause of Christ. Eventually a church without readers or with readers with the tastes just listed will become a marginalized, easily led group of Christians impotent to stand against the powerful forces of secularism that threaten to bury Christian ideas under a veneer of soulless pluralism and misguided scientism. In such a context, the church will be tempted to measure her success largely in terms of numbers—numbers achieved by cultural accommodation to empty selves. In this way, as Os Guinness has reminded us, the church will become her own grave digger; her means of short-term "success" will turn out to be the very thing that marginalizes her in the long run.[17]

Casting Out the Empty Self

I'm afraid there are no quick solutions to the problem of the empty self, and we cannot simplify its impact on the Christian mind. I devote a good deal of chapter eight to how we can change the local church in order to defeat the empty self and develop a Christian intellectual life both personally and in our corporate presence in the world. But for now, I want to list briefly suggestions that in one way or another focus on developing a set of habits that are conducive to the development of the Christian mind in order to replace the habits of the empty self that are inimical to the Christian life. The battle here will be won or lost in the area of habits.

1. Admit the problem. First, we must admit that this is a problem and we need to inform others about it. We do ourselves or our God no good if we hide from the fact that the empty self threatens all of us. Any movement that brings about lasting changes begins with consciousness raising. Start talking with your Christian friends about the value of the Christian mind. Mention the empty self in your Sunday school class, your home Bible study, and so on. Talk to your children about developing their intellectual abilities for the service of Christ and His people. Before a problem can be solved, it must be carefully defined and clearly acknowledged.

2. Choose to be different. Second, at some point we need to make a fundamental decision that we will be different no matter what the cost. We Christians simply must admit that we have allowed our culture to squeeze us into its mold. We must stand against the culture (including inappropriate tendencies in the evangelical subculture), resist the empty self, and eschew the intellectual flabbiness that goes along with it. Motivation is a key here. I am no expert on motivation, but I do have one piece of advice, derived from almost thirty years of ministry: Expose yourself to ideas with which you disagree and let yourself be motivated to excel intellectually by the exposure. Listen to talk shows, read the editorial page, and walk around a local university and look at bulletin boards or read the student newspaper. Get into discussions with people at work with whom you differ. The point is to spend time around those who do not simply reinforce your own ways of looking at things. There are two advantages to this. For one thing, we can learn from our critics. For another, such exposure can move us to realize just how serious the war of ideas really is and how inadequately prepared we are to engage in that contest.

3. Change your routine. Third, for one week, note two things on a sheet of paper. First, observe your energy rhythms. When is your energy at a low point during the day and when is it vigorous? Second, note what you tend to do when you get home from work or just after you have finished eating dinner. Often, when our energy is low or when we get home from work or finish dinner, we go into a passive mode and turn on the television. I believe that an intellectual life is easier to develop if a person learns to limit television watching and spends more time getting physical exercise. I don't think I have to defend limiting television watching in this regard, but what about exercise? Your mind becomes more alert and you have more energy to be proactive and to read if you are in good shape.[18] I tell my graduate students that if they want to get the most out of the intellectual opportunities of graduate school, then they must learn to use low-energy times, or moments like after work or dinner, as occasions to engage in physical exercise. Try something. After dinner go for a walk instead of turning on the TV. When you get back, sit down for thirty minutes to an hour and read an intellectually challenging book. The important thing here is to get out of passive ruts, especially those passive couch potato moments, and replace old habits with new ones that create energy to read, reflect, and be more proactive.

4. Develop patience and endurance. Fourth, learn how to suffer and develop patient endurance. A life of intellectual cultivation takes effort. And it can be painful. The mind is like a muscle: it needs to be stretched beyond itself. I often read books that are a little over my head so I can develop my intellectual strength. Also, it often takes time to work through an important topic with sufficient care and attention. One needs to take a long-term perspective toward reading and study. But such a perspective will require endurance in staying put in a chair, with pen in hand, long enough to read deeply and widely. This requires a spirit of quietness and an absence of distraction. If you are fidgety and have to get up every fifteen minutes, you must get control of yourself. And gaining such control will require self-denial, suffering, and endurance. The intellectual life is both a means to and a result of a life of discipline, self-control, and endurance.

The best way to develop these traits is to practice the spiritual disciplines, especially solitude and fasting. Through solitude, I am learning to be quiet, alone, and focused. Through fasting, I am learning to say no to immediate gratification and bodily distraction and control myself. The spiritual disciplines can facilitate endurance, patience, discipline, and self-control—virtues that constitute the soil in which the cultivation of the Christian mind takes place. Richard Foster's *Celebration of Discipline* and Dallas Willard's *The Spirit of the Disciplines* are excellent guides to these spiritual disciplines.

5. Develop a good vocabulary. Fifth, keep a dictionary handy and get in the habit of looking up words that you don't understand. The development of a good vocabulary is an important tool in the cultivation of the Christian mind. The ubiquitous and egregious (look them up!) avoidance of the dictionary today is no help to the person who wishes to love God with his or her mind.

6. Set some intellectual goals. Finally, it is important for you to set some study goals on a yearly basis. I suggest you team up with another person in your church who has similar study interests and commit yourselves to a mutually accountable reading program. For six years now, I have met every Friday morning for breakfast with a study partner. My friend and I read books in philosophy, psychology, contemporary culture, spiritual formation, and so on. We meet to discuss our reading. Also, we each subscribe to important Christian periodicals (for example, *Christianity Today*) and regularly browse in secular and Christian bookstores. We come together and share our discoveries each week, and our times together are rich! Find a plan that works for you and just do it!

Two Thieves of the Christian Mind

The empty self is a general foe of the Christian mind. But two specific thieves rob many people of the fruitfulness and flourishing that is part of a developing Christian intellectual life. In wrapping up this chapter, I shall discuss each thief in turn.

Thief 1: The Odd Bedfellows of Inferiority and Pride

1. Inviting these bedfellows to be guests: Many times adult learners have a deep sense of insecurity about their own mental abilities.

Defensiveness and a false sense of pride can arise to protect one from feeling embarrassed about not knowing something. Intellectual embarrassment is one of the worst forms of humiliation—no one wants to come off as stupid or uninformed.

I think our adult Sunday school classes have unintentionally contributed to this false sense of pride. I have spoken in hundreds of churches and have regularly observed Sunday school classes which divide into small groups to reflect on a passage or discuss an idea. Later, when the groups recombine to share their observations with the entire class, group feedback is almost always affirming no matter how inaccurate or poorly reasoned a point is. Over the years, this creates a feeling of safety in the class but at the price of generating both a false sense of pride and the mistaken notion that all opinions are equal, whether spontaneous and quickly conceived or the result of detailed study prior to class time. It also keeps adults from learning how to receive criticism for their ideas in the interest of truth and stifles growth in the ability to respond nondefensively.

If we don't work on this in the safety of the company of our own brothers and sisters, we will come off as small, reactionary, and inarticulate in the public square. We need to give one another permission to express inadequately thought-out points to each other and create the expectation that we can learn to argue with one another, critique and defend ideas, or leave class with more work to do on a subject. All of this is in the interest of learning to reason carefully to get to the truth of what we study together.

This may be a bit threatening at first, but over the long haul it will produce a church filled with people who are more secure about what they believe and why. The very forms that define our periods of study together often institutionalize false pride and a lack of intellectual growth. There is absolutely nothing wrong with admitting you don't know something or that you're currently inadequately equipped to think a topic through. What is unacceptable, however, is running from this fact and thereby giving up on intellectual and spiritual growth in the interest of avoiding embarrassment or possible rejection. We all need help in this area, and we should care enough about truth and reason to give that help. Even if we agree with one another's conclusions, we need to dedicate ourselves for Christ's sake to refusing to allow each other to reach those conclusions with poor argumentation and sloppy treatment of data.

Another form of inferiority comes from the simple fact that we are evangelicals. For some time now, our culture has told us that conservative Christians are intellectually inferior, that the Christian faith is irrational, and so forth. And we constantly watch our views caricatured as the news media, hostile university professors, and others regularly build straw men out of Christian positions and proceed to destroy those straw men. When a community is repeatedly told that it is ignorant, it will come to believe that message whether or not it is true.

2. Asking them to leave: What should we do about this problem? I think we need to work harder at holding forth and celebrating our past and contemporary Christian thinkers. We need to know who they are. Do you know who the top Christian intellectuals are today in various fields? Are these people and their work placed before our children as examples to be emulated? We do this for Christian sports heroes, missionaries, and public speakers, so why not do it for our intellectuals?

The effect of identifying and celebrating our Christian intellectuals before one another cannot be overestimated. Social historian John G. Gager has pointed out that even though the early church was a minority movement that faced intellectual and cultural ridicule and marginalization, it maintained internal cohesion and a courageous witness thanks in no small measure to the powerful role in the broader Christian community of Christian intellectuals and apologists.[19] The early church knew who her intellectuals and apologists were, and this gave them confidence and a feeling of strength.

In the same way, we must identify, celebrate, utilize, and make role models out of our Christian thinkers. And we need to celebrate the absolutely unequaled history of the intellectual life in the Christian church. If an alternative community of atheists, Buddhists, or anything else can rival the rich cultural and intellectual leadership in church history, let someone come forth and demonstrate it. The intellectual life is our heritage as Christians, and it is time to remind ourselves of this.

Thief 2: Keeping a Sense of Control

1. The fear of losing control: I once told my children that if they ever got to the point where they thought it was unreasonable to believe that Christianity was true, then they should abandon the faith. Does that sound risky? It is, but what is the alternative? Should we tell our children to set their minds aside totally and accept the Christian faith *without* using their intelligence? It can be risky to encourage people to develop their minds and allow reason to help them decide what they believe and why. No one can predict where such an approach will lead in a specific individual's life. It's easy to lose control of the outcome.[20] If your church is Reformed, charismatic, or whatever, and if your church actually equips people to think widely and deeply about their own theological beliefs, there is no guarantee that they will all come down where the church leaders are on a specific topic. For some, this can create an uncomfortable heterogeneity; it forces us to work harder at drawing lines between what sort of theological diversity a church will or will not tolerate within its membership.

2. Commitment to truth and reason: The fears just mentioned are easy to understand. However, we cannot let our fears dictate to us our approach to Christian growth and ministry. We need to keep two things firmly planted in the center of our minds. First, we simply must reaffirm our commitment to truth and right reason and be confident that our Christian beliefs both warrant that commitment and will flourish in light of it. As Roger Trigg has noted, "Any commitment, it seems, depends on two distinct elements. It presupposes certain beliefs [to be true] and it also involves a personal dedication to the actions implied by them."[21] We are committed to Christianity in general, or some doctrinal position in particular, because we take that commitment to express what is true. And we are committed to the importance of our God-given faculty of mind to aid us in assessing what is true.

3. Consequences of abandoning a commitment to truth and reason: Second, we need to remember the consequences of abandoning a fundamental commitment to truth and reason. A people that does not care about these will be easily led to behave in certain ways by rhetoric, image, narcissistic self-infatuation, and so on. This is extremely dangerous. Further, if our allegiance to Christianity is not based on the conviction that it is true and reasonable, then we are treating the faith as a mere means to some self-serving pragmatic end, and that demeans the faith. For example, if we are more concerned with practical application from the Bible than with having good reasons for thinking we have correctly interpreted it, then our bottom line will be that the Bible exists as a tool to make us a success, and we do not exist to place ourselves under what it really says.

In medicine, we all know what a placebo is. It is an innocuous substance that doesn't really do anything to help an illness. But the patient's false belief that it works brings some mental relief. Unfortunately, a placebo works due to the naive, misinformed, false beliefs on the part of the patient. Sadly, the placebo effect is not limited to medicine. Many people have worldview placebos — false, naive, misinformed beliefs that allow them to live in a safe fantasy world of their own mental creation. To see why this is sad, consider the fictitious story of Wonmug.

Wonmug was a hopelessly dumb physics student attending a large western university. He failed all of his first-semester classes, his math skills were around a fifth-grade level, and he had no aptitude for science. However, one day all the physics students and professors at his college decided to spoof Wonmug by making him erroneously think he was the best physics student at the university. When he asked a question in class, students and professors alike would marvel out loud at the profundity of the inquiry. Graders gave him perfect scores on all his assignments when in reality he deserved an F. Eventually, Wonmug graduated and went on for his Ph.D. The professors at his university sent a letter to all the physicists in the world and included them in the spoof. Wonmug received his degree, took a prestigious chair of physics, regularly went to Europe to deliver papers at major science conferences, and was often featured in *Time* and *Newsweek*. Wonmug's life was pregnant with feelings of respect, accomplishment, expertise, and happiness. Unfortunately, he still knew absolutely no physics. Do you envy Wonmug? Would you wish such a life for your children? Of course not. Why? Because his sense of well-being was built on a false, misinformed worldview placebo.

Often, life is a struggle. We grow sick, lose our jobs, experience fragmented relationships with others, and eventually die. We want to know if there is anything real upon which to base our lives. Is there really a God and what is He actually like? What does God believe about the things that matter most? Is there any purpose to life and, if so, what is it? Why was I thrust into this world? Are values objective and real, or arbitrary and invented? Is there life after death? In what ways can I really count on God, and are there any true, effective ways to get close to Him? When we ask these questions, we don't just want answers that help us merely because we believe them. We want to be comforted because our answers to these questions are really true. For the wise person of virtue, a life well lived is based on the truth, not on a placebo.

But if truth really matters after all, then it follows that rationality also is crucial to a life well lived. Why? Because if we want a life built on truth, we want to be sure that our worldview consists of the highest percentage of true beliefs and the lowest percentage of false ones. The only way available to us for making sure this is the case with our own belief system is through the careful use of our faculty of reason. In the ordinary decisions of daily life, we try to base our beliefs and actions on the best evidence we can get. From sitting on a jury to buying a new house, we try to base our decisions on a careful assessment of all the relevant evidence we can get. Who would respect someone who voted in a jury trial or decided which house to buy with no regard to the evidence relevant to these decisions? If someone used blind faith and bought the first house he or she saw with a For Sale sign in front of it, but made no effort to get information about the house and neighborhood, we would consider that person foolish. Why? Because when we use our reason and base decisions on the best assessment of the evidence we can make, we increase our chances that our decisions are based on true beliefs.

Now if this is the case for day-to-day issues, why should we suddenly abandon the importance of reason and evidence when it comes to religion? We should not. Any religious belief worthy of the name should be accepted because we take the belief to be true and do so by the best exercise of our mental faculties we can muster. In the long run, it is better to risk losing control, face our doubts, be patient, and do the best job we can of using our minds to get at the truth. Not only is the Christian faith secure enough to withstand such an approach, but the faith actually encourages it.

CONCLUSION

If we are going to make progress in our Christian lives, then we must defeat the empty self and take back what insecurity and fear of losing control have taken from us. This is the first step toward making progress in cultivating the Christian mind as part of an overall spiritual journey pleasing to God and good for others and ourselves. But just exactly how does one develop a more careful intellect? How can a person learn to think better and be more assured that his or her beliefs are, in fact, true? To these questions we now turn.

CHAPTER FIVE

Clearing the Cobwebs from My Mental Attic

X

*He [Christ] wants a child's heart,
but a grown-up's head.*

C. S. LEWIS[1]

K

*Ought not a Minister to have, First,
a good understanding, a clear apprehension,
a sound judgment, and a capacity of reasoning
with some closeness?*

JOHN WESLEY[2]

K

*Study is a specific kind of experience
in which through careful observation
of objective structures we cause thought processes
to move in a certain way. . . . When done with concentration,
perception and repetition, ingrained habits of thought
are formed.*

RICHARD FOSTER[3]

I ATTENDED THE UNIVERSITY OF MISSOURI AND RECEIVED A B.S. IN CHEM-
istry in 1970. The vast majority of my course work consisted of math, physics, and chemistry. In a typical science course, we would cover around three hundred pages of textbook per semester. I read very little prose and spent most of my time solving mathematical problems associated with my chemistry, physics, and math textbooks. I roomed with a literature major my freshman year, and it was not uncommon for him to have fifteen hundred pages of assigned reading in one course. Intellectually speaking, our college experience was very different until my conversion to Christ in the fall of my junior year.

As a new convert, I entered a world entirely new to me, a world filled with philosophical, theological, biblical, ethical, political, and historical ideas. As my tender, newly regenerated soul began to grow close to Christ, I began to care deeply about ideas in those areas, so I started reading anything I could get my hands on. At first, the reading was hard for me because I was unprepared for it. My scientific training had been valuable in many ways, but reading a book on theology is very different from solving problems in organic chemistry. I simply was not in the habit of reading demanding prose in the humanities about broad ethical, theological, or philosophical themes. But I persevered, and in the process I cleared away some of the cobwebs that covered vast regions of my mental attic.

Nothing that is worth doing is pleasurable or easy in the early stages of learning how to do it. But through regular practice, patient endurance, and proper mentoring, skills emerge and habits are formed that enable a person to be good at the activity in focus. This is clearly the case in learning to play golf, hit a baseball, or read in completely new areas of study. It is no less true of becoming a deep, careful thinker in general. If we are to love God adequately with the mind, then the mind must be exercised regularly, trained to acquire certain habits of thought, and filled with an increasingly rich set of distinctions and categories. There is no simple way to do this, and it would be presumptuous to attempt to describe fully how to develop a mature mind in one short chapter. Still, there are certain aspects of intellectual cultivation that we can discuss briefly yet profitably. My intent here is to help you get started. In this chapter, we will probe two of these aspects: forming habits of the mind and principles of reasoning.

FORMING HABITS OF THE MIND

The Formation of Virtue

A mature person has a tightly integrated, well-ordered soul. A carefully developed mind is a crucial part of a well-ordered soul. A mind that is learning to function well is both part of and made possible by an over-all life that is skillfully lived. You cannot learn to use your mind well for Christ's sake by just reading a logic book or taking more adult educa-tion courses. You must order your general lifestyle in such a way that a maturing intellect emerges as part of that lifestyle. If you want to develop a Christian mind, you must intend to order your overall form of life to make this possible. You cannot just read a book or two and add this to a lifestyle otherwise indifferent to the intellect.

Moreover, learning to be a careful Christian thinker results in an entire way of being present in the world. To see what I mean by this, recall from chapter three that what a person spends time learning will affect the way that person sees, hears, thinks, and behaves. A trained lawyer actually hears things on the evening news, sees things in the newspaper, and approaches conversations with others in ways that would be unavailable to her if she had gone into psychology or busi-ness. A person with a well-developed lawyer-type mind will have a distinctive way of being present in the world. This is also true of a per-son who is cultivating a careful Christian mind. That person will be present to the world in a distinctively Christian intellectual way. He will notice certain things others miss, read things (for example, theol-ogy, church history) others eschew, and so forth. To develop a Christian mind skillfully, you must want to *be* a certain sort of person badly enough that you are willing to pay the price of ordering your lifestyle appropriately. Of course, some Christians are called to a vocation of being a Christian intellectual in one way or another—a Christian philosopher or New Testament scholar, for example. This requires a more intense, focused ordering of one's life than is needed for those without this calling. But every believer, regardless of vocational call-ing, needs to cultivate a Christian mind.

Virtues and the Good Life

A life so ordered to facilitate intellectual growth is characterized by a certain set of virtues that makes such growth possible. A virtue is a skill, a habit, an ingrained disposition to act, think, or feel in certain ways. Virtues are those good parts of one's character that make a person excellent at life in general. As with any skill (for example, learning to swing a golf club), a virtue becomes ingrained in my personality, and thus a part of my very nature, through repetition, practice, and training. If I want to develop the virtue of compassion, I must regularly practice acts of mercy, self-sacrifice, and kindness. Knowing what these virtues are will give you something specific at which to aim in your efforts to cultivate your mind.

Certain virtues are especially relevant to the development of an intellectual life.[4] Moreover, these virtues are not isolated from each other. They are deeply interrelated. Growth in one virtue can aid maturity in another skill and vice versa. If you want a maturing Christian mind, you'll need to cultivate these virtues through regular practice. Five groups of virtues are especially important for cultivating a Christian mind.

FIVE GROUPS OF VIRTUES

The Virtue of Wisdom

The first group contains *truth seeking, honesty,* and *wisdom.* The Christian mind is committed to seeking and finding the truth even if that truth is not what one wanted to hear. The Christian seeks to know and do the truth. In fact, in a certain sense the believer's commitment to the truth is even more basic than his or her dedication to the Christian faith in general or some doctrinal position in particular: If one came to believe that Christianity or some doctrinal belief were false, then one ought to give up the belief in question. By way of application, we should learn to listen to what our critics say about us even if we don't like the way they express their views. A wife or husband should try to get at the truth of a spouse's criticisms even if it was expressed angrily and inappropriately. Practice this in all areas of your life to cultivate the habit of wanting the truth.

Honesty is closely related to truth. The Christian mind is honest about what it does and does not believe. The thinking Christian tries to be honest to himself or herself and to others. An important part of honesty is proportionality. Proportionality is the measure of the degree to which one ought to accept a belief or the degree to which a specific argument actually supports that belief. We ought to proportion our degree of belief to the degree for which we have grounds for accepting it. Many times we think that believing something with less than complete certainty means we really do not believe it. But this is not true. If you believe something, you must be at least slightly more certain that it is true than you are that it is false—you must be more than fifty-fifty regarding the belief. And your certainty about the belief can grow.

This growth ought to be based on and proportional to the rational considerations relevant to the belief. It is unproductive to try to believe something beyond your grounds for believing it and dishonest to act as if you believe something more strongly than you do. Overbelief is not a virtue. For example, I am far from certain on many Christian beliefs I hold. I lean toward the view that the days of Genesis are vast periods of time and not literal twenty-four-hour periods. But about two days of the week I flip-flop and accept the literal view. Based on my study, I cannot convince myself either way, and I'm about sixty-forty in favor of the old-earth position. Other beliefs of mine have grown in certainty over the years—that God really exists, for example. We should be honest with ourselves about the strength of our various beliefs and work on strengthening them by considering the issues relevant to their acceptance.

We should also be honest about what arguments are and are not good in supporting our beliefs. Recently, I heard a guest minister preach a sermon about condom distribution in the public schools. He began by acknowledging that he was against this practice and went on to lecture on the various arguments for and against it. At one point he criticized as inadequate an argument used by many Christians against condom distribution. He was not promoting condom distribution, he was demoting a bad argument against it. What happened after the service was very sad. A number of people criticized him behind his back because, on their view, he had come down in favor of condom distribution. But this was clearly wrong. He had simply criticized one argument raised against condom distribution. His point was this: God is not honored when His people use bad arguments for what may actually be correct conclusions. Proportionality involves distinguishing a conclusion from arguments used to reach it and recognizing that rejecting certain arguments is not the same as rejecting a conclusion. Because of minds not trained to be sensitive to proportionality, people in the congregation could not hear what the minister said and missed a great chance to learn something.

Wisdom is also related to truth seeking. Wisdom is the wise use and application of knowledge. It involves knowing how to use good means to accomplish worthy ends in a skillful manner. The New Testament clearly teaches that the more one is willing to obey and apply the truth, the more one will be in a position to gain knowledge about more truth. For the Christian, seeking the truth is no mere abstract activity unrelated to life. The more we practice living what we already know, the better we will be at learning more. Some Christians misunderstand the nature of wisdom, preferring practical wisdom and disdaining theoretical knowledge. However, since wisdom is the application of knowledge, you cannot be practically wise without being theoretically informed. Truth seeking, honesty and proportionality, and wisdom are important virtues to cultivate if a growing Christian mind is to become a reality.

A second group of virtues contains *faith* (trust) and *hope*. One must have peace and serenity of mind in order to develop a life of understanding, reflection, and meditation. An anxious, depressed, distracted soul is not conducive to intellectual growth. We Christians trust and hope that truth is good and worth having because we are confident in the God of truth. In my opinion, this is one reason why intellectual growth and cultural flourishing are often a result of the Christian penetration of a society. Trust and hope in God help build confidence that truth is a valuable thing to have because it is ultimately good. A confident mind is a mind free to follow the truth wherever it leads, without the distracting fear and anxiety that come from the attitude that maybe we're better off not knowing the truth. This is one reason why Christians need not fear the honest examination of their faith.

A lack of faith and hope creates a distracted mind incapable of intellectual growth and devotion to God. Noise and busyness can rob one of serenity of mind as well. If you truly desire to develop a Christian mind, then you must squarely face this fact: The mind cannot grow without reflection and meditation on what has been studied, and reflection and meditation require periods of quiet and solitude on the one hand and simplicity of life on the other. You must order your life so as to remove as far as possible, given your other commitments, unnecessary modern gadgets and distractions to maintain focus and quiet in your life. Take the phone off the hook regularly. Don't just rely on your answering machine, because even a ringing phone will rouse your curiosity about the identity of the caller and distract you. Don't spend all your time in front of a computer or the television. If you can afford it, pay to have your taxes done or your yard mowed. Do what you can to free yourself from unnecessary distractions. As an application, you may want to draw up a list of ways you can simplify your life and create more time for quiet reflection.

Humility and the associated traits of *open-mindedness, self-criticality*, and *nondefensiveness* form the third group of virtues relevant to the intellectual life. We must be willing to seek the truth in a spirit of humility with an admission of our own finitude; we must be willing to learn from our critics; and we need to learn to argue against our own positions in order to strengthen our understanding of them. I once heard a Christian college professor tell a group of parents that the purpose of a Christian college is to challenge the students' faith. I piped up in disagreement and argued that the purpose (among other things) was to strengthen and develop their faith, and one way to do this was to face questions honestly. The purpose of intellectual humility, open-mindedness, and so forth is not to create a skeptical mind that never lands on a position about anything, preferring to remain suspended in midair. Rather, the purpose is for you to do anything you can to remove your unhelpful biases and get at the truth in a reasoned way. A proper development of this group of virtues can aid in that quest.

Here is something to practice. When your view is criticized or even ridiculed on television, a radio talk show, or in a newspaper editorial, don't just react angrily. Take a moment to jot down on paper the person's main thesis and how that thesis was supported. Then do two things. First, assume the person is expressing at least some good points and try to identify them. This assumption may be false, but the search for common ground with intellectual opponents is a good habit. In the process of identifying these good points, try to argue against your own view. Second, try to state on paper exactly how you would argue against the view being expressed in an intellectually precise yet emotionally calm way. This exercise may take a few minutes, but if repeated regularly it will aid you in developing this third group of virtues.

Fourth, the Christian mind requires *ardor, vigilance*, and *fortitude*. The Christian thinker should be a passionate person filled with ardor or zeal—zeal for God and truth. This zeal expresses itself in a passion to know and do the truth and to live a religiously reasonable form of life. It also helps make possible the vigilance necessary to stick to a life of study when it is not convenient or not particularly valued by those around you. Often a topic of study requires the patient development of a long, complicated chain of arguments before the issue can be understood, and vigilance is needed to see it to completion. An impatient generation looking for instant solutions and quick answers will be a generation of shallow slogans.

Fortitude or courage is also needed, and this comes from confidence in God's providential care of His children, including His availability to comfort them even in the face of martyrdom. The Christian mind requires the courage to face the truth and to stand up for it even when doing so is not popular. Bravery does not imply the absence of fear, but the ability to rise above and not be controlled by it. The person with an articulate, well-reasoned Christian worldview will be attacked if he or she defends unpopular Christian positions in the public square. Fortitude will be needed to enable one to continue to hunger for, cling to, and propagate the truth in such circumstances. Joseph Pieper astutely observes that fortitude contains two elements: endurance and attack.[5] The courageous person, especially one with intellectual courage, must learn to endure suffering and hardship in the interests of the truth and to continue attacking harmful falsehoods even if that is risky and painful.

A person must have motivation to develop zeal, vigilance, and courage. One of the best ways to gain this motivation is to put yourself in a slightly threatening yet not overwhelming situation in which you must defend your views. Regularly, when I teach an adult education class in a church, I require class members to develop a ten-question survey and interview five different people they do not know to be Christians—at a mall, at work, or somewhere else. Inevitably, two things happen. First, the class members gain firsthand exposure to the menagerie of ideas held by those in their own community. Second, they realize how ill-prepared they are to articulate and defend their own beliefs. Such exposure creates an initial hunger to grow in diligence as a learner and to be more courageous about what one believes.

The final virtue I shall mention is *fidelity to God and dedication to His cause in the world as one's chief end.* The Christian intellectual is here to serve a Name, not to make one. Unfortunately, I have seen too many Christian thinkers who have a certain texture or posture in life that gives the impression that they are far more concerned with assuring their academic colleagues that they are not ignorant fundamentalists than they are with pleasing God and serving His people. Such thinkers often give up too much intellectual real estate far too readily to secular or other perspectives inimical to the Christian faith. This is why many average Christian folk are suspicious of the mind today. All too often, they have seen intellectual growth in Christian academics lead to a cynical posture unfaithful to the spirit of the Christian way. I have always been suspicious of Christian intellectuals whose primary agenda seems to be to remove embarrassment about being an evangelical and to assure their colleagues that they are really acceptable, rational people in spite of their evangelicalism. While we need to be sensitive to our unbelieving friends and colleagues, we should care far less about what the world thinks than about what God thinks of our intellectual life. Fidelity to God and His cause is the core commitment of a growing Christian mind. Such a commitment engenders faithfulness to God and His people and inhibits the puffiness that can accompany intellectual growth.

Study as a Spiritual Discipline
Dallas Willard defines a spiritual discipline as "an activity undertaken to bring us into more effective cooperation with Christ and His Kingdom."[6] In any human endeavor, repetitive exercise and practice bring skill and excellence. Sometimes a particular activity is good because it accomplishes a specific result. Swinging a baseball bat is good if it produces a base hit. However, that same activity can also be done, not for the result alone, but for the training it offers. A person can repeatedly swing a bat in a batting cage for the purpose of training, and not to increase his output of base hits. And other good results can follow from such training besides the one usually or normally intended; for example, regular trips to a batting cage can get a person in good overall condition besides helping him get base hits.

The same thing is true of study. We often correctly approach study specifically for some direct end—preparing a lesson or learning a topic covered in a book. But study should also be approached as a set of training activities, as spiritual and intellectual exercises. Study is a discipline that strengthens the mind and enriches the soul. Sometimes I study a book for the sheer value of engaging my intellect in a stretching, strenuous activity. At other times, I read to help myself cultivate the intellectual virtues listed above. Seen as a discipline, study becomes a means of building my character, ingraining habits of thought and reflection, and reinforcing in my own soul the value of the life of the mind. We study, then, not simply to gain knowledge about the topic of study, but as a broader spiritual discipline. By way of application, it is important to read books from time to time as a form of spiritual discipline and intellectual exercise, even if the topic of the book does not address one of your immediate, felt needs. If all you do is read simple books or those that overemphasize stories or practical application, you'll never learn to think for yourself as a mature Christian, nor will you develop a trained mind.

The Importance of English Grammar and Syntax

Jane Healy observes that "the way people use language is braided together tightly with the way they think."[7] Healy is right. While we do not need to think in language (a child can think prior to language acquisition, and, in fact, since language is a vehicle for thought, language presupposes thought and not vice versa), nevertheless, language development is critical for cultivating a careful, precise, attentive mind.[8] Most people today do not use good grammar or syntax in sentence construction. Interestingly, the demise of grammar and syntax reflects a change in the main way language is currently used.

Today, we primarily use language to express emotions, create experiences, or get someone to do something, like buy a product. Careful thought is not always relevant to these modern appropriations of language. How many television commercials actually persuade us to buy something on the basis of an articulate defense of a product! The devaluation of grammar correlates closely with a devaluation of the mind, truth, and thought. When a main purpose of language is the careful, precise expression of thought, grammar and syntax become critical because they make such expression of thought possible.

If we Christians are to develop our minds, we must take greater care to improve our syntax and grammar, and we must expect this from each other. From years of experience grading student papers, I can tell you that if a student's grammar is poor, he or she has a difficult time developing a coherent line of thought clearly and carefully. Let's give ourselves permission to correct one another's grammar with a gentle, nonarrogant spirit in our fellowship meetings. Isn't a developed intellectual love for God worth the price of an initial embarrassment at such correction? After all, the alternative is to continue to allow one another to speak incorrectly and fail to realize the intellectual benefits that come from the correct use of language.

Having seen the importance of a Christian mind, and having (hopefully) been persuaded of the importance of good thinking, ordered language, and good grammar, you may be asking, "Okay, what is well-reasoned thinking?" Let's look now at the principles that govern reasoning and why they are important to the mind.

PRINCIPLES OF REASONING

Why Logic?

Besides cultivating virtue, taking study as a spiritual discipline, and being more disciplined about your grammar and syntax, you should be acquainted with certain logical tools that constitute the very nature of thought. Even young children use these tools without knowing the names for them. In this section, I want to examine briefly some of the more important principles of argument. If you really want to develop your intellectual skills, you should memorize these and practice using them and recognizing their presence in things you hear or read. For a more thorough discussion of principles of reasoning and argument, consult any standard introductory logic text.[9]

We Christians must never forget that our God is a God of truth, reason, and logic. He speaks wisdom to His children, invites them to reason and argue with Him logically, and demands that they present in logical fashion the reason why they believe. The image of God within us includes the faculty of abstract reasoning and logical thought. In Romans, the apostle Paul presents in a careful, logical fashion a host of Old Testament texts about the nature of sin, judgment, and justification. In public debate, Jesus Himself regularly used careful logic to refute opponents' arguments and present them with a carefully reasoned alternative. When John Wesley told a group of ministers to become proficient in logic as a part of their calling, he was expressing a deep understanding of the Christian faith as that faith is depicted in the Bible and throughout church history.

In logic, an *argument* is defined as a group of statements containing premises and a conclusion in which the former are claimed as support for the latter. Using an argument is not the same as being argumentative. In using an argument, one simply supports a conclusion with premises. Being *argumentative* is a defensive personality defect. Christians are required by God to argue, *not* to be argumentative (1 Peter 3:15).

Arguments are either *deductive* or *inductive*. In a valid deductive argument, *if* the premises are true, then the conclusion *must* be true. For example, "(1) All dogs are ducks, (2) All ducks are cats, (3) Therefore, all dogs are cats" is a valid deductive argument. In spite of the fact that premises 1 and 2 are false, *if* they were true, the conclusion would have to be true.

In an inductive argument, the premises do not guarantee but merely provide support or grounds for the truth of the conclusion. An inductive argument with true premises does not guarantee but only *makes probable* the truth of its conclusion. It would be possible to have a good inductive argument with true premises and a false conclusion. For example, "(1) Ninety-five percent of people who receive the antibiotic get well, (2) We are about to give John the antibiotic, (3) Therefore, John is about to get well" is a good inductive argument. Premises 1 and 2 do in fact provide good support for the conclusion, even though the premises could be true and the conclusion false.

Deductive arguments can be either *valid* or *invalid*. As we have seen, if a deductive argument is valid, its conclusion must be true if its premises are true. An invalid deductive argument is one in which the premises could be true but the conclusion false. For example, "(1) All dogs are mammals, (2) All cats are mammals, (3) Therefore, all dogs are cats" is invalid because it contains true premises and a false conclusion. A *sound* argument is a deductive argument with true premises (and therefore, a true conclusion), and this is what we want to employ as best we can. A *syllogism* is a deductive argument that consists of exactly two premises and one conclusion.

The argument above about dogs and cats is a syllogism (an invalid one). Since these terms may be new to you, we'll follow this general introduction with a discussion of important principles of reasoning, followed by a list of certain fallacies of reasoning that occur regularly.

A BRIEF LESSON IN LOGIC

Principles of Reasoning and Argument

A number of principles of reasoning and argument are crucial yet easy to grasp and, in fact, can be taught profitably to children.

1. Three important syllogisms: There are several different types of syllogisms, but the three below are easy to spot and occur all the time in our thinking and arguing. Let P and Q in the following stand for any two sentences. (*Modus ponens* is a Latin term meaning "in the mood of affirming"; *modus tollens* means "in the mood of denying.")

Modus Ponens (MP)	Modus Tollens (MT)	Disjunctive Syllogism (DS)
1. If P then Q	1. If P then Q.	1. Either P or Q.
2. P	2. Not Q.	2. Not P.
3. Therefore, Q.	3. Therefore not P.	3. Therefore, Q.

Take a look at MP and MT. Note that premise 1 is the same in both syllogisms: "If P then Q." In an "if-then" sentence like this, P is called the antecedent and Q the consequent. Here is an example of MP *(modus ponens):*

1. If you believe in Jesus Christ, then you are saved.
2. You believe in Jesus Christ.
3. Therefore, you are saved.

You will observe that premise 2 ("You believe in Jesus Christ") is actually an affirmation of the antecedent of premise 1 (the antecedent is what comes after "if" in premise 1). MP is a valid deductive argument form: If the premises are true, then the conclusion must be true. However, there is sometimes invalid reasoning associated with MP called *the fallacy of affirming the consequent:*

1. If P then Q.
2. Q.
3. Therefore, P.

Note that premise 2 makes the mistake of affirming the consequent of premise 1 instead of the antecedent; that is, it asserts Q instead of P.

This is a fallacy because such an argument could have true premises and a false conclusion, as follows: (1) If it is raining outside (P), then it is wet (Q), (2) It is wet (Q), (3) Therefore, it is raining (P). But it may be wet due to a sprinkler system and not because it is raining.

Here is an example of MT *(modus tollens):*

1. If atheistic evolution is true, then organisms are simply physical systems.
2. It is not true that organisms are simply physical systems (for example, they may have souls).
3. Therefore, it is not the case that atheistic evolution is true (it is false).

Note that premise 2 correctly consists in a denial of the consequent of premise 1. As with MP, there is sometimes invalid reasoning associated with MT called *the fallacy of denying the antecedent:*

1. If P then Q.
2. Not P.
3. Therefore, not Q.

For example:

1. If Jones took the car, then he went to the store.
2. It is not true that Jones took the car.
3. Therefore, it is not true that Jones went to the store.

Here, 1 and 2 could be true, but 3 is false. Maybe Jones went to the store in a taxi.

Finally, here is an example of a disjunctive syllogism:

1. Either Jones left the house or he is at home.
2. It is not true that Jones left the house.
3. Therefore, he is at home.

In premise 1, we are presented with an option: either Jones left his house or he is at home. One of these is true because the dilemma is an exhaustive one and there are no third options. One of these alternatives must be true. So, if it isn't true that Jones left the house, he has to be at home.

Medieval theologians noted that even dogs appear to behave as if they understand disjunctive syllogisms. They observed that when a dog chased a rabbit down a road that suddenly forked, either the rabbit went left or it went right. If the dog sniffed the left fork with no success (it discovered that the rabbit had not taken the left fork), *it would not sniff the right fork.* Rather, it *would immediately run down the right fork,* apparently because it already knew that's where the rabbit went.

In Deuteronomy 30:15-19 (NASB), Moses presents a disjunctive syllogism. See if you can find the two premises and the conclusion:

> See, I have set before you today life and prosperity, and death and adversity. . . . But if your heart turns away and you will not obey, . . . I declare to you today that you shall surely perish. . . . So choose life in order that you may live.

2. Necessary and sufficient conditions and counterexamples: While we are on the subject of "if-then" statements, it is absolutely crucial to learn to distinguish the difference between necessary and sufficient conditions. A *necessary condition* is one that must prevail before a second condition can occur. If P is a necessary condition for Q, then if Q is true, P must be true, but P alone may not guarantee the truth of Q. (Example: reread the sentence above, asserting the following conditions: P = Doug Geivett is alive; Q = Doug Geivett is married.) To refute a claim that P is necessary for Q, simply give a counterexample in which Q is true and P is false (in which case P could not be necessary for Q). For example, if someone claims that a necessary condition for practicing science is that you are studying something that can be directly observed, then we can refute this claim by citing examples of scientific practice that do not involve studying something that can be directly observed (the death of the dinosaurs, electrons). In English, a necessary condition is often introduced by the words "only if," "entails that," "implies that."

A *sufficient condition* is one that is adequate for another condition to succeed. If P is a sufficient condition for Q, then if P is true, Q must be true, but there may be other ways for Q to be true besides the truth of P. (Example: P = Doug Geivett is married to Diane; Q = Doug

Geivett is married.) To refute a claim that P is a sufficient condition for Q, simply give a counterexample in which P is true and Q is false (in which case P could not be sufficient for Q). For example, if someone claims that a sufficient condition for practicing science is that you are studying something that can be directly observed, then we can refute this claim by citing examples of nonscientific practice that do involve studying something that can be directly observed (for example, doing a word study in literature where you directly observe an author's uses of a term). In English, a sufficient condition is often introduced by the words "if," "in case," "provided that," "given that." In an "if-then" statement, the antecedent is the sufficient condition and the consequent is the necessary condition. Sometimes in logic, "if-then" is symbolized by the sign ⊃. A useful device for remembering which is the necessary and which is the sufficient condition in an "if-then" statement is to remember "SUN," because such a statement in logic looks like this: S⊃N.

Let's test your understanding. Of the following pairs, which is the necessary and which is the sufficient condition (answers are in the note)? Pair 1: P = The apple is red; Q = The apple is colored. Pair 2: P = The box is shaped; Q = The box is square. Pair 3: P = Jones is a human; Q = Jones is a person.[10]

3. The law of identity: Sometimes people make reductionist claims that one thing is nothing but (is identical to) something else — for example, that the soul is nothing but the brain, that sex is nothing but a certain bodily activity, that religious experience is nothing but a psychological phenomenon. The law of identity helps us evaluate such claims. Bishop Joseph Butler (1692-1752) once remarked that everything is itself and not something else. This simple truth has profound implications. Suppose you want to know whether J. P. Moreland is Eileen Spiek's youngest son. If J. P. Moreland is identical to Eileen Spiek's youngest son, then in reality, there is only one thing we are talking about: J. P. Moreland who is Eileen Spiek's youngest son. Furthermore, J. P. Moreland is identical to himself; he is not different from himself. Now if J. P. Moreland is not identical to Eileen Spiek's youngest son, then in reality we are talking about two things, not one.

This illustration can be generalized into a truth about the nature of identity: For any *x* and *y*, if *x* and *y* are identical (they are really the same thing, there is only one thing you are talking about, not two), then any truth that applies to x will apply to y and vice versa. This suggests a test for identity: if you could find one thing true of x not true of y, or vice versa, then x cannot be identical to (be the same thing as) y. If there is something true of a state of my brain (for example, it has electrical activity, weight, is composed of chemicals) that is not true of a state of my mind, say a thought (thoughts don't have weights and aren't built out of chemical or electrical components), then the state of my brain is not the same thing as the state of my mind.

4. Self-refutation: Whenever you are listening to someone argue for a position on something, always pay attention to whether or not the person is asserting something that is self-refuting. What is self-refutation? A statement is about a subject matter. "All electrons have negative charge" is about the subject matter called electrons. Some statements refer to themselves, that is, they include themselves in their own field of reference. "All English sentences are short" refers to all English sentences whatsoever, including that very sentence itself. Sometimes a statement refers to itself and fails to satisfy its own criteria of rational acceptability or truthfulness. "No English sentence is longer than three words," "I do not exist," and "There are no truths" are self-refuting. They refer to themselves and they falsify themselves. Self-refuting statements are necessarily false; that is, they cannot possibly be true.

Here are some common self-refuting assertions:

- "I believe that no one can believe something that cannot be tested by the five senses or by science." (The belief itself cannot be so tested.)
- "All morality is relative to private taste, so you morally ought to be more tolerant of others." (How can I have an objectively true moral duty to be tolerant if all duties are merely relative to private tastes?)
- "All attitudes and behaviors are caused by our genes, so we are not responsible for them and people ought to stop passing judgment on others, for example, on homosexuals." (If all behavior is beyond judgmental evaluation because it is determined by things—genes—over which I have no control, then this should apply to homophobia, child molestation, and everything else, and not merely to someone's favorite hobby-horse like homosexual freedoms.)

What would you say about this statement: "There are no moral absolutes." Is it self-refuting?[11] For the answer, see note 11.

5. Three important concepts: Before we turn to a list of frequently occurring fallacies of reasoning, it is important for us to get before our minds three logical concepts that are sometimes confused: *contradictory, contrary*, and *converse*. Contradictory statements are those that necessarily have the opposite truth values—one is true and the other false. For example, these two statements are contradictory: "All S are P" (all men are mortal) and "Some S are not P" (some men are not mortal). So are these: "Some S are P" (some dogs are brown) and "No S are P" (no dogs are brown). In each pair, the two propositions contradict each other and one is true while the other is false.

The relation "being contrary" refers to two very specific types of propositions: "All S are P" (all dogs are mammals) and "No S are P" (no dogs are mammals). When we say that the propositions "All S are P" and "No S are P" are contraries, we mean that they cannot both be true. At least one of them must be false (in fact, both may be false as in "All dogs are brown" and "No dogs are brown").

Finally, two propositions relate to one another as converses when their subject and predicate terms are switched. In logic, there are four very special forms of propositions that are given the names A, E, I, and O: A = All S are P (converse = All P are S), E = No S are P (converse = No P are S), I = Some S are P (converse = Some P are S), and O = Some S are not P (converse = Some P are not S). Note that in each case, the converse simply switches the subject and predicate terms S and P. When you convert an E or I statement, the new statement is logically equivalent; that is, the converted statement will have the very same truth value (true or false) as the original statement. "No S are P" (an E statement) is logically equivalent to "No P are S." If one is true, the other will be true; if one is false, the other will be false. "Some S are P" (an I statement) is logically equivalent to "Some P are S." However, when you convert an A or O statement, you do not get a logically equivalent result. One of the statements could be true, for example, and the converse false as with "All dogs are mammals" (a true A statement) and its converse, "All mammals are dogs" (a false A statement), or "Some birds are not crows" (a true O statement) and its converse, "Some crows are not birds" (a false O statement).

Important Informal Fallacies

In addition to good principles of reasoning and argument, everyone should learn to spot certain informal fallacies of reasoning in his or her own communication as well as others'. Here are some of the most important informal fallacies.[12]

1. Appeal to pity: In an appeal to pity, the premises of an argument are logically irrelevant to the conclusion, but they are psychologically moving in such a way that the conclusion may seem to follow. In an appeal to pity, the arguer attempts to evoke pity from the reader or listener in support of a conclusion. For example, "If abortion is forbidden, then the rich will still be able to secure safe abortions but the poor will either have back-alley abortions or keep producing children to draw more welfare."[13] Here an appeal is made to our sense of pity for the poor, heightened by our sense of disgust with the rich in contrast to the poor, and the conclusion reached is that abortion should be morally permissible. But the question of the moral permissibility of abortion is an issue of the moral status of the fetus, not a question of how we feel about the rich or poor in this context. Consider a parallel counterargument: "If handguns are not kept legal, then the poor either will have to use black-market, illegal guns that could misfire and be a danger to the shooter, or else stop stealing and remain poor while the rich will still be able to secure good handguns." The fact that this argument is such a poor one shows the folly of using an appeal to pity.

2. Appeal to the people: In this fallacy, one argues that if you want to be accepted, included in the group, loved, or respected, then you should accept conclusion X as true. Here the arguer incites group emotions or the enthusiasm of the crowd, appeals to people's vanity or snobbery, or challenges people to jump on the bandwagon to support a conclusion. For example, "Everyone who is really with it and modern in orientation recognizes that condoms ought to be distributed in the schools, so you should get with it and accept the same verdict." Or, "Modern, cultured people are not so narrow to think that one religion is the absolute truth, so you Christians should stop claiming that Christ is the only way to God." This type of argument is wielded widely among teenagers, and unfortunately, sermons sometimes employ this form of fallacious reasoning to "establish" what in fact may be a true conclusion. Remember, a fallacious argument may or may not have a true conclusion. Either way, such an argument fails to establish that conclusion properly.

3. **Ad hominem** *argument:* In this fallacy, one argues against an opponent's position by attacking the other arguer and not the argument. For example, "Your argument against affirmative action could not possibly be a good one because you are a white male." Here is another one: "Newt Gingrich has argued for lowering taxes. What a joke! Gingrich is just a rich Republican who could never understand what it means to have compassion on those less fortunate than he." Again: "Why don't pro-lifers adopt babies if they're so concerned about abortion. Their position is nothing but hypocrisy! And men have no right to speak about abortion since they can't get pregnant." Sometimes it can be relevant to attack a person if the person's character or credibility is relevant to the truth of his or her claims, for example, in evaluating the testimony of a witness in court. In such a case, no *ad hominem* fallacy is committed.

4. Genetic fallacy: This fallacy occurs when someone confuses the origin of an idea with the reasons for believing the idea and faults the idea because of where it came from (for example, because of who said it or how the idea first came to be believed) and not because of the adequacy of the grounds for the idea. For example, "The idea of God originated out of fear of the dark and a terror of death, so it is not reasonable to believe in God." This is not how the idea of God originated, but even if it were, that fact would be utterly irrelevant in judging whether or not one ought to believe in God. Again: "You are a Christian and not a Buddhist because you were raised in a Christian country and your parents taught you to be a Christian. Therefore, there is no good reason to prefer Christianity to Buddhism." The fallacy of this argument should be apparent. When we answer the question, *"Why* do you believe in *x?"* we need to keep separate a psychological or originating "why" from a rational "why." A psychological or originating "why" is a request to give the motive for a belief or to state how you came to have the belief in question ("my parents taught it to me"). As interesting as these issues are, they must be kept distinct from the request to cite the reasons you have for thinking that some belief is true. Motives are one thing, rational grounds and evidence are another.

5. Straw man: This fallacy is committed when an arguer distorts an opponent's position for the purpose of making it more easy to destroy, refutes the distorted position, and concludes that his opponent's actual view is thereby demolished. For example, "All creationists think that the world began in 4004 B.C., that Noah's ark contained every single pair of species we see today, and that no evolutionary change has occurred, period. Moreover, the only reason creationists appeal to miracles is to cover their ignorance of scientific causes. They believe in a god-of-the-gaps. These ideas cannot withstand rational scrutiny, so creationism ought to be rejected." This argument draws the conclusion that creationism in any form ought to be rejected by refuting claims that virtually no creationist would accept. Here is another example: "Everything needs a cause, God is a thing; therefore, God needs a cause." This argument is a straw man because it ignores the nature or identity of God.

   6. Red herring: This fallacy gets its name from a procedure for training dogs to follow a scent. A red herring would be dragged across the trail with the intent of leading the dog astray with its potent scent. Well-trained dogs do not follow red herrings but stick to the original scent. In logic, a red herring fallacy takes place when someone diverts the reader's or listener's attention by changing the subject to some different and irrelevant issue. The arguer finishes by either drawing a conclusion about this different issue or by simply presuming that a conclusion has been established.

   Here is a common red herring: "Pro-choice is something all Americans should accept. Unfortunately, the religious right wants to invade our bedrooms and force their narrow-minded, mean-spirited views on others. Loosen up, religious right! You should learn to be more compassionate for those less fortunate than you!" The argument begins with a conclusion to be established, namely, that all Americans should be pro-choice. But the argument quickly gets off track and follows a red herring—it turns into an argument about the personality traits of those in the religious right and draws a conclusion about the people so characterized. What happened to the original issue? Along the way, the argument got off track and followed a red herring.

   7. Begging the question: There are different versions of begging the question, but a major form of this fallacy occurs when a disputant uses his conclusion as one of the premises employed to establish that conclusion. The conclusion is simply asserted as one of the premises in the argument used to justify that conclusion. Often, this fallacy is concealed by stating the proposition in question one way when it is a premise and another way when it is the conclusion. For example: "Capital punishment is *wrong* because it is an example of doing something we have *no business doing*, namely, taking a person's life." Here the conclusion "Capital punishment is wrong" includes the term "wrong." The premise used to argue for this conclusion is actually just a different way of stating the conclusion itself. This is masked, however, because the proposition uses "no business doing" when it is stated as a premise. It should be clear, however, that "no business doing" is just another way of saying "wrong."

Here is another example: "I know the Bible is completely true and trustworthy because it is the Word of God and as the Word of God the Bible teaches the complete truthfulness of everything it asserts." The conclusion (that the Bible is completely true and trustworthy) is correct, but the argument used to establish that conclusion begs the question. Can you think of a better argument for the conclusion that does not beg the question?[14]

CONCLUSION

Much more could be said about the topics of this chapter than space has allowed. For example, there are more informal fallacies than I have listed above. But this chapter provides you with enough material to allow you to form some concrete goals and practices in developing a better Christian mind.

In part one, we looked at why we modern evangelicals have lost the emphasis on the intellectual life characteristic of our ancestors and affirmed in the Bible. We also saw from Holy Scripture and from the way the mind works that developing a careful Christian mind is not an option for someone serious about Christian discipleship and mature human flourishing. In part two, we looked at some suggestions for how one can actually go about developing a Christian mind. In part three, we will turn to a different area of reflection. We will look at different aspects of a properly functioning Christian mind to see different areas of life in which a growing Christian mind is essential, beginning with evangelism in chapter six.

WHAT A MATURE CHRISTIAN MIND LOOKS LIKE

X

CHAPTER SIX

Evangelism and the Christian Mind

X

*Western civilization is for the first time in its history
in danger of dying. The reason is spiritual. It is losing
its life, its soul; that soul was the Christian faith. . . .
We do apologetics not to save the church
but to save the world.*

PETER KREEFT AND RON TACELLI[1]

K

*So [the apostle Paul] was reasoning in the synagogue
with the Jews and the God-fearing* Gentiles,
*and in the market place every day
with those who happened to be present.*

ACTS 17:17 (NASB)

RECENTLY, SYNDICATED COLUMNIST THOMAS SOWELL WROTE THE FOLLOWING:

Many studies have shown how ignorant our high school and even college graduates are of basic knowledge that was once taken for granted. What is even more alarming is how lacking they are in the ability to think systematically. Such elementary things as defining terms and going step-by-step from evidence to conclusions have given way to emotional rhetoric and automatic responses to buzzwords and visions. As someone who has taught at several colleges, I am all too painfully aware of the erosion of thinking over the years. But even after leaving the classroom, I have continued to encounter the same mindlessness everywhere. For example, an environmentalist to whom I presented certain facts responded by saying, "But they are raping the planet!" "What specifically does that mean?" I asked. He was as speechless as someone who had just played the ace of trumps and was then told that that was not enough to win.[2]

Sowell's point is a serious one that has dramatic implications for the way we Christians usually present the gospel to unbelievers. Because of the mindlessness of our culture, people do not persuade others of their views (religious or otherwise) on the basis of argument and reason, but rather, by expressing emotional rhetoric and politically correct buzzwords. Reason has given way to rhetoric, evidence to emotion, substance to slogan, the speech writer to the makeup man, and rational authority (the right to command compliance and to be believed) to social power (the ability to coerce compliance and outward conformance). The way we reach decisions today, the manner in which we dialogue about issues, and the political correctness we see all around us are dehumanizing expressions of the anti-intellectualism in modern society when it comes to broad worldview issues. Rhetoric without reason, persuasion without argument is manipulation. Might—it is wrongly believed—makes right.

When was the last time you saw or read in media coverage of the abortion controversy any attempt at all to clarify and state the crucial arguments offered by each side? Instead, a media already widely sympathetic with the pro-choice position continues to use rhetoric to "persuade" people to see abortion rights in favorable ways. One example of this is the constant use of the labels "pro-choice" and "anti-abortion." Apart from the inaccuracy of these labels, pro-life advocates are not against abortion per se, but are *for life*, a fact that would be evident if an abortion technique were developed that saved the life of the child and allowed it to be put up for adoption. This media practice amounts to nothing less than subliminal propaganda that is swallowed all too easily by a nation of empty selves.

No movement, political, religious, or otherwise, can survive with dignity or flourish in a culture if it allows the following to arise:

- A culture where its viewpoint is considered irrational by a significant number of people and is not adequately represented among the intellectual leaders who shape the plausibility structure of that culture.
- A culture in which the movement itself enlists others to join, not primarily in terms of the importance of the ideas and the truth that defines that movement, but in terms of the satisfaction of felt needs for those who sign up.
- An atmosphere wherein the movement does not mobilize a growing number of its soldiers to be articulate advocates and defenders of its ideology who can engage in debate in the public square.

It saddens me to say that Sowell's remarks, along with the observations just expressed, accurately describe many of the current approaches to evangelism employed by the evangelical community. I should know. One of my spiritual gifts is evangelism, and I have been involved in it for twenty-seven years. I have trained thousands of people to communicate the gospel to others, and I have given evangelistic talks in most of the states in this country. I say this not to boast, but to assure you that I am no ivory tower academic (whatever that means). I am a practitioner. In the last quarter of a century I have seen a slow, steady erosion of apologetical reasoning and argument as part of the texture of our evangelism. Instead, evangelism is increasingly associated with the things Sowell bemoans: rhetoric, Christian buzzwords, and an overdone appeal to felt needs. In the very way we do evangelism, we have inadvertently let the world squeeze us into its mold.

A few years ago, I was in the Baltimore airport waiting to get on a plane to the Midwest. I overheard three women talking next to me. One woman was explaining to the others why she had left Catholicism and become a Baptist. Her "reasons" were that she liked the people, the music, and the feeling she got in the Baptist church, and she found the minister's sermons interesting and pleasurable to hear. Now, these are all wonderful, but they do not justify changing one's basic religious commitment. Conspicuous by its absence was one single reference to the woman's attempt to compare Catholic and Baptist theology to see which was more likely to be true. Reason played the same role in this woman's religious life that it did in the environmentalist's commitment in Sowell's article. If reason plays no practical role in such religious decisions as choosing a denomination or becoming a Christian in the first place, why should we expect it to inform subsequent decisions within the religious life?

Given the contemporary cultural climate, it is easier to get people to buy a product, join a movement, or accept a set of ideas if you use rhetoric, appeal to emotions and felt needs, and set aside a rational presentation of the topic at hand. But the short-term "successes" of such an approach can dull us to the long-term harm that will be done by taking this easy way out. As British sociologist and theologian Os Guinness has argued, the Devil will allow short-term success in evangelism and church growth if the means used to achieve it ultimately contribute to the marginalization of the church and her message.[3] In this case, the church becomes her own gravedigger. By eschewing the role of reason in evangelism, and substituting in its place an overemphasis on a simple gospel appeal directed at felt needs, short-term gains are to be expected in a culture of empty selves. But who can deny that while our numbers have grown, *our impact has not been proportionate to our numbers?*

There is too much at stake for this situation to continue. What is needed is a rethinking of the very nature of evangelism, more specifically, of the role of reasoning and argument in the way we do evangelism. In what follows, I will describe the role of reason in evangelism and offer some examples of how to use reasoning in persuading others of the truthfulness of the gospel in particular or the Christian worldview in general.

APOLOGETICS AND EVANGELISM

Evangelism and Apologetics

Apologetics is the primary form through which the Christian mind expresses itself in the task of evangelism. *Apologetics* comes from the Greek word *apologeomai*, whose root meaning is "to defend something." *Apologetics* can be defined as *that New Testament ministry which seeks to provide rational grounds for believing Christianity in whole or in part and to respond to objections raised against Christianity in whole or in part.* So understood, apologetics is a ministry designed to help unbelievers to overcome intellectual obstacles to conversion and believers to remove doubts that hinder spiritual growth.

In chapter two, we saw that there is a biblical basis for the use of the mind in doing apologetics. First Peter 3:15 commands us to be ready to give a reasoned defense to someone who asks us for a credible reason why we believe what we do. Jude 1:3 admonishes us to *"contend earnestly"* for the faith. "Contend earnestly" carries with it the idea of engaging in a contest, a struggle, a conflict, or a debate by the pious in the heroic struggle for religious truth, justice, and virtue. The term clearly includes the idea of an intellectual struggle, an idea also expressed by Paul when he said spiritual warfare involves "destroying speculations and every lofty thing raised up against the knowledge of God, . . . taking every thought captive to the obedience of Christ" (2 Corinthians 10:5). Spiritual warfare is a struggle with persons, demonic and human, and the primary way persons influence other persons is through the ideas they get others to accept. Thus, intellectual tools and reasoning are an important part, though not the whole of spiritual warfare. The other primary components are spiritual preparedness, discernment, courage, and wisdom.

We see examples of apologetics everywhere in the Scriptures. In Acts, Paul argued, reasoned, presented evidence, and tried rationally to persuade others to become Christians (Acts 14:15-17; 17:2-4, 16-31; 18:4; 19:8-9). He brought to center stage the truth and reasonableness of the gospel, *not* the fact that it addresses felt needs. Though both are important, there is a clear Pauline emphasis placed on the former. Jesus Christ Himself regularly engaged in logical debate and rational argument with false, destructive ideologies in His culture, and on several occasions He told people to believe in Him, not simply on the basis of His words, but because of the evidence of His miracles.

In this way, Jesus and Paul were continuing a style of persuasion peppered throughout the Old Testament prophets. Regularly, the prophets appealed to evidence to justify belief in the biblical God or in the divine authority of their inspired message: fulfilled prophecy, the historical fact of miracles, the inadequacy of finite pagan deities to be a cause of such a large, well-ordered universe compared to the God of the Bible, and so forth. They did not say, "God said it, that settles it, you should believe it!" They provided a rational defense for their claims.

It is sometimes said that Genesis does not try to "prove" the existence of God, it merely assumes it. But this is inaccurate. True, Genesis does not argue against atheism because atheism was not a major ideology among the pagan nations surrounding Moses and Israel. But those nations did believe in fickle, finite, immoral deities. In fact, a widespread pagan belief was the idea that each spring the gods copulated, their seed fell to the ground, and that was why crops sprouted and grew each year. Based on that belief, yearly pagan rituals included frenzied orgies to induce the gods to copulate and insure a new season of crops. Genesis takes this view to task and presents a testable claim: The God of Israel delegated to living things the intrinsic power to reproduce after their own kinds, an odd and foreign idea to the nations of the ancient Mideast. But this claim carried with it a test. If the pagans ceased their orgies, then no crops would grow if their views were correct and the gods needed inducement to copulate. But if the biblical view were correct, crops would continue to arise.

The General Value of Apologetics

I am not suggesting that the only thing in Scripture relevant to evangelism is rational argument and apologetics. However, I am suggesting that *apologetics is an absolutely essential ingredient to biblical evangelism.* And it is easy to see why. An emphasis on reasoning in evangelism makes the truthfulness of the gospel the main issue, not the self-interested "fulfillment" of the listener. Felt needs are important, but if they are made the issue, Christianity will be seen as just another means of helping the convert overcome his problems, along with his therapist and workout routine. Let me repeat—there is a place for a simple gospel presentation and for addressing people's felt needs in our evangelistic strategy. But these should never be the tail that wags the dog, at least not if our evangelism is to express biblical teaching and common sense. If the truth of a message is important, apologetical reasoning will be a crucial part of evangelism because it places the emphasis where it should be—on the truth of the message.

None of this means you must have a Ph.D. before you can share the faith with an unbeliever. In the gospels, people touched by Jesus bore testimony to Him immediately without training. But these gospel examples are not there to teach us how to do evangelism—the book of Acts does that. They're there to show that all manner of people were coming to faith in Jesus and to provide testimony about who Jesus was. Clearly, a new Christian should witness for Christ as opportunity presents itself, irrespective of the amount of training acquired. But it does not follow that a maturing Christian, five, ten, or twenty years old in the Lord, should still be unskilled in reasoning on behalf of the gospel.

Will this approach to evangelism take work? You bet it will. We'll have to do a lot of reading, studying, and thinking. But if someone can spend several hours a day learning to swing a golf club, at least the same effort would not be inappropriate for someone who wants to be a more effective witness for Christ.

A life of study and intellectual growth enhances one's effectiveness in personal evangelism in many ways. Yesterday, my friend Dan Yim reminded me of one of those ways. Many times we want to communicate the gospel to friends, coworkers, or relatives. But this can create tension and a certain unnaturalness when we are with them, because we feel pressured to find some seam in the conversation from which we can artificially redirect the discussion to our testimony or something of the sort. If a person has a secular/sacred dichotomy in his life due to a lack of a carefully thought-out, integrated Christian worldview, then the gospel will have to be forced into an otherwise secular discussion. But if a person has developed a Christian mind, she can relax because she has an understanding of and a Christian view about a number of "secular" topics. In such a situation, it would be hard to have a normal conversation without Christianity coming up naturally and in a way relevant to the topic of discussion. Moreover, a well-developed mind can see connections between what a friend is saying and other issues of which the friend may not be aware. For example, a friend may be espousing moral relativism yet inconsistently hold that we all have an absolute duty to save the environment. If a person sees the connections, she can simply ask well-placed questions that naturally lead to a discussion of broader worldview issues, including God and our relationship to Him. In such a case, the pressure is off because a person has the intellectual categories necessary to make natural connections between Christianity and a host of regular conversation topics. There is no need to try to find a crack in the discussion to insert a gospel presentation utterly unrelated to the flow of conversation. What a joyful fruit of the intellectual life this is!

Apologetics and Children

Two hundred years ago, the great spiritual master and Christian activist William Wilberforce (1759-1833) wrote a book about the nature of real Christianity and authentic spiritual growth. In a modern book about the spiritual life, especially the cultivation of spirituality in children, I doubt that the first issue addressed would be apologetics! But this is precisely what was at the forefront of Wilberforce's mind. His statement is so powerful, I will cite it in full:

> In an age in which infidelity abounds, do we observe them [parents] carefully instructing their children in the principles of faith which they profess? Or do they furnish their children with arguments for the defense of that faith? They would blush on their child's birth to think him inadequate in any branch of knowledge or any skill pertaining to his station in life. He cultivates these skills with becoming diligence. But he is left to collect his religion as he may. The study of Christianity has formed no part of his education. His attachment to it—where any attachment to it exists at all—is too often not the preference of sober reason and conviction. Instead his attachment to Christianity is merely the result of early and groundless possession. He was born in a Christian country, so of course he is a Christian. His father was a member of the Church of England, so that is why he is, too. When religion is handed down among us by hereditary succession, it is not surprising to find youth of sense and spirit beginning to question the truth of the system in which they were brought up. And it is not surprising to see them abandon a position which they are unable to

defend. Knowing Christianity chiefly by its difficulties and the impossibilities falsely imputed to it, they fall perhaps into the company of unbelievers.[4]

Having witnessed hundreds of evangelical children hit the college campus, I can attest to the fact that we need to follow Wilberforce's advice and start early in teaching them the reasons for their faith. Make no mistake about it. Young children can ask profound intellectual questions about God and religion. And if we do not take them seriously and work to provide them with good answers, it will impact the vibrancy of their Christian commitment sooner or later.

Just last night I received a phone call from a woman in our neighborhood I'll call Beth. Beth has a son in high school who is a friend of my youngest teenage daughter, Allison. Beth became a Christian five years ago, and her son is a believer too. Unknown to me, a friend of Beth's had recommended she read an apologetic book I wrote a few years ago entitled *Scaling the Secular City*. Yesterday, someone told Beth that Allison's father was the author of the book. She called me to ask some apologetical questions.

The conversation was quite interesting. She opened up on the phone about a frustration and a fear. The frustration was that she still had a large number of nonChristian friends and relatives who regularly asked her hard questions about her faith that she was not able to answer. She felt fear because the spiritual life of her son, like most teenagers, was something she could not take for granted, and her son regularly asked her questions about Christianity that she could not address. She feared not only for her son's spiritual growth but also that he would not respect her own dedication to Christ if she did not take hard questions seriously enough to find out answers. Her son had pointed out that she had time to do a number of hobbies, watch television, and so on, so that if getting good answers to certain questions mattered to her, she would have gotten them by now. He concluded that her faith must not matter that much to her, because she had not taken the time to wrestle with issues that might show her faith was false. I encouraged her to continue growing and to be intentional about making progress in learning apologetical answers to various questions. My experience leads me to believe that Beth's situation is not unique.

Beth's call reminded me that it is important to develop our Christian minds by learning why we believe what we believe. This is an important aspect of our spiritual lives. As we grow in our apologetical knowledge and skills, our faith becomes more steady, powerful, and confident. We also grow in our courage and boldness as witnesses for Jesus Christ. And we learn to be attractive, nondefensive ambassadors for Christ who are prepared to give an answer to someone who asks us what we believe and why.

This chapter has demonstrated the importance of the transformation of our minds toward Christlikeness as it relates to evangelism. An important foundation for evangelism is the ability to answer questions, much like Beth's need just mentioned. We now turn to the relationship between the Christian mind and apologetic reasoning to see how developing such skills is related to our spiritual growth.

CHAPTER SEVEN

Apologetic Reasoning and the Christian Mind

X

The Christian affirmation is . . .
that the Trinitarian structure which can be shown to exist in the
mind of a man and in all his works is, in fact, the integral
structure of the universe, and corresponds, not by pictorial
imagery, but by necessary uniformity of substance,
with the nature of God, in whom all that is exists.
DOROTHY SAYERS, IN *THE MIND OF THE MAKER* [1]

K

To think secularly is to think within a frame of reference bounded
by the limits of our life on earth: it is to keep one's calculations
rooted in this-worldly criteria. To think Christianly is to accept all
things with the mind as related, directly or indirectly, to man's
eternal destiny as the redeemed and chosen by God.
HARRY BLAMIRES, *THE CHRISTIAN MIND* [2]

K

It is important to see that apologetics is not an activity reserved
for philosophers who also happen to be religious believers. Much
that passes as philosophy of religion is really apologetics as
practiced by individuals who reject tenets of religious belief. I do
not say this to be critical of philosophers of religion who may also
happen to be atheists. My point is that philosophers who reject the
Christian religion do not suddenly become, by virtue of this fact
alone, more objective or rational or open-minded than
philosophers who are Christians or Jews.
RONALD H. NASH, *FAITH AND REASON* [3]

137

W E HAVE SEEN THE IMPORTANCE OF REASON AND APOLOGETICS IN EVAN-
gelism. In this chapter I want to present briefly three examples of
such apologetic reasoning in action, as it encounters skepticism, scientism, and moral relativism. I select these three issues because Christians
encounter them frequently; they are important issues in their own right,
and they provide clear, accessible examples of the art of apologetical
reasoning.

No one person is adequate for this task, and that is why we need
each other. But I think the discussion that follows clearly shows how we
can all benefit from learning how to do apologetics.

ANSWERING THE SKEPTIC

What Is Skepticism?

We have all met skeptics who in one way or another have raised doubts
about what we can know or reasonably believe. When you assert something, the skeptic responds with "Says who?" or "How do you know?"
There are many different forms of skepticism, and I cannot describe
and critique all of them here. For our purposes, let us define the skeptic as someone who does not believe that people have knowledge or
rationally justified beliefs. Some skeptics are global skeptics: they hold
their skepticism about all beliefs whatever. Others are local in orientation. They may allow for knowledge in certain areas, like science or
mathematics, while confining their skepticism to, say, ethical or religious claims.

Skepticism and the Problem of the Criterion

In 1984, E. Calvin Beisner wrote a perceptive article in *Discipleship
Journal* in which he claimed that Christians interested in refuting skepticism should learn about what is sometimes called *the problem of the
criterion.*[4] Beisner was right. So we begin our critique by clarifying the
problem of the criterion. We can distinguish two different questions relevant to the human quest for knowledge. First is, What is it that we
know? This is a question about the specific items of knowledge we pos-

sess and about the *extent* or *limits* of our knowledge. And second: How do we decide in any given case whether or not we have knowledge in that case? What are the criteria for knowledge? This is a question about our *criteria* for knowledge.

Now suppose we want to sort all of our beliefs into two groups—the true or justified ones and the false or unjustified ones—in order to retain the former and dispose of the latter in our entire set of beliefs. Such a sorting would allow us to improve our rational situation and grow in knowledge and justified belief. But now a problem arises regarding how we are to proceed in this sorting activity. It would seem that we would first need an answer to at least one of our two questions. But before we can answer our first question about the extent of our knowledge, we would seem to need an answer to our second question about our criteria for knowledge. Yet before we can answer the second question, we seem to require an answer to our first question. This is the problem of the criterion.[5] If we don't know how we know things, how can we know anything at all or draw limits to human knowledge? But if we don't know some things before we ask ourselves how we can have knowledge in the first place, on what basis will we answer that question?

There are three main solutions to the problem. First, there is *skepticism*. The skeptic claims, among other things, that no good solution to the problem exists and, thus, there is no knowledge. The next two solutions are advocated by those who claim that we do have knowledge. *Methodism* (not the religious denomination) is the name of the second solution, and it has been advocated by philosophers such as John Locke and René Descartes. According to methodism, one starts the enterprise of knowing with a criterion for what does and does not count as knowledge; that is, we start with an answer to question two and not question one. Methodists claim that before I can know some specific proposition P (for example, there is a tree in the yard), I must first know some general criterion Q and, further, I must know that P is a good example of or measures up to Q. For example, Q might be "If you can test some item of belief with the five senses, then it can be an item of knowledge," or perhaps "If something appears to your senses in a certain way, then in the absence of reasons for distrusting the lighting or your senses, you know that the thing is as it appears to you."

Unfortunately, methodism is not a good strategy because it leads to a vicious infinite regress. To see this, note that in general, methodism implies that before I can know anything (P), I must know two other things: Q (my criterion for knowledge) and R (the fact that P satisfies Q). But the skeptic can ask how it is that we know Q and R and the methodist will have to offer a new criterion Q' that specifies how he knows Q and another new criterion R' that tells how he knows that Q satisfies Q'. Obviously, the same problem will arise for Q' and R', and a vicious regress is set up.

Another way to see this is to note that there have been major debates about what are and are not good criteria for knowledge. Seventeenth-century thinker John Locke offered something akin to the notion that an item of knowledge about the external world must pass the criterion of deriving that item of knowledge from simple sensory ideas or impressions (roughly, testing it with the senses). By contrast, Locke's counterpart René Descartes offered a radically different criterion: the item of knowledge must be clear and distinct when brought before the mind. If we are methodists, how are we to settle disputes about criteria for knowledge? The answer will be that we will have to offer criteria for our criteria, and so on. It would seem, then, that methodism is in trouble.

There is a third solution to the problem known as *particularism*, which is advocated by philosophers such as Thomas Reid, Roderick Chisholm, and G. E. Moore. According to particularists, we start by knowing specific, clear items of knowledge: for example, that I had eggs for breakfast this morning; that there is a tree before me or, perhaps, that I seem to see a tree; that $7 + 5 = 12$; that mercy is a virtue; and so on. I can know some things directly and simply without needing criteria for how I know them and without having to know *how* or even *that* I know them. We know many things without being able to prove that we do or without fully understanding them. We simply identify clear instances of knowing without having to possess or apply any criteria for knowledge. We may reflect on these instances and go on to develop criteria for knowledge consistent with them and use these criteria to make judgments in borderline cases of knowledge, but the criteria are justified by their congruence with specific instances of knowledge, and not the other way around.

For example, I may start with moral knowledge (murder is wrong) and legal knowledge (taxes are to be paid by April 15) and go on to formulate criteria for when something is moral or legal. I could then use these criteria for judging borderline cases (intentionally driving on the wrong side of the street, for example). In general, we start with clear instances of knowledge, formulate criteria based on those clear instances, and extend our knowledge by using those criteria in border-line, unclear cases.

Rebutting the Skeptic

The skeptic can raise two basic objections against the particularist. First, the particularist allegedly begs the question against the skeptic by simply assuming his answer to the point at issue—whether we have knowledge. The skeptic asks, how does the particularist know that we have this knowledge? Isn't it possible in the cases cited above that the particularist is wrong and only *thinks* he has knowledge?

Particularists respond to this objection as follows. First, regarding begging the question, if the skeptic doesn't offer a reason for his skepticism (and just keeps asking, "How do you know?" each time the particularist makes a knowledge claim), his skepticism can be ignored because it is not a substantive position or argument. If, on the other hand, his skepticism is the result of an argument, then this argument must be reasonable before it can be held as a serious objection against knowledge. However, if we did not know some things, we could not *reasonably doubt* anything (for example, the reason for doubting my senses now is my knowledge that they have mislead me in the past). Therefore, unbridled skepticism is not a rationally defensible position, and it cannot be rationally asserted and defended *without presupposing knowledge*.

Second, the skeptic tries to force the particularist to become a methodist by asking the "how do you know?" question since the skeptic is implying that before you can know, you must have criteria for knowledge. And the skeptic knows he can refute the methodist. But the particularist will resist the slide into methodism by reaffirming that he can know some specific item without having to say how he knows it. For example, the particularist will say, "I know that mercy is a virtue and not a vice even if I don't know how it is that I know this. But, Mr. Skeptic, why think that I have to know how I know this *before* I can know it?"

Further, the particularist argues that just because it is logically possible that he is mistaken in a specific case of knowledge, that does not mean he is mistaken or that he has any good reason to think he is wrong. And until the skeptic can give him good reason for thinking his instances of knowledge fail, the mere logical possibility that he is wrong will not suffice. Suppose I claim to know about the time and event when I first went to Disneyland several years ago. In response, the skeptic tries to show I don't really know this by raising the possibility that I might have been born five seconds ago with a memory and that my memory is deceiving me. The particularist will respond this way: Just because the statement "J. P. Moreland was born five seconds ago with a memory" is not a logical contradiction (like "J. P. Moreland is and is not a human being") and could be true as a bare, logical possibility, that does not mean we have good reasons for actually believing the statement is correct. The particularist will insist that unless there are good reasons for believing the skeptic's claim (and the skeptic doesn't give such reasons), the bare possibility that it might be true is not sufficient to call into question what I actually know about my Disneyland visit.

The particularist and skeptic have very different approaches to knowledge. For the skeptic, the burden of proof is on the one who claims to know something. If it is logically possible that one might be mistaken, then knowledge is not present because knowledge requires complete, 100 percent certainty. Of the two main tasks in the quest for knowledge (obtaining true or justified beliefs and avoiding false or unjustified beliefs), the skeptic elevates the latter and requires that his position be *refuted* before knowledge can be justified. To refute something is to show that it is wrong. The skeptic thinks avoiding error is better than gaining truth and thinks he must be shown wrong before anyone can claim to know anything.

The particularist elevates the value of gaining as many truths as are available in the world and tries to *rebut* the skeptic. To rebut something is not to show that it is wrong, but simply to show that the skeptic has not adequately shown that it is true. After all, the particularist recognizes that we all know many things before we ever talk to skeptics. He places the burden of proof on the skeptic and requires the skeptic to show that his skepticism is true and should be taken seriously before he allows the skeptic to bother him about knowledge. The particularist does not need to refute the skeptic (show skepticism is false), he merely needs to rebut the skeptic (show that the skeptic has not adequately made his case for skepticism). Given that the skeptic cannot consistently argue for his skepticism, there is no reason to deny what is obvious to all of us: that we do know many things.

One Skeptic's Story

Once I was strolling through an open area at a large mall and I overheard two men sitting on a bench arguing about morality. It was evident that one was a Christian who was trying to convince his skeptical friend that abortion was wrong. Unfortunately, the Christian was getting the worst end of the dialogue because he could not get past his friend's constant questioning about how we know anything at all is right or wrong. I stopped, introduced myself, mentioned that I had inadvertently heard their discussion, and asked if I could join in, because the topic was of great interest to me. Happily, they were quite warm to the idea.

Daniel (the skeptic) told me he thought it was wrong to force our moral views on anyone else because no one really knows right from wrong anyway. He asserted that no one could really claim to know anything at all. I asked Daniel if he knew there were no moral truths that could be known, and he responded by saying that he didn't know this, he just thought it was true. I asked him if he knew if he thought this or did he just think that he thought it. Being a bright person, he knew (!) that I was backing him into an infinite regress of "thinking that he thought that he thought that . . ." So he bit the bullet and said he knew he thought that no one knew any moral truths.

I pointed out that we had established that he himself had at least some knowledge, and I went on to ask why he thought no one had any moral knowledge. I adopted the particularist standpoint and asserted a number of moral truths that we all know: torturing babies is wrong, fairness and kindness are virtues, hatred is a vice, what Hitler did to the Jews in World War II was immoral. I also reminded him that he himself seemed to accept at least one item of moral knowledge: It is wrong to force our moral views on others! I then shifted the burden of proof onto Daniel and asked him why in the world anyone should think that we don't know these things to be true because we do, in fact, know them.

Daniel seemed a bit embarrassed, but he managed to come up with a response: No one could tell him how we know these things and, further, there were several moral areas (like when to allow a terminally ill relative to die) where it was hard to draw the line between right and wrong. I told Daniel that there was no good reason to think that someone had to know *how* he knew something before he could know it. Many people, I said, never have the time to think about how they know certain things, but they know them nonetheless. I also showed him that there was no good reason to think that someone had to have a detailed moral answer to all hard, borderline cases (like certain end-of-life situations) before he could claim to know that torturing babies was wrong!

As the conversation went on, Daniel's friend, Greg, was deeply encouraged in his faith (as he told me later when Daniel left for a moment). Daniel won most of their arguments, and he was encouraged to see a Christian lovingly, gently, and intelligently point out to Daniel where his thinking was flawed. After around an hour, we actually got Daniel to admit to the existence of knowable moral absolutes and were able to open Daniel up to the pro-life position and to the gospel. Daniel said this had been the first time in his life that a Christian had been able to respond to his skepticism. It was a joy to be prepared to engage Daniel and Greg in this way. My previous studies had paid off (except I went home empty-handed because I forgot what I had gone to the mall to purchase!).

ANSWERING SCIENTISM

Two Forms of Scientism

We have all met people who think you can't know something unless you can prove it scientifically. Since most religious or ethical claims cannot be tested in the lab, it is asserted that they can't be known. Such people embrace what is known as *scientism*. Scientism is the view that science is the only paradigm of truth and rationality. If something does not square with currently well-established scientific beliefs, if it is not within the domain of things appropriate for scientific investigation, or if it is not amenable to scientific methodology, then it is not true or rational. Everything outside of science is a matter of mere belief and subjective opinion, of which rational assessment is impossible. Science, exclusively and ideally, is our model of intellectual excellence.

Actually, there are two forms of scientism: *strong scientism* and *weak scientism*. Strong scientism is the view that some proposition or theory is true or rational if and only if it is a scientific proposition or theory. That is, if and only if it is a well-established scientific proposition or theory that, in turn, depends upon its having been successfully formed, tested, and used according to appropriate scientific methodology. There are no truths apart from scientific truths, and even if there were, there would be no reason whatever to believe them.

Advocates of weak scientism allow for the existence of truths apart from science and are even willing to grant that they can have some minimal, positive rationality status without the support of science. But advocates of weak scientism still hold that science is the most valuable, most serious, and most authoritative sector of human learning. Every other intellectual activity is inferior to science. Further, there are virtually no limits to science. There is no field upon which scientific research cannot shed light. To the degree that some issue or belief outside science can be given scientific support or can be reduced to science, to that degree the issue or belief becomes rationally acceptable. Thus we have an intellectual, and perhaps, even a moral obligation to try to use science to solve problems in fields heretofore untouched by scientific methodology. For example, we should try to solve problems about the mind by the methods of neurophysiology and computer science.

Note that advocates of weak scientism are not merely claiming that, for example, belief that the universe had a beginning, supported by good philosophical and theological arguments, gains *extra* support if it also has good scientific arguments for it. This claim is relatively uncontroversial because, usually, if some belief has a few good supporting arguments and later gains more good supporting arguments, then this will increase the rationality of the belief in question. But this is not what weak scientism implies, because this point cuts both ways. For it will equally be the case that good philosophical and theological arguments for a beginning will increase the rationality of such a belief that was initially supported only by scientific arguments. Advocates of weak scientism are claiming that fields outside science gain if they are given scientific support and not vice versa.

If either strong or weak scientism is true, this would have drastic implications for those who try to integrate their scientific and theological beliefs. *If strong scientism is true, then theology is not a rational enterprise at all and there is no such thing as theological knowledge. If weak scientism is true, then the conversation between theology and science will be a monologue with theology listening to science and waiting for science to give it support.* For thinking Christians, neither of these alternatives is acceptable.

What's Wrong with Scientism?

Note first that strong scientism is self-refuting. You will recall from chapter five that a proposition (or sentence) is self-refuting if it refers to and falsifies itself. For example, "There are no English sentences" and "There are no truths" are self-refuting. Strong scientism is not itself a proposition of *science*, but a proposition of *philosophy about science* to the effect that only scientific propositions are true and/or rational. In other words, strong scientism is a philosophical claim, *not* a scientific one. And strong scientism is itself offered as a true, rationally justified position to believe. Propositions that are self-refuting do not just happen to be false propositions that could have been true. Self-refuting propositions are *necessarily false;* that is, it is not possible for them to be true. What this means is that, among other things, no amount of scientific progress in the future will have the slightest effect on making strong scientism more acceptable.

There are two more problems that count equally against strong and weak scientism. First, scientism (in both forms) does not adequately allow for the task of stating and defending the necessary presuppositions for science itself to be practiced (assuming scientific realism). Thus, scientism shows itself to be a foe and not a friend of science.

Science cannot be practiced in thin air. In fact, science itself rests on a number of substantive philosophical theses that must be assumed if science is even going to get off the runway. Each of these assumptions has been challenged, and the task of stating and defending these assumptions is a task of philosophy, not science. The conclusions of science cannot be more certain than the presuppositions it rests on and uses to reach those conclusions.

Strong scientism rules out these presuppositions altogether because neither the presuppositions themselves nor their defense is a scientific matter. Weak scientism misconstrues their strength in its view that scientific propositions have greater rational authority than those of other fields like philosophy. This would mean that the conclusions of science are more certain than the philosophical presuppositions used to justify and reach those conclusions, and that is absurd. In this regard, the following statement by John Kekes strikes at the heart of weak scientism:

> A successful argument for science being the paradigm of rationality must be based on the demonstration that the presuppositions of science are preferable to other presuppositions.

That demonstration requires showing that science, relying on these presuppositions, is better at solving some problems and achieving some ideals than its competitors. But showing that cannot be the task of science. It is, in fact, one task of philosophy. Thus the enterprise of justifying the presuppositions of science by showing that with their help science is the best way of solving certain problems and achieving some ideals is a necessary precondition of the justification of science. Hence philosophy, and not science, is a stronger candidate for being the very paradigm of rationality.[6]

Here is a list of some of the philosophical presuppositions of science:

- the existence of a theory independent, external world
- the orderly nature of the external world
- the knowability of the external world
- the existence of truth
- the laws of logic
- the reliability of our cognitive and sensory faculties to serve as truth gatherers and as a source of justified beliefs in our intellectual environment
- the adequacy of language to describe the world
- the existence of values used in science (for example, "test theories fairly and report test results honestly")
- the uniformity of nature and induction
- the existence of numbers and mathematical truths

There is a second problem that counts equally against strong and weak scientism: *the existence of true and rationally justified beliefs outside of science.* The simple fact is that true, rationally justified beliefs exist in a host of fields outside of science. Strong scientism does not allow for this fact, and it is therefore to be rejected as an inadequate account of our intellectual enterprise.

Moreover, some propositions believed outside science ("red is a color," "torturing babies is wrong," "I am now thinking about science") are better justified than some believed within science ("evolution takes place through a series of very small steps"). It is not hard to believe that many of our currently held scientific beliefs will and should be revised or abandoned in one hundred years, but it would be hard to see how the same could be said of the extrascientific propositions just cited. Weak scientism does not account for this fact. Furthermore, when advocates of weak scientism attempt to reduce all issues to scientific ones, this often has a distorting effect on an intellectual issue. Arguably, this is the case in current attempts to make the existence and nature of mind a scientific problem.[7]

The Scientist's Story

One evening an engineering friend in my church named Tom invited me to a party at his house. His boss had been a senior engineer for twenty-five years and had gone back to school to finish a Ph.D. in physics. Tom warned me that he had invited his boss to the party because he hated Christianity and regularly mocked the faith at work. Tom had taken the liberty of telling his boss that I would be there and could answer some of his questions. It sounded like I was in for an interesting evening to say the least.

I arrived at the party on time and was at the hors d'oeuvres table when Tom's boss arrived. Tom brought him over and introduced us to each other. When I extended my hand to Mr. Smith (not his real name), he started attacking my Christian beliefs without a moment's hesitation.

"I used to think that religion and philosophy were important, but I now recognize that they are just superstition," he asserted. "Science is the only area where we have knowledge. If you can quantify something or test it in the lab, then you can know it. Otherwise, it's just one person's opinion against another's. To me, the sole value of religion is that believing it helps some people who need that sort of thing, but religious beliefs are neither true nor rational because they are not scientifically testable."

I let him go on for what seemed like the longest ten minutes of my life. In the most gracious way I could muster, I finally got a chance to respond: "I have a few questions for you, Mr. Smith. I am puzzled as to how I should understand what you have asserted for the last ten minutes. You have not said one single sentence from science and nothing you have asserted is the least bit scientifically testable or quantifiable. In fact, you have spent all of your time making *philosophical* assertions *about* science and religion. Now, I get the distinct impression that you want me to take your ten-minute monologue as something that is both true and rational. But how can this be, given your scientism, because you do not believe that philosophical assertions are either true or rational? On the other hand, if you don't think your own assertions are either true or rational, why have you been boring us with emotive expressions of autobiography for the last ten minutes? After all, some of the finger foods are getting cold."

My response must have shocked Mr. Smith because he literally muttered a few things under his breath and changed the subject. I wouldn't let him off the hook. "I have another question, Mr. Smith. As you know, there have been different definitions of truth offered by various thinkers. Can you give me one single scientific test that offers a definition of truth itself or that shows me that there is such a thing? I take truth to be a correspondence between a statement and the external world. If I say grass is green and, in fact, grass is green, my assertion is true. But what kind of scientific test will enable me to know what truth itself is or that we have it? What about the other assumptions of science? Can you give me a scientific proof that these assumptions are correct or reasonable to believe?"

Before my very eyes, Mr. Smith's entire demeanor changed. He was accustomed to bullying Christians and it wasn't working now. The rest of the evening we were able to discuss the gospel and a number of other related issues. I stayed in touch with Tom for the next year and not once during that time did Mr. Smith ever again attack Christianity at work.

ANSWERING MORAL RELATIVISM

What Is Moral Relativism?

Moral relativism is widely espoused in this country. This moral thesis holds that everyone ought to act in accordance with the agent's own society's code (or perhaps, with the agent's own personal code). What is right for one society is not necessarily right for another. For example, society A may have in its code "Adultery is morally permissible" and society B may have "Adultery is morally forbidden." In this case, adultery is permissible for members of A and forbidden for those in B.

Put differently, moral relativism implies that moral propositions are not simply true or false. Rather, the truth values (true or false) of moral principles themselves are relative to the beliefs of a given culture. For example, "murder is wrong" is not true plain and simply; it is "true" for culture A but, perhaps, "false" for culture B. The point here is not just that there is a certain relativity in the *application* of moral principles. For example, two cultures could both hold that "one should maintain sexual fidelity in marriage" but apply this differently due to factual differences about what counts as a marriage (for example, one wife or several wives). Factual diversity can lead to differences in the way a moral rule is applied.

Moral relativism goes beyond this type of diversity and asserts that the truth values of moral principles themselves are relative to a given culture. For example, whether or not one ought to maintain sexual fidelity could be true relative to one culture and false relative to another culture. There is a difference between individual moral relativism (also called *subjectivism*) and cultural moral relativism (also called *conventionalism*). Subjectivism says the truth of moral rules is relative to the beliefs of each individual; conventionalism makes moral truth relative to entire cultures or societies.

Five Objections to Moral Relativism
Because of the seriousness of the criticisms raised against it, the majority of moral philosophers and theologians do not embrace moral relativism. *First*, it is difficult to define what a society is or to specify in a given case what the relevant society is. Consider societies A and B above. If a man from A has extramarital sex with a woman from B in a hotel in a third society, C, which holds a different view from either A or B, which is the relevant society for determining whether the act was right or wrong?

Second, a related objection is the fact that we are often simultaneously a member of several different societies that may hold different moral values: our nuclear family; our extended family; our neighborhood, school, church, or social clubs; our place of employment; our town, state, country, and the international community. Which society is the relevant one? What if I am simultaneously a member of two societies and one allows but the other forbids a certain moral action? What do I do in this case?

Third, moral relativism suffers from a problem known as the reformer's dilemma. If normative relativism is true, then it is logically impossible for a society to have a virtuous, moral reformer like Jesus Christ, Gandhi, or Martin Luther King, Jr. Why? Moral reformers are members of a society who stand outside that society's code and pronounce a need for reform and change in that code. However, if an act is right if and only if it is in keeping with a given society's code, *then the moral reformer himself is by definition an immoral person*, for his views are at odds with those of his society. Moral reformers must always be wrong because they go against the code of their society. But any view that implies that moral reformers are impossible is defective because we all know that moral reformers have actually existed!

Put differently, moral relativism implies that neither cultures (if conventionalism is in view) nor individuals (if subjectivism is in view) can improve their moral code. The only thing they can do is change it. Why? Consider any change in a code from believing, say, racism is right to racism is wrong. How should we evaluate this change? All the moral relativist can say is that, from the perspective of the earlier code, the new principle is wrong, and from the perspective of the new code, the old principle is wrong. In short, there has merely been a change in perspective. No sense can be given to the idea that a new code reflects an improvement on an old code because this idea requires a vantage point outside of and above the society's (or individual's) code from which to make that judgment. And it is precisely such a vantage point that moral relativism disallows.

Some relativists respond to this by claiming that moral reformers are allowed in their view because all moral reformers do is make explicit what was already implicit but overlooked in the society's code. Thus, if a society already has a principle that persons ought to be treated equally, then this implicitly contains a prohibition against racism even though it may not be explicitly noted. The moral reformer merely makes this explicit by calling people to think more carefully about their code. Unfortunately, this claim is simply false. Many moral reformers do in fact call people to alter their codes. They do not merely make clear what was already contained in preexisting codes.

Other relativists claim they can allow for the existence of moral reformers by recognizing that societies may contain, implicitly or explicitly, a principle in their code that says, "follow the advice of moral reformers." But again, this response does not work. For one thing, what does it mean to call these reformers "moral" if they do not keep the rest of their society's code, which, by definition, they do not keep? If, on the other hand, the reformer does keep and believe in the rest of his or her society's code, how could a change in that code count as a moral improvement? A reformer could have the *power* to bring change, but how could he or she have the moral *authority* to do so? And why call the change a moral improvement? Second, moral reformers can exist without any such principle being in a society's code, so the presence or absence of such a principle is irrelevant. Third, what if there are two or more moral reformers operating at the same time? Which one do we follow? Finally, the presence of such a principle in a society's code would place all the other moral principles in jeopardy, for they would be temporary principles subject to the whims of the next moral reformer. In fact, before someone could honestly follow a principle in the society's code, that person would have to make a good faith effort to ensure that a moral reformer had not changed that part of the code that day.

Fourth, some acts are wrong regardless of social conventions. Advocates of this criticism usually adopt the standpoint of particularism (see the earlier discussion of skepticism) and claim that all people can know that some things are wrong, such as torturing babies, stealing as such, greed as such, and so forth, without first needing criteria for knowing how it is that they do, in fact, know such things. Thus, an act (torturing babies, for example) can be wrong and known to be wrong even if society says it is right, and an act can be right and known as such even if society says it is wrong. In fact, an act can be right or wrong even if society says nothing whatever about that act.

Fifth, if moral relativism is true, it is difficult to see how one society could be justified in morally blaming another society in certain cases. According to moral relativism, I should act in keeping with my society's code and others should act in keeping with their societies' codes. If Smith does an act that is right in his code but wrong in mine, how can I criticize his act as wrong?

One could respond to this objection by pointing out that society A may have in its code the principle that one should criticize acts of, say, murder, regardless of where they occur. So members of A could criticize such acts in other societies. But such a rule further reveals the inconsistency in normative relativism. Given this rule and the fact that normative relativism is true and embraced by members of A, those in A seem to be in the position of holding that members of B ought to murder (since B's code says it is right) and I ought to criticize members of B because my code says I should. Thus, I criticize members of B as immoral and at the same time hold that their acts should have been done. Further, why should members of B care about what members of A think? After all, if normative relativism is true, there is nothing intrinsically right about the moral views of society A or any society for that matter. For these and other reasons, moral relativism must be rejected.

The Moral Relativist's Dilemma—in Stereo

One afternoon I was sharing the gospel in a student's dorm room at the University of Vermont. The student began to espouse ethical relativism: "Whatever is true for you is true for you and whatever is true for me is true for me. If something works for you because you believe it, that's great. But no one should force his or her views on other people since everything is relative."

I knew that if I allowed him to get away with ethical relativism, there could be for him no such thing as real, objective sin measured against the objective moral command of God, and thus no need of a Savior. I thanked the student for his time and began to leave his room. On the way out, I picked up his small stereo and started out the door with it.

"Hey, what are you doing?" he shouted.

"What's wrong with you?" I queried. "Are you having problems with your eyes? I am leaving your room with your stereo."

"You can't do that," he gushed.

"Well," I replied, "since I lift weights and jog regularly, I think I can in fact do it without any help. But maybe you meant to say, 'You *ought not* do that because you are stealing my stereo.' Of course, I know from our previous conversation that this is not what you mean. I happen to think it is permissible to steal stereos if it will help a person's religious devotions, and I myself could use a stereo to listen to Christian music in my morning devotions. Now I would never try to force you to accept my moral beliefs in this regard because, as you said, everything is relative and we shouldn't force our ideas on others. But surely you aren't going to force on me your belief that it is wrong to steal your stereo, are you?

"You know what I think? I think that you espouse relativism in areas of your life where it's convenient, say in sexual morality, or in areas about which you do not care, but when it comes to someone stealing your stereo or criticizing your own moral hobbyhorses, I suspect that you become a moral absolutist pretty quickly, don't you?"

Believe it or not, the student honestly saw the inconsistency of his behavior and, a few weeks later, I was able to lead him to Jesus Christ.

SUMMARY

John Stott has reminded us of the importance of intellectual activity for sparking revival. History testifies to the power of people's thoughts to shape their actions. People die for ideas. Says Stott,

> Every powerful movement has had its philosophy which has gripped the mind, fired the imagination and captured the devotion of its adherents. One has only to think of the Fascist and Communist manifestos of this century, of Hitler's *Mein Kampf* on the one hand and Marx's *Das Kapital* and *The Thoughts of Chairman Mao* on the other.[8]

Stott is right on the money.

It is no accident that the flourishing of evangelistic activity in the 1960s and 1970s was woven around the writings of C. S. Lewis, Josh McDowell, and Francis Schaeffer. Today we need a revival of evangelistic fervor and spiritual power. And an absolutely crucial element that must take place before we will see this revival is a renaissance of apologetics and intellectual activity in the evangelical church. My prayer is that I will live to see that renaissance become a reality.

CHAPTER EIGHT

Worship, Fellowship, and the Christian Mind

X

Lord and Savior, true and kind, be the master of my mind;
Bless and guide and strengthen still all my powers
of thought and will. While I ply the scholar's task,
Jesus Christ be near, I ask; Help the memory,
clear the brain, knowledge still to seek and gain.

BISHOP H. G. C. MOULE —CHURCH OF ENGLAND BISHOP

K

Take my intellect, and use
Every Power as thou shalt choose.

FROM THE HYMN "TAKE MY LIFE AND LET IT BE"

K

If there is a religion in the world which exalts the office
of teaching, it is safe to say that it is the religion
of Jesus Christ. . . . A religion divorced from earnest
and lofty thought has always, down the whole history
of the Church, tended to become weak, jejune and
unwholesome, while the intellect, deprived of its
rights within religion, has sought its satisfaction without,
and developed into a godless rationalism.

JAMES ORR[1]

IN 1989, THE CALIFORNIA SCIENCE CURRICULUM FRAMEWORK AND Criteria Committee authored a document entitled "The California Science Framework," which set guidelines for teaching science in California's public schools. The document effectively established Darwinian naturalism as the state's official educational viewpoint and marginalized creationists or anyone else who disagrees with evolution. In one particularly demeaning passage of the Framework, advice is given to teachers who are approached by children raised in religious homes who object to evolutionary teaching on that basis:

> At times some students may insist that certain conclusions of science cannot be true because of certain religious or philosophical beliefs that they hold. . . . It is appropriate for the teacher to express in this regard, "I understand that you may have *personal reservations* about accepting this scientific evidence, but it is *scientific knowledge* about which there is *no reasonable doubt* among scientists in their field, and it is my responsibility to teach it.[2]

Note carefully that the California board of education regards religious, that is, Christian, beliefs as personal, private, subjective opinions to be contrasted with the true, public, objectively rational affirmations made by scientists. Where do secular people get this image of Christian doctrine? May I suggest that they get it from watching the Christians they meet, and more specifically, from watching the role that reason and truth play in the evangelical community. Unbelievers watch us while we are at work and they notice the forms that our worship and fellowship take. If unbelievers do not see a vibrant intellectual life when they observe Christians at work, or engaged in fellowship and worship, are they to be blamed if they conclude that truth and rationality do not matter much to us?

In Promethean fashion, philosopher of science Rom Harre has laid down this gauntlet:

I believe that the scientific community exhibits a model or ideal of rational cooperation set within a strict moral order, the whole having no parallel in any other human activity. And this despite the all-too-human characteristics of the actual members of that community seen as just another social order. Notoriously the rewards of place, power and prestige are often not commensurate with the quality of individual scientific achievements when these are looked at from a historical perspective. Yet that very community enforces standards of honesty, trustworthiness, and good work against which the moral quality of say Christian civilization stands condemned.[3]

Are you listening? Harre is claiming that, judged by the standards of rational cooperation, honesty, trustworthiness, and good work, the scientific community must be seen as *morally superior* to the church or any other rival community. I do not think Harre is right, but the simple fact that he would think he could get away with making a claim like this tells us that, for many readers, the assertion has a ring of plausibility about it. What is going on here? Could Harre be observing the same Christian practices seen by the California State Board of Education?

These remarks are angering, saddening, and egregious. God created us to be rational creatures. We have a religious duty to think and to think well. Scripture regularly admonishes us not to "be as the horse or the mule, which have no understanding" (Psalm 32:9). The psalmist cries out to God with the confession that I was senseless and ignorant; I was a brute beast before you (Psalm 73:22). This chapter explores ways in which the life of the mind enriches and informs worship, fellowship, and vocation.

WORSHIP

What Is Worship?

Whereas edification focuses on benefiting believers, worship is directed at God. The essence of worship is the intentional ascription of worth, service, and reverence to the Lord. Worship can take place in public or private, in individual or corporate ways. In fact, for the integrated believer, in one way or another, everything in life can be understood as an act of worship. In this sense, worship is expressed in one's overall approach to life and in every area of life (Romans 12:1). Worship creates a home for the soul as it learns to rest in God. As Isaiah 26:3 (NASB) promises, The steadfast of mind Thou wilt keep in perfect peace, Because he trusts in Thee. This is good news in a culture where the average person changes his or her geographic home about every four years.

A more specific form of worship occurs in specific acts of praise and exultation, especially in the assembly with the people of God. Of special importance to this latter understanding is the conscious expression of worship *in* the very act of study in high school or college or *in* and *through* the vocation a believer selects. I will say more about vocation later in the chapter. For now, I will limit my remarks about worship to individual or corporate expressions of reverence and worth to God.

Worship and the Nature of God

There is another aspect of worship that is extremely important. To grasp this aspect, consider a young man who respects and, in a certain sense, reveres a sports figure precisely because that figure is good at what he does. In this case, the sports figure is a worthy object of that respect and reverence. If the sports figure were in reality a complete joke at his sport, then while it would be permissible for the young man to *like* the sports figure, it would be inappropriate for the young man to *revere* him. A person ought to proportion his respect and reverence to the actual worthiness of the object of that respect and reverence. If a second sports figure came along who was superior in skill to the first hero, the young man would owe the second athlete more reverence than he gives the inferior athlete. Even if a second athlete never came along, the young man should not give *total* reverence to his hero because he doesn't deserve it. This becomes obvious when we realize that if a superior athlete were to enter the scene or if the revered hero were to improve his skills over the years, then the young man would be obliged to give more respect to the new hero or to the same hero now improved.

These insights about respect have dramatic implications for our worship of God. Theologians describe God as a maximally perfect being. This means that God is not merely the greatest, most perfect being who happens to exist. *He is the greatest being that could possibly exist.* If God were merely the greatest being who happens to exist, it would be possible to conceive of a case where a greater god could come along (even if such a being did not actually exist) or where the real God grew in His excellence. In these cases, our degree of worship ought to increase and, therefore, a God who just happened to be the greatest being around (and who could be surpassed in excellence) would not be a worthy object of *total* worship. Fortunately, the God of the Bible is a maximally perfect being; that is, He is the greatest being that could possibly exist. It is impossible for a greater being to supersede God or for God Himself to improve Himself in any way. Thus, God is owed our supreme, total worship. This is why Scripture calls idolatry the activity of giving more dedication to something finite than to God. *God is worthy of the very best efforts we can give Him in offering our respect and service through the cultivation of our total personality, including our minds.*

Seen in this light, dedication to intellectual growth is not merely to be done for the edification of the worshiper, but as an act of service rendered to God. Halfhearted study in high school or college represents a failure to grasp the fact that loving God with the mind is part of worship. Such halfhearted study is an unworthy offering to the Lord.

With this as a background, let us look at how we can better bring our minds into our corporate and individual acts of adoration and praise. Worship should never be reduced to an act of intellect—it involves all that we are—but the intellect is more central to worship than we often realize.

Corporate Worship
Far too often, we are allowed to leave our minds at the door when we come to worship God in the assembly of His people. This is simply unacceptable and beneath God's dignity as a maximally perfect being. What we need to do is plan more carefully and think harder about how we can engage the intellects of our brothers and sisters as part of our collective offerings of praise to our Father. In the next chapter, I will offer my advice for making the local church a more effective home for cultivating the Christian mind. There I will address the nature of sermons as something that needs to be changed. For now, I shall offer four biblical insights that, if followed, will over time mature a congregation's intellectual engagement in worship.

1. Insights from John 4:24: The first insight is derived from a study of John 4:24: "God is spirit, and those who worship Him must worship in spirit and truth." This verse is well known, as is the incident in which it is embedded: Jesus' encounter with the Samaritan woman at the well. The immediate context of verse 24 is the woman's misunderstanding of the nature of worship. Perhaps in an attempt to bring out their ethnic differences, the woman claims that for the Samaritans, worship is to be practiced on Mount Gerizim in Samaria while purebred Jews assert that the place of worship is Jerusalem. She obviously wanted Jesus to take a side in the dispute.

Verse 24 is Jesus' answer to the woman. The second half of the verse is widely discussed by Christians today. Jesus taught that we are to worship in spirit and in truth. By this, Jesus meant that *the worship that really counts is not based on external conformance to custom.* Instead, it is to be rooted in the inner being; it should be sincere and earnest; and it ought to be in accordance with the true nature of God, His revelation, and His acts. The first half of the verse is not as widely discussed, yet it is clear that "God is spirit" forms the foundation upon which Jesus' entire response is built. What does this phrase mean and why is it so relevant to the nature of genuine worship?

In John's writings, we often encounter a word or phase that has a dual meaning, both of which are intended by the author. For example, in John 3:7 Jesus says we must be "born *anothen*." The Greek term *anothen* can mean either "again" or "from above," and it appears that the ambiguity is intentional: *both* meanings are intended. I think the same thing is going on with "God is *pneuma* [spirit]." Before I state the dual meaning of *pneuma*, it is important to observe that the word is placed first in the Greek text of the verse, which literally reads "spirit is God." In Greek, when an author wanted to emphasize an adjective (in this case, "spirit"), he would place it at the first of the sentence. So the verse says something like this: "It is of first importance to recognize that God's very nature is that of spiritual being."

In addressing the woman's confusion, Jesus meant two things by "spirit." First, God is an immaterial, spiritual being, not a material object. Since material objects like idols are located at specific places, it makes sense to localize worship where those idols are. But since God is an omnipresent spirit, He is not confined to one place and, thus, geographical location is not crucial for worship, given God's spiritual nature. As David reminds us in Psalm 139:7-12, there is nowhere we can go where God is not present.

The second meaning of "spirit" in the passage is more relevant to our topic. Throughout the Old Testament, when God is referred to as spirit it is often to emphasize that He is a living, active being who initiates toward His creatures and gives them life. Thus, in Genesis 1:2 it is the Spirit of God who hovers over the waters. In John's writings, this same meaning is frequently associated with God as a spirit. For example, in John 6:63 it is the Spirit who gives life, and in John 7:37-39 it is the Spirit who produces rivers of living water in the lives of God's children. What does this have to do with worship? Simply this: *Worship is not under the control of human beings, nor is the form it takes up to their whims. Rather, worship is a response to a God who initiates toward His people, gives them life, and shows Himself active on their behalf.*

An important application follows from this insight. Frequently, our worship services place worship prior to the teaching of the Word. Now there is nothing wrong with this in itself. However, if worship is response, then if a service starts with worship, the people of God have not been given something to which to respond. In my view, we ought to vary the order of our services from time to time. Regularly, we ought to begin our services with a time of teaching followed by congregational testimonies about how God has used the sermon topic in people's lives. Once God's people have their minds filled with truths about God, His Word, and His ways, and once they have had a chance to meditate for a moment on these truths and the way they have been applicable to someone else's life, then the congregation is prepared to respond in worship. This makes sense from what we learned in chapter 3 about the role of the mind in directing the other faculties of the soul. The emotions and will can be more sincerely and intentionally directed toward God if the mind has been given the chance to recall, understand, or reflect on truth.

2. The parallel between marriage and worship: A second and closely related insight about the mind and worship comes from reflecting on the close biblical parallel between sexual intimacy in marriage and worship among God's people. It is no accident that idolatry is called adultery throughout the Bible. In an interesting way, the people of God are married to the Lord. He is our bridegroom and the church is His bride. To go after false gods is to play the harlot. In Ephesians 5:31-32, the apostle Paul compares the sexual one-flesh relationship between a man and a woman in marriage to Christ's relationship with the church. In an ideal sexual act in marriage, there is union, openness, mutual adoration and tenderness, and a degree of intimacy not found in other aspects of the marriage relationship. This same endearing intimacy is to be characteristic of the church's relationship to the Lord Jesus.

If sexual union is to approximate the ideal God intended, then a husband and wife ought to warm up to each other prior to that union by thinking true, good, tender, affectionate thoughts about one another, by focused communication and so forth. It would be hard for an act of sexual union between husband and wife to be what God intended if the two simply jumped in bed together, quickly had intercourse, and then went their separate ways. Yet this is exactly analogous to what we do Sunday after Sunday when we come together in worship. People get out of their cars, enter the assembly room, talk or read the bulletin, and then they are expected to jump into worship immediately as the first hymn is sung. What we need to do is think more carefully about how to use the ten or twenty minutes from the time people enter the sanctuary until the formal service starts to help people transition from the Sunday morning rush to a time of intimacy with God and His people. This time should be a period of warmup for worship, learning, and fellowship.

There are many ways to do this, but here is one suggestion. Whoever is preaching that morning should have a feel for the sermon topic and the main theme of the service. That person could easily develop (or have someone else develop) a one-page handout to be given to each person entering the sanctuary. The handout should have various exercises designed to prepare people for the theme of the morning. It could reproduce a paragraph from an editorial in the newspaper and ask for a response from the worshiper. It could lead a brief word study by listing a key word from the sermon text and five or six other verses with that word. It could print a written prayer on the sermon theme or ask the worshiper to write a prayer on a certain topic. The point in all of this is to capitalize on the time before the service starts by engaging people's minds, feelings, and wills to warm them up for corporate worship and prepare them to think about the topic for the morning.

3. Hymns and intellectual engagement in worship: A third way to enhance people's intellectual engagement in worship involves the way we use hymns. The Scriptures affirm several legitimate purposes for singing (reaffirmation of doctrine, expression of love or pain to God, intensifying our solidarity as a corporate body) and many different forms of music to use in worship. Some churches struggle to strike a balance between contemporary praise songs and more traditional hymns of the faith. In my view, both have an important place in the service, and each congregation will find its own balance between the two genres. While there are exceptions to the rule, generally, praise songs are better than traditional hymns at getting people to express repeatedly simple truths to God and to enter emotionally into such acts of expression. By contrast, traditional hymns are usually more suited for affirming and expressing doctrinal and theological truths. I suggest that we be more intentional about using traditional hymns according to the purpose for which they are best suited. Instead of just opening the hymnal and singing a traditional hymn, I think the worship leader should spend more time introducing the hymn. Occasionally, something about the hymn writer or the historical context of the hymn should be given or the congregation should be briefly instructed in and directed to ponder certain theological themes in different verses of the hymn prior to its singing. If we do this from time to time, we will sing fewer hymns together, but what we do sing will be more meaningful. The great hymns of the faith are filled with good theology and careful language, and we should engage people's minds more directly in employing this genre in our worship.

4. Supplication as persuasion: Fourth, we should use our minds more carefully in supplication before God. Martin Luther said that "in 'supplication' we strengthen prayer and make it effective by a certain form of persuasion."[4] For Luther, *supplication is a form of reasoning with God*, and in this point he was correct. The Scriptures regularly depict supplication as a way of approaching God in which the worshiper brings his "case" before God (Jeremiah 12:1, 20:12). The Hebrew word for "case" is *rib*, and it means a reasoned legal case brought before a judge of some kind. In supplication, we carefully think through our requests and the reasons for them before we approach God. We then reason that case before His throne and trust that He will take our case into consideration.

Too often our congregational prayers are vague, rambling, poorly reasoned, and incoherently expressed. I don't know how many times I have heard God addressed as Father and moments later, the Father is being thanked for dying on the cross! Apart from the fact that this is a heresy known as Patripassianism (the view that God the Father died on the cross), it reveals a wandering mind on the part of the prayer leader.

It is appropriate to address the entire Godhead or any specific member of the triune God, but we should be clear in our own mind whom we are addressing, and if we turn to address a different member of the Trinity, we ought to be clear about that too! C. S. Lewis put his finger on the underlying cause of much of our rambling prayers in Screwtape's advice to his nephew, the demon Wormwood. Wormwood is to have his Christian patient

> remember, or to think he remembers, the parrot-like nature of his prayers in childhood. In reaction against that, he may be persuaded to aim at something entirely spontaneous, inward, informal, and unregulated, and what this will actually mean to a beginner will be an effort to produce in himself a vaguely devotional mood in which real concentration of will and intelligence have no part.[5]

There is too little concentration of will and intelligence in our public (not to mention private) prayers. Since supplication is a form of reasoned persuasion before God, we ought to be more thoughtful about supplication in the assembly. Sometimes this will require a worship leader to write out a carefully crafted prayer to be read in the congregational prayer time.

Individual Worship

Individual devotion, adoration, and praise are enriched by intellectual engagement no less than is corporate worship. Much could be said about the development of intellectual engagement in personal worship, but I shall limit my remarks to one important dimension of this topic: learning how to read well.

1. Devotional reading: There are two very different types of reading, each with its own style and characteristic effects: devotional and intellectual reading. The distinction between these is not one of different types of books read, but of different ways of reading. In devotional reading, one reads quietly, slowly, and with a sense of spiritual attentiveness and openness to God. The goal of devotional reading is not so much gathering new information or mastering content, though that may indeed happen. The goal is to deepen and nourish the soul by entering into the passage and allowing it to be assimilated into one's whole personality.

Certain books have a distinctive spiritual texture to them and are best suited as objects for the devotional style of reading—books like Thomas à Kempis's *The Imitation of Christ*, Brother Lawrence's *The Practice of the Presence of God*, or Richard Foster and James Smith's collection of essays entitled *Devotional Classics*. These and similar writings contain such a psychological depth and spiritual richness *that the very act of reading them correctly* can change one's life. *Lectio divina* is the name of a devotional, prayerful reading technique applied to the Bible. Deriving from ancient roots in church history, this type of scriptural reading has impacted people for centuries.

Certain steps are required in order to enter correctly into the process of devotional reading.[6] First, you must get into a position of being ready to listen with the heart to the Holy Spirit as His quiet voice speaks to you about what you are reading. Before a devotional reading of *The Imitation of Christ* or prior to practicing *lectio divina* on a gospel text or a psalm (the four gospels, the Psalms, and the Wisdom Literature, especially Proverbs and Ecclesiastes, are the best texts for this type of reading), sit quietly, confess any sin that comes to mind (and promise to make reconciliation if that is needed), and express tender devotion to God with whatever sincerity you can muster at this stage of the process. Then invite God to speak to your heart about what you are reading.

Second, with a spirit of expectancy and an attitude of openness and vulnerability, read the selected text slowly, calmly, and with an open, vulnerable heart. The goal here is not to read a lot of material, but to enter into a small portion of a book or of the Scripture. While reading, seek to monitor what is happening inside your own soul. Do not try to master the passage, but allow the passage to master you. Third, throughout the process of reading, you may sense the need to stop, to meditate and contemplate a specific meaning in the text, and to enter into a dialogue with God about that meaning.

Finally, it is important to recognize that this type of slow, contemplative reading will frequently be met with hindrances that distract or discourage you. Especially discouraging is the sense that the text is not as moving as you had hoped. The proper response when this happens is to stop reading, allow yourself to feel whatever is going on inside, offer the situation to God, and rededicate yourself to continuing to learn how to get better at this type of reading. With practice and persevering dedication, you will benefit deeply from such contemplative openness before God.

2. Three tips for intellectual reading: Intellectual reading is an attempt to grasp the concepts, structure, and arguments that form the content of the thing being read. The goal is to learn something new, to master specific content, to develop one's intellectual categories, and to grow in one's ability to think. Space forbids me to describe this sort of reading in detail, but I will mention three tips for developing skills here.

First, the mind works from the *whole to the parts to the whole*. When you start to read a book or begin a new area of study, the first thing you should try to do is get an overview of the main issues in that book or area of thought. For example, in reading a book, you should begin with the book jacket or the introduction in order to get before your mind a statement of the book's primary thesis and the main issues to be discussed. Next, spend five minutes studying the table of contents. Use a pen and note on the page any observations about structure you can see (for example, that chapters one to three seem to go together and chapters four to five contain answers to the problems surfaced in the first three chapters).

For college students or those with easy access to a good library, if you are really going to dissect a book, obtain a few book reviews of the work prior to your own reading. In graduate school, when I bought my textbooks for the semester, I would go immediately to the library, ask the librarian for help in locating reviews of my textbooks (they are trained at doing this), and xerox and read them.

A good book review does two things: it gives you the big picture about a book's major thesis and its overall structure, and it evaluates the strengths and weaknesses of the book. Both can be helpful to have in mind before you begin to read. Your purpose in all of this is to get a tentative grasp of the whole of the book and at least a small feel for how the author develops his or her thesis.

After these initial steps, you begin to read the book with pen in hand. You move from your tentative guess at the book as a whole to an examination of the book's parts. If possible, never read a serious book without something with which to write. Your goal in reading is to surface the structure of each chapter. I will address this aspect of reading shortly, but for now, I want to emphasize that once the book's parts have been read, you should reexamine your initial guess at the overall thesis and structure of the book and revise where necessary.

In approaching a new, relatively unfamiliar area of study (for example, end-of-life ethics, the role of women in the church), start with a brief introduction to the subject matter. I try to read a dictionary or encyclopedia article if possible, or an introductory textbook in the area. Often, a librarian can help you find a magazine or journal article that summarizes the main issues in the area of study. Again, your goal is to obtain an initial set of categories that can help you be more informed in noticing things you may otherwise miss when you set out to analyze more carefully a detailed text in the area of investigation.

In addition to the movement from whole to parts to whole, it is important to focus on *structure* at each step, especially when actually reading each chapter in the book. I usually write in the left-hand margin, every two to three paragraphs, a summary of the main arguments in the text. I am very careful to note in the margin any change in the structure. For example, I ask these kinds of questions: Is the author continuing to develop the same point of discussion treated in the preceding paragraphs? Has the text shifted to making a new point parallel to the one just made or are we now reading criticisms and rebuttals of the main thesis? What you are after is a chapter filled with marginal notes that form an outline of the flow of that chapter.

After I read a subsection in a chapter (usually marked off by an actual subheading in the text), I return to the page where that subsection began and write a two- or three-sentence summary of the main point of the subsection. When I have finished the entire chapter, I look at all of my subsection summaries and write a summary of the entire chapter at the top of the first page of that chapter. You want to mark up the book in such a way that if you return to it months later, you can look at your marginal notes and get a feel for the main flow of the chapter's structure and its content.

I use two notational devices to help me learn a chapter's structure. First, if an author is offering arguments for his or her thesis, I put a "+1," "+2," and so forth in the margin where each specific argument begins. If the author states three such arguments in five pages, I will be able to locate those arguments by looking at my marginal notations. I note arguments against the author's thesis with "-1," "-2," and so on. If the author offers two counterarguments against the first assault of his or her claims (which was marked with a "-1"), I note those counterarguments with "- -1" and "- -2." The goal is to keep track of the arguments and counterarguments that compose the structure of the debate in the text itself.

Second, if I write a marginal note that contains my own thoughts about an issue instead of representing a summary of the text itself, I put the remark in parentheses and begin it with "N.B.," which is the abbreviation for the Latin term *nota bene*, which means "take note." For example, "(N.B. Rachels fails to recognize that intention is the very essence of a moral act and this is where his argument goes wrong.)" This allows me to keep track of when I am inserting my own thoughts and when I am summarizing the text itself.

Here is a final tip for learning how to read better. Inside the front cover of the book I construct my *own index*. As I read a book, if I come upon a topic of special interest to me, I turn to the blank pages at the front of the book and write down a key term or phrase ("Darwin's view of the soul," "predestination and moral responsibility"), followed by the corresponding page number(s) in the text. Every time that topic is in view, I write those page numbers down. This gives me my own index for a book based on the things to which I want later access.

In developing the art of intellectual reading as part of personal worship, it is important to keep three things in mind. First, do not measure the value of such reading by the *immediate* practical application or spiritual enlivening that comes from an hour or two devoted to analyzing a chapter or two of a book. Often, it takes several chapters for an idea to be developed with sufficient care and depth to offer something to apply to one's life and thought. Sometimes you need to be patient and stay with a line of thought for several weeks before things get clear to you. Intellectual reading is never a quick fix, and its value is measured in the long-term maturity that comes from practicing this type of reading.

Second, get into the habit of reading books that are somewhat beyond your ability to grasp. If you spend all of your time reading material that requires little intellectual effort, you will not stretch your mind and grow appreciably in your thinking ability.

Finally, when you undertake to read a book seriously, you cannot treat that book as a novel to be read for recreation. Compared to intellectual reading, recreational reading is fairly passive, can be done quickly, and does not require a great deal of work or engagement on the part of the reader. In intellectual reading, you simply must stay alert, use a pen, make notes regularly, and remember to look for three things: Structure! Structure! Structure! If you do not walk away from an occasion of reading with a better grasp of the flow of argument in what has been read, you have not practiced intellectual reading successfully.

Excellence in Our Worship

I live about twelve miles from Disneyland, and I have a season pass that entitles me to visit the park several times each year. Disneyland is no mere theme park. Compared to other parks of amusement, Disneyland is just different. From the restaurants and shrubbery to the Indiana Jones ride, the park exudes excellence. For example, Disneyland employs one crew to do nothing but change light bulbs throughout the park year-round. The crew has a catalog listing the life expectancy of the thousands of light bulbs in the park, and they make sure to change each and every bulb at 80 percent life expectancy so no one ever sees a burned-out bulb! I have been to Disneyland around one hundred times and have never, ever seen a burned-out bulb.

If Disney can impart this sort of spirit of excellence to its bulb changers, we Christians can afford to do no less when it comes to worshiping the living God. We need to increase our expectations of excellence when it comes to corporate and private worship. And if we do, the proper cultivation of the mind will be a crucial dimension of our excellence in worship. Loving and worshiping God includes the total personality, including the mind. We worship God with our minds when we struggle to read something so we can love and serve Him better, when we understand the contents of the hymns we sing, when we activate our minds and make them ready to hear before given something to which to respond in the worship service. Without the bulb changers, Disneyland would be just another amusement park. Without an intellectual component, worship becomes a less than total expression of adoration to a God who deserves a lot more effort than Disney insists on at its park.

In a way, worship is an aspect of our fellowship with a personal God. So it should come as no surprise that if there is an intellectual component to our fellowship with God, there should be an intellectual dimension to our fellowship with others in the body of Christ. If this is right, then a cultivation of a developed, Christian mind should both enrich and serve as at least one goal of Christian fellowship. Let's see just how and why this is so.

Fellowship

Aristotle on Friendship

We begin our investigation of the Christian mind and fellowship not with Holy Scripture but with the Greek thinker Aristotle (384-322 B.C.), and specifically, with his view of friendship.[7] According to Aristotle, there are three kinds of friendship: friendships based on usefulness and advantage, those based on pleasure, and those based on goodness and virtue. The first two, says Aristotle, do not involve people who genuinely feel an affection for one another per se. Such "friends" are attracted to each other solely as a means of some advantage or pleasure that each individual can get out of the friendship. We are all too familiar with this type of friendship, and while there is nothing wrong with deriving pleasure or advantage from friendships, if these were the only reasons we had for developing relationships with others, we would have no deep or genuine friendships at all.

The third type of friendship is quite profound. Here friendships are formed around a common vision of virtue and the good life, and friendship serves to sustain, foster, and strengthen each friend in his or her commitment and progress in a life well lived. At first, Aristotle thought that the city-state was the main place to foster such a commitment to the good life, but he quickly came to see that such a commitment was virtually absent in the state. So Aristotle turned to a community of friends within the city-state as the place for fostering commitment to virtuous, wise living.

Aristotle Was Seeking *Koinonia*

Aristotle was quite right in much of what he said, but without the revelation found in the Word of God he could not find the proper vehicle for fostering the good life: fellowship in the body of Christ. Aristotle's concept of friendship is deepened and fulfilled in the New Testament concept of fellowship. The word *fellowship* comes from the Greek word *koinonia*, which has as a root meaning "to hold something in common." In the New Testament it primarily means to have a share in the gospel cause through financial participation in support of the spread of the gospel (see Philippians 1:5). It is legitimate to expand the meaning of fellowship beyond financial participation, but one thing about New Testament fellowship is critical for our understanding. It does not refer to people getting together simply to enjoy one another, though, of course, there is nothing wrong with that! Rather, very much like Aristotle's third type of friendship, *New Testament fellowship is a means for developing commitment to and advancing the spread of the kingdom of God and the gospel of Christ.* While New Testament fellowship is valuable for its own sake, nevertheless, it must always be a means to these ends as well. When we meet for fellowship, we should have something in mind and ought intentionally to seek to foster our mutual commitment to advancing the cause of Christ and the spread of the gospel.

Fellowship and the Christian Mind

A very important application follows from this understanding of fellowship. Apologetics in particular, and the life of the mind in general, are crucial aspects of New Testament fellowship. We are to meet together to stimulate our mutual commitment to growth in the body of Christ and to the advance of the cause of Christ in the struggle for the minds and hearts of men and women. We are to encourage each other in our pursuit of the good life, the imitation of Christ in our individual and communal forms of life. *New Testament fellowship should be guided by a clear conception of the good life in the New Testament, especially the gospel. This must include a conception of how to grow in that good life, how to spread and defend it among unbelievers, and how to protect ourselves from being conformed to godless ways of thinking, feeling, and behaving. If this is so, then the mutual stimulation of the Christian mind will be a foundational characteristic of New Testament fellowship as we seek to equip each other to be better proclaimers and defenders of the gospel and the Christian worldview in which it is embedded.*

We need consciously to develop fellowships of the mind, forms of gathering in which we express a joint commitment to study, learn, evangelize, defend the gospel, and penetrate the pagan culture with the radical ideas in the New Testament. For six years, I have met for breakfast every Friday morning (except for vacations) with my dear friend Bill Roth to read through the great devotional classics in the history of the church. We are committed to praying for each other, to entering more deeply into life in the kingdom of God, and to developing a more articulate and effective ministry of spreading the gospel in our respective spheres of influence.

We need Christians who share the same vocation—businesspersons, homemakers, health care professionals—to band together in groups to study and encourage each other to penetrate their professions with the gospel and a Christian worldview. We need men and women to gather for weekly breakfasts or house-church meetings and commit themselves to reading serious books, to developing their understanding of theology and of the structures of thought in the culture they are seeking to reach, to mutual pursuit of life in the kingdom of God and to the spread of the gospel.

Frankly, too much of what passes for fellowship today is trite conversation that has no clear goal for its purpose. And when we do meet to study something, all too often we gather to study things that are based in self-help and narcissism and not in trying to be better equipped to spread the gospel of Christ! Christian artists should gather regularly to develop a common view of art and its role in a Christian worldview, and they should seek to discover ways to use art appropriately for the advancement of the cause of Christ.

And what I have said about artists should be applied to other natural groupings of people with a common vocation in the body of Christ. Why? Because such groups hold a career in common, and specific forms of fellowship should be fostered to encourage one another to be more effective in penetrating that vocation for Christ. Vocation is an important sphere of a believer's life. It is to that subject that we now turn.

Vocation and an Integrated Christian Worldview

X

One may justly say that our Public School tradition
has actively encouraged an attitude to life
which makes a strong distinction between
the theoretical and the practical,
and which gives to ideas and ideals
the status of leisure-time interests not to be taken
too seriously and on no account to
be related to practical affairs.
HARRY BLAMIRES, *THE CHRISTIAN MIND*[1]

K

What we do when we weed a field is not quite different
from what we do when we pray for a good harvest.
C.S. LEWIS, *GOD IN THE DOCK*[2]

VOCATION AND DISCIPLESHIP

As a disciple grows, he or she learns to see, feel, think, desire, believe, and behave the way Jesus does in a manner fitting to the kingdom of God and the disciple's own station in life. With God's help, I seek to live as Jesus would if He were me. That is, how would Jesus live if He were a philosophy professor at Biola University married to Hope and father of Ashley and Allison? That question and concept I keep before me constantly as I seek to follow Him. Admittedly, it is a huge target and I don't always hit the mark — just ask Hope, Ashley, and Allison — but I try not to let my imperfections or failures cause me to lose sight of the target! Let's look now at what the target of discipline in our vocational life might look like.

Implications of the Nature of Discipleship

Two important implications flow from the nature of discipleship. For one thing, the lordship of Christ is holistic. The religious life is not a special compartment in an otherwise secular life. Rather, the religious life is an entire way of life. To live Christianity is to allow Jesus Christ to be the Lord of every aspect of my life. There is no room for a secular/sacred separation in the life of Jesus' followers.

Secondly, discipleship is not a job, it's a vocation! Further, as a disciple of Jesus, I do not have a job, I have a vocation; and if I go to college, I go to find and become excellent in my vocation, not simply to find a job. A job is a means for supporting myself and those for whom I am responsible. For the Christian, a vocation (from the Latin *vocare*, "to call") is an overall calling from God. Harry Blamires correctly draws a distinction between a general and a special vocation:

> The general vocation of all Christians — indeed of all men and women — is the same. We are called to live as children of God, obeying His will in all things. But obedience to God's will must inevitably take many different forms. The wife's mode of obedience is not the same as the nun's; the farmer's is not the same as the priest's. By "special vocation," therefore, we designate God's call to a man to serve him in a particular sphere of activity.[3]

We often neglect His concept of vocation in our models of discipleship. Therefore I want to focus our discussion on this notion of a special vocation that, hereafter, I will refer to simply as a vocation. A vocation includes a job but is much, much more. It is the specific role I am to play in life, and it includes the sum total of the natural talents, spiritual gifts, and historical circumstances providentially bestowed on me by God. An important part of a believer's vocation is his or her major in college or main form of work as a career. If we are to be integrated, holistic Christians who make an impact on the world, we need to learn how to be Christian doctors, schoolteachers, lawyers, businesspersons, and so forth.

A few weeks ago I talked to Jack, a recent college graduate who had been heavily involved in a parachurch ministry in college. His major was cultural anthropology. After discussing his college studies with him for about thirty minutes, I quickly saw that Jack's professors were extremely hostile to Christianity in the way they trained people in their department. Jack was committed to sharing his faith, to sexual purity before marriage, and to having a regular quiet time. But some of the things he believed—including moral relativism regarding the nature of sexuality and the permissibility of same-sex marriage—were simply not consistent with a life of dedication to Christ. The model of spiritual growth he had followed in college was not holistic, and Jesus was not the Lord of his vocation. This type of thing should not happen to someone as devoted to Christ as Jack was. His problem was not a bad heart, it was a misinformed picture of commitment to Christ.

If we are to be Christians in our vocations, we will have to develop a Christian mind in and about those vocations and we must train our children to go to college with the same mind-set. To understand what I mean here, we need to draw a distinction between intrinsic and extrinsic issues in vocation. An extrinsic issue is one that is part of my general Christian vocation but has nothing specifically to do with my particular career. We evangelicals have done a decent job at working on these extrinsic issues. For example, we have sought to train people to share their faith at work and to be godly examples in the way they conduct themselves. But note carefully that neither of these, evangelism and godly living, has anything specifically to do with, say, being a physical education teacher as opposed to being an elementary school teacher. What we desperately need is a renewed commitment to training people about intrinsic issues: *learning to think and live Christianity regarding issues specific to what I do in my career.*

In order to "get at" such a model of holistic discipleship, I want to focus on what I believe is the "heart of the matter." If Jack, the student just mentioned, had possessed a truly integrated Christian worldview, I don't think he would have bought into the moral relativism his anthropology professors were pushing. To get a broader idea of what I mean, let's look at several more examples of how critical it is to develop such a worldview about issues intrinsic to different fields of study or careers.

Developing an Integrated Christian Worldview

1. June is a biblical exegete who teaches at Bible Study Fellowship. In her deep study and teaching of the Scriptures, she becomes aware of how much her own cultural background shapes what she can see in the biblical text, and she begins to wonder whether meanings might not reside in the interpretation of a text and not in the text itself. She also wonders if certain methods of interpretation may be inappropriate given the nature of the Bible as revelation.

2. Bill is a child psychologist who volunteers at a large Midwestern church. In his professional life he reads literature regarding identical twins who are reared in separate environments. He notes that they usually exhibit similar adult behavior. Bill then wonders if there is really any such thing as freedom of the will, and if not, what he should make of moral responsibility and punishment. You can conclude for yourself whether his answer to such important questions might affect his counseling in the church.

3. Diane is a political science and history teacher at a high school in rural East Texas. She reads John Rawls's *Theory of Justice* and grapples with the idea that society's primary goods could be distributed in such a way that those on the bottom get the maximum benefit even if people on the top have to be constrained. She wonders how this compares with a meritocracy wherein individual merit is rewarded regardless of social distribution. Several questions run through her mind: What is the state? How should a Christian view the state and the church? What is justice, and what principles of social ordering ought we to adopt? Should one seek a Christian state or merely a just state?

4. Julie is a counselor who learns of specific correlations between certain brain functions and certain feelings of pain, and she puzzles

over the question of whether or not there is a soul or mind distinct from the brain.

5. A missionary named Louise notes that cultures frequently differ over basic moral principles. She wonders whether or not this proves that there are no objectively true moral values that transcend culture. Her biblical training says there are, but in the field she has met other Christian missionaries who claim otherwise. Louise wonders how to sort out such differences.

6. Frank, a Dallas businessman, notices that the government is not adequately caring for the poor. He discusses with a friend the issue of whether or not businesses have corporate moral responsibilities or whether only individuals have moral responsibility. He wonders, as a Christian, whether there are answers about such things from a biblical perspective.

7. Mike, an engineer, learns Euclidean geometry and some of its alternatives and goes on to ask if mathematics is a field that really conveys true knowledge about a subject matter or if it merely offers internally consistent formal languages expressible in symbols. If the former, then what is it that mathematics describes? If mathematical entities exist and are timeless, in what sense did God create them?

8. Rick is a recent convert to the Christian faith and a sophomore majoring in education. In his most important education class he is asked to state his philosophy of education. In order to do this, he must state his views of human nature, truth, how people learn, the role of values in education, and so on. Rick wonders how his newfound Christian convictions inform these issues.

In each of these cases, there is a need for the person in question, if he or she is a Christian, to think hard about the issue in light of developing a holistic Christian worldview. When one addresses problems like these, there will emerge a number of different ways that theology can interact with an issue in a discipline or career outside theology.

Five Models of Integration

Here are some of the different ways such interaction can take place.

A. Issues in theology and another discipline may involve two distinct, nonoverlapping areas of investigation. For example, debates about angels or the extent of Christ's atonement have little to do with organic chemistry. Similarly, it is of little interest to theology whether a methane molecule has three or four hydrogen atoms in it. In such cases theological truth has little to offer the discipline in question and vice versa. It is important to recognize this because there are many issues in our vocations that Christians and nonChristians will view in the same way, and there is no clear way in which Christianity informs that issue. Manufacturing a product, teaching first grade, or giving a flu shot to a patient will involve skills and information about which a Christian worldview is simply silent. In these cases, we are free in Christ to adopt whatever views or approaches we judge to be reasonable and appropriate.

B. The complementary view: Issues in theology and another discipline may involve two different, complementary, noninteracting perspectives about the same reality such that the whole truth is a combination of both perspectives. Suppose you were going to describe an apple. You could choose to take a color perspective and describe the color of the apple's skin, insides, and stem. Or you could take a shape perspective and describe the shape of the apple. This would give two different descriptions of the apple: "The red thing on the table" and "The round thing on the table." Each perspective is true and the whole truth is a combination of both.

Moreover, neither perspective "interacts" with the other one. What does this mean? It means that no amount of new information about the color of the apple will threaten or reinforce the shape description of the apple. If you suddenly revised your color description to "the green thing on the table," this would not require you to describe the apple as square or triangular because the color and shape perspectives do not directly affect each other. Likewise, sociologists can describe some aspects of church growth in terms of group homogeneity, size of parking lot, geographical location of the church, demographics, etc. But a theologian could also describe the growth due to these factors in terms of God's providential increase of a congregation.

Again, we can say that God brings the rain but scientists can offer complementary descriptions of this fact in scientific terms. When God employs the laws of nature to accomplish some intent of His, the complementary view often works. It fails, however, when God brings about some effect in a direct, miraculous way. For example, there will be no complementary perspective in scientific terms for what caused Jesus to rise from the dead. If you are trying to decide what to believe about some issue in your vocation, it may well be that a Christian perspective on the issue is a different, complementary perspective from the economic, psychological, scientific, or other perspective offered by a theory in your vocation.

In a case like this, a Christian has no obligation to try to refute the vocational theory because the whole truth of the matter is a combination of both perspectives. A doctor could believe that God heals people both in direct, miraculous ways and in indirect, providential ways. That doctor could also believe that certain biological processes are means of healing. In the miraculous case, there will be no adequate biological description of the entire cause of healing since it was due, at least in part, to a direct, miraculous act of God. However, in the case of the "normal" healing, the biological description of these processes is complementary to a theological description of God's indirect, providential healing such that the whole truth is a combination of both. Here, the Christian doctor has no obligation to try to refute the biological theory to leave room for God since both perspectives complement each other.

C. Issues in theology and another discipline may directly interact in such a way that either area of study offers rational support for the other or raises rational difficulties for the other. Sometimes a discovery in your vocation adds support to some aspect of Christian teaching. For example, some psychologists claim the traditional family does a better job of producing healthy, well-functioning children than alternative lifestyles. Some economists assert that, other things being equal, to the degree that people lead morally upright lives and embody a wide range of virtues, the economy will be healthier. Certain scientists have argued that the big bang theory supports the biblical doctrine that the world had a beginning due to the creative power of a supernatural person outside the world.

On the other hand, there may be theories in some discipline that, if correct, would tend to count against Christian ideas. Certain ideas about the age of the universe are hard to harmonize with the notion that it was created a few thousand years ago in six literal twenty-four-hour days. In neurophysiology and psychology, some have argued that homosexual behavior is completely determined by genetic factors outside of one's control and, thus, homosexuality is neither immoral nor something for which one is responsible. In education, some contend that the state, not the family or church, has ultimate authority to socialize children and teach them moral values.

Note carefully that I am not agreeing with the cases just cited. I am simply pointing out that Christians working in these fields are presented with challenges to Christian teaching and they should try to remove the problem for the body of Christ. Perhaps our understanding of Christian teaching is mistaken, maybe the evidence for the theory challenging Christian teaching is weak and the wrong implications have been drawn from it. In general, your vocation or college major may provide cases where ideas are either supportive or challenging to Christian positions on a given issue. In cases like these, you should use your mind well and help the church integrate her teachings with the issue in question.

D. Theology tends to support the presuppositions of another discipline and vice versa. Some have argued that many of the presuppositions of science (for example, the existence of truth; the rational, orderly nature of reality; the adequacy of our sensory and cognitive faculties as tools suited for knowing the external world) make sense and are easy to justify given Christian theism, but are at odds with and without ultimate justification in a naturalistic worldview. Similarly, some have argued that philosophical critiques of skepticism and defenses of a correspondence theory of truth (roughly the idea that truth is the correspondence between a proposition and a state of affairs in the world; for example, the proposition "grass is green" is true just in case there is a state of affairs in the world—grass being green—to which the proposition corresponds) offer justification for some of the presuppositions of theology.

E. Theology fills out and adds details to general principles in another discipline and vice versa, and theology helps one practically apply principles in another discipline and vice versa. For example, theology teaches that fathers should not provoke their children to anger, and psychology can add important details about what this means by offering information about family systems, the nature and causes of anger, etc. Psychology can devise various tests for assessing whether one is or is not a mature person, and theology can offer a normative definition to psychology as to what a mature person is. For example, Scripture teaches that a spiritually mature person is not regularly filled with anxiety (Matthew 6:25-34) and regularly focuses his or her efforts on building up other people (Matthew 16:24-27, Philippians 2:3-4, 1 Thessalonians 5:11). This is a normative characterization of a mature person; that is, it tells us what a mature person *ought* to look like. Armed with this characterization, a psychologist could devise tests to determine the degree to which these traits are manifested in a person, how they can be fostered in different personality types, and what kinds of things hinder their development.

INTEGRATION AND VOCATION

We have seen examples of the need for Christians to think carefully and integratively about their vocation, and we have looked at different ways that a Christian worldview can interact with a specific vocational issue. I now want to suggest five different intrinsic issues that we Christians need to address as we attempt to think through our vocations in light of our Christian worldview. Before I do, however, it is important to realize that not all fields of study in college nor all career paths are equally in need of thinking Christianity. For example, a Christian psychologist, history teacher, or doctor will need to be more carefully integrated as a Christian than, say, a Christian civil engineer or truck driver.

I am not saying it is unimportant for Christian truck drivers to seek to live and think Christianity in their line of work. But different vocational areas do not interact with a Christian worldview in the same way. A good rule of thumb is this: *The more a field is composed of ideas about the nature of ultimate reality, what and how we know things, moral values and virtues, the nature and origin of human beings, and other issues central to mere Christianity, the more crucial it will be to think carefully about how a Christian should integrate his discipleship unto Jesus with the ideas and practices in that field.* But a word for my truck driver brothers and sisters out there: I'm not letting you off the hook! Remember this: truck driving is a business, so it's important for you to have a good grasp on Christian business ethics and to practice these ethics as you seek to follow Christ in your chosen field.

Five Specific Areas

Having said that, here are five specific areas of integration relevant to Christian discipleship in a vocation:

- What are the ethical issues involved in my vocation and how do they relate to my ethical beliefs as a Christian? As a businessperson, what is my view of corporate moral responsibility? Do corporations as wholes have moral responsibility, or only individuals (for example, the CEO)?

- What does my field say about what is and is not real, about what is true and false, and how do I understand that as a Christian? For example, should a Christian counselor believe that the mind is really the brain and that moral behaviors are determined by our genes? Should a Christian in any of the sciences be a theistic evolutionist?
- What does my field say about the nature and limits of knowledge? If I am an engineer, should I believe that the only thing we can know is what can be measured and tested in a science laboratory? If I am a parent, should I be supportive of values clarification in the public schools? Doesn't values clarification communicate that we really don't have moral knowledge, only moral opinions? And doesn't such a view create problems when it claims that what is really relevant for a student's moral development is not that his or her moral views are correct but that he or she "sincerely" expresses his or her own feelings?
- What methodology for gathering data does my field require before someone is allowed to assert his or her views about something? For example, we are often led to believe that if we do not have a scientific study on something, we just cannot claim to know anything about the topic in question. But can't someone also use common sense, Scripture, or other forms of reasoning besides a scientific study to justify a position on some topic? Does your field tend to limit proper methodology in a way you find unreasonable as a thinking Christian?
- Are there any specific virtues that seem to be especially relevant to your work?

Specific Examples

Here are some examples of more specific questions for certain vocations:

Health care professions: What is the nature of medicine? Are certain virtues and values part of the very nature of medicine so that if professionals are not trained in these virtues and values, they are not practicing medicine but only technology? What is the purpose of medicine? What is the nature of the patient/professional relationship (a covenant or a contract)?

Sports and coaching: What is the difference between play/recreation and entertainment, and between a celebrity and a hero? In what sense are and ought sports figures to be heroes? Why should we value health, and what value should we place on it? Should winning be the main or at least an important goal for sports participation at various ages?

Business: What is the purpose of a corporation, and do corporations have moral responsibility? What are the justification for and limitations on capitalism? What is money? How should we think about employee rights, conflicts of interest (whistle-blowing, loyalty to the firm versus other loyalties), truth and disclosure in advertising, responsibilities to the environment, affirmative action?

Bluecollar work: What role should beauty play versus practicality, efficiency, and economic frugality in building something? How does a theology of the body, the Incarnation itself, and Jesus' vocation as a carpenter compare with a Greek view of the mind/body distinction (where mental activity was considered more important than working with one's hands), and how does the Christian view impact the dignity of bluecollar work?

Homemaking/child raising: What are the different learning styles exemplified by children, and what are the processes of childhood development? Are these *descriptive* (they merely describe what usually is the case) or *normative* (they prescribe what *ought to be* the case)? What is the value of self-esteem and how should it be developed? What role should self-interest play in motivating a child to achieve? Arguably, being a "teenager" is a modern Western phenomenon. If this is correct, then it is probably not a normal or necessary part of maturation. What are the implications of this for child raising? What is the purpose of education? What should be the state's role in teaching values/virtues to children in the public schools?

These questions are not easy, and there is no guarantee that we will all agree about how to answer them. But we need to do a better job of making these kinds of issues central to our parachurch and local church discipleship training. If X stands for my vocation or college major, then my Christian duty and privilege is to develop an articulate, well-informed philosophy of X that serves as a basis for my living as a Christian X and for penetrating X with a Christian worldview. Parachurch ministries should develop discipleship strategies and materials that mentor college students in their majors. Churches should provide Sunday school classes and other training venues that are broken down into vocational groupings, and Christian intellectuals should be utilized in this aspect of discipleship training. We should have vocational testimonies from time to time from the pulpit (for example, "Here is how I am seeking to be an integrated, thinking, Christian businessperson"). In these and other ways, we can stimulate one another to loving and serving Christ in our whole lives.

SUMMARY

I originally wrote this chapter during the summer Bob Dole and Bill Clinton were running for president. One night the evening news presented a poll according to which the majority of Americans believed that Bill Clinton had lied about certain issues, committed adultery, and exemplified a weak character in general. Yet his popularity was close to an all-time high. According to the poll, most Americans are not particularly concerned with character issues. Instead, their primary concern is whether or not a presidential candidate understands and promises to *meet the voters' felt needs*. (The poll was borne out, by the way, in the November 1996 elections.) In my opinion, this poll expresses the approach to life characteristic of the empty self (described in chapter four) now ubiquitous in our culture.

If this is true, then there has never been a greater opportunity for Christians to be different from the broader culture and to make a difference. But this will not happen if we do not take specific steps to develop a more thoughtful, intellectually deep, and spiritually rich life of the mind in our worship, fellowship, and vocation. It will also not happen if we do not take a hard look at reforming our understanding of what a local church is and how it is to go about its activities. In the final chapter of this book, I offer a manifesto for reforming the local church.

GUARANTEEING A FUTURE FOR THE CHRISTIAN MIND

X

Recapturing the Intellectual Life in the Church

X

When faced with a crisis situation, we evangelicals usually do one of two things. We either mount a public crusade, or we retreat into an inner pious sanctum.

MARK NOLL[1]

K

Generally speaking, the church does not seem to be doing very well in meeting the need at present. We have spoken earlier about its great expansion in numbers in recent decades. A great body of disciples is emerging in South America and Africa. It may be for them to show the way for humankind as they walk fully in the yoke with Jesus. But they will never do this or even solve the problems of their own peoples, if they take the spiritual attainments of the Western church as the height of Christian possibility.

DALLAS WILLARD[2]

K

Even a bad shot is dignified when he accepts a duel.

G. K. CHESTERTON[3]

S AINT PAUL TELLS US THAT THE CHURCH — NOT THE UNIVERSITY, THE media, or the public schools — is the pillar and support of the truth (1 Timothy 3:15). But you would never know it by actually examining our local church practices week by week or by observing the goals and objectives set by many parachurch ministries. As we near the end of the second millennium in the era of our Lord, we evangelicals need to ask ourselves three very important and painful questions.

First, why is our impact not proportionate to our numbers? If the evangelical community is even one-third the size polls tell us it is, we should be turning this culture upside down. Second, why are ministers no longer viewed as the intellectual and cultural leaders in their communities that they once were? Compared to pastors of the past, contemporary ministers have lost much of their *authority* among both unbelievers and the members of their own flocks. Third, how is it possible for a person to be an active member of an evangelical church for twenty or thirty years and still know next to nothing about the history and theology of the Christian religion, the methods and tools required for serious Bible study, and the skills and information necessary to preach and defend Christianity in a post-Christian, neopagan culture?

I cannot offer a full response to these questions here, even if I were adequate for the task (which I am not). But twenty-six years of ministry have convinced me of this: *Among a small handful of factors foundational to such a response is the hostility or indifference to the development of an intellectual life in the way we go about our business in the church.* Having planted two churches and four Campus Crusade ministries from scratch, pastored in two other congregations, and spoken in hundreds of churches during the last quarter century, I have become convinced that we evangelicals neither value nor have a strategy for developing every member of our congregations to one degree or another as Christian thinkers. To convince yourself of this you need only look regularly at the types of books that show up on the Christian booksellers' top-ten list. Since the 1960s, we have experienced an evolution in what we expect a local church pastor to be. Forty years ago he was expected to be a resident authority on theology and biblical teaching. Slowly this gave way to a model of the pastor as the CEO of the church, the administrative and organizational leader. Today the ministers we want are Christianized pop therapists who are entertaining to listen to.

In the midst of all this, the church has become primarily a hospital to soothe empty selves instead of a war college to mobilize and train an army of men and women to occupy territory and advance the kingdom until the King returns. Of course, the church should actually be *both* hospital and war college and, in fact, much, much more. But there is no question that we are not succeeding in mobilizing such an army and training them with the intellectual and spiritual skills necessary to enter deeply and profoundly into the spiritual life and to destroy speculations and every lofty thing raised up against the knowledge of God. A church incompetent cannot effectively be a church militant. And make no mistake, like it or not, we are in a war for the hearts, minds, and destinies of men and women all around us.

Because the stakes are so high, we simply cannot afford to tolerate this situation any longer. I am not suggesting that we evangelicals are not making progress or doing well in a number of areas. But neither is my head in the sand. We must recommit ourselves to developing richer, deeper, more powerful churches for Jesus Christ and the good of others and ourselves. And as philosopher Roger Trigg points out, it is a matter of common sense that "Any commitment, it seems, depends on two distinct elements. It presupposes certain beliefs [to be true] and it also involves a personal dedication to the actions implied by them."[4] This means that we must become convinced that change is needed and we must be willing to pay the price to bring about that change.

Change is not valuable for its own sake, and I have no interest in novelty just to be novel. Many of the things we do in the local church are good and should remain a part of our philosophy of ministry. *But no business, movement, or group will survive and flourish if its resistance to relevant and important change is rooted in the idea that we should keep doing something simply because that's the way we've always done it.* The purpose of this chapter is to rouse discussion among us and to provide some practical suggestions with which to experiment in our churches. If you don't agree with the ideas and suggestions to follow, then at least argue about them among your brothers and sisters. Find out where and why you think I am wrong and come up with better suggestions.

I offer one word of caution before we proceed. If what I am about to say is true, then we need to change a number of things we are currently doing in the church. Unfortunately, people can get hurt in the way we bring about change, and it is all too easy to look for people to blame for things that are going wrong. These harmful approaches and attitudes are foreign to the spirit of Christ, so read what follows with a tender spirit as well as with a tough mind.

REFURBISHING THE LOCAL CHURCH

Philosophy of Ministry

1. No senior pastors: Any local church or any individual believer should have a philosophy of ministry—that is, a view about the purpose, objectives, structures, and methods of ministry that ought to characterize a local church ministry. In my view, any philosophy of local church ministry ought to be clear about three very crucial ideas. First, the local church in the New Testament contained a plurality of elders (see Acts 14:23, 20:28; Philippians 1:1; Hebrews 13:17). The New Testament knows nothing about a senior pastor. In my opinion, the emergence of the senior pastor in the local church is one of the factors that has most significantly undermined the development of healthy churches.

Think about it. More and more people go into the pastorate to get their own significance needs met, and congregations are increasingly filled with empty selves, as we saw in chapter four. Given these facts, the senior pastor model actually produces a codependence that often feeds the egos of senior pastors while allowing parishioners to remain passive. None of this is intentional, but the effects are still real. The senior pastor model tends to create a situation in which we identify the church as "Pastor Smith's church" and parishioners come to support *his* ministry. If a visitor asks where the minister is, instead of pointing to the entire congregation (as the New Testament would indicate, since we are all ministers of the new covenant), we actually point to Pastor Smith. On the other hand, poor Pastor Smith increasingly gets isolated from people and peer accountability, and eventually, he dries up spiritually if he is not careful.

The local church should be led and taught by a plurality of voices called elders, and these voices should be equal. If so-called lay elders (I dislike the word *lay!*) do not have the seminary training possessed by those paid to be in "full-time" local church ministry, then the church needs to develop a long-term plan to give them that training in the church itself or elsewhere. No one person has enough gifts, perspective, and maturity to be given the opportunity disproportionately to shape the personality and texture of a local church. If Christ is actually the head of the church, our church structures ought to reflect that fact, and a group of undershepherds, not a senior pastor, should collectively seek His guidance in leading the congregation.

2. What the pastoral staff and elders should be doing: Second, Ephesians 4:11-16 may well be the most critical section in the entire New Testament for informing the nature of local church leadership. In that passage, the apostle Paul tells us that God has given the church evangelists and pastors-teachers (among other persons) who have a very specific function in the body. Their job description is to equip others for ministry, not to do the ministry themselves and have others come and passively support them. For example, the test of the gift of evangelism is not how effective you are at winning others to Christ, but rather, your track record at training others to evangelize. The senior pastor model tends to centralize ministry around the church building and the pastor himself. Where he is, is where the action is. We bring people to him to evangelize, to counsel, and so forth. On this view, there is little need actually to equip parishioners to develop their own gifts, talents, and ministries because their job is to support *the* minister.

But according to Ephesians 4, this tradition has it backwards. New Testament ministry is *decentralized*, and *the function of pastors-teachers is to equip others to do the ministry*. If we were more serious about this approach, we would do a better job of providing theological, biblical, philosophical, psychological, and other forms of training in our churches because without it, the ministers (that is, the members of the church) would not be adequately equipped to do the ministry.

3. The distinction between forms and functions: Third, we need to make a careful distinction between forms and functions in the church.[5] *A New Testament function is an absolute biblical mandate that every church must do*—for example, edify believers, worship God, evangelize the lost, and so forth. Functions are unchanging nonnegotiables.

By contrast, *a form is a culturally relative means of fulfilling biblical functions*. Forms are valuable as a means to accomplish those functions and should be constantly evaluated, kept, or replaced in light of their effectiveness. Examples of forms are the existence of youth directors,

Sunday school classes, vacation Bible schools, the order used in the worship service along with the kinds of music utilized, and so forth. We must keep in mind that we are *free*—genuinely and honestly free in Christ—to adjust our forms any way we wish, under the constraints of common sense, biblical teaching, and effectiveness. If the way a specific church conducts Sunday school classes is not effective in fulfilling the function of teaching people in the faith, then we should change it.

Serious harm has been done to our churches by confusing forms and functions and by clinging to the former just because we have always done them a certain way. We have no right to adjust our functions, but we have a duty to examine constantly our forms. A church that does not do this will have a lot to answer for at the judgment seat of the Head of the church.

Before I offer several suggestions for refurbishing the local church that, in one way or another, express these three core components of philosophy of ministry, I want to summarize more precisely what I am claiming. The local church ought to be led by a plurality of elders whose main job is to develop the ministries of others. They are to see to it that members of the body discover their spiritual gifts and natural talents and receive the training and equipping necessary to be good at their ministries individually and corporately. The elders are free to do whatever is necessary to the forms in the church in order to succeed in equipping the saints to accomplish biblical functions for the church. *If this is correct, then the church must see herself as an educational institution, and the development of the Christian mind will be at the forefront of the church's ministry strategy of equipping the saints.*

Practical Suggestions

Here are a number of practical suggestions for making this philosophy of ministry a reality in the local church. I have actually done most of these in my own ministry and have witnessed their effectiveness firsthand.

1. Sermons: We must overhaul our understanding of the sermon along with our evaluation of what counts as a good one. The filling station approach (people come each week to get filled up until next week) is itself running out of gas. Yet we persist in viewing the sermon as a popular message that ought to be grasped easily by all who attend and evaluated solely on the basis of its pleasurableness, entertainment value, and practical orientation. Unfortunately, twenty years of exposure to these types of messages result in a congregation filled with people who have learned very little about their religion and who are inappropriately dependent upon someone else to tell them what to believe each week.

I do not dispute that sermons should be interesting and of practical value. But when most people say they want a sermon to be practical, I don't think they really mean how-tos and religious formulas as opposed to reasoned sermons that argue a case and actually cause people to learn something new. After all, most practicing Christians sense deep in their hearts that they know far too little about their faith and are embarrassed about it. *They want to be stretched to learn something regularly and cumulatively over the years by the sermons they hear.* What people really want when they say they desire practical sermons is this: They want passion and deep commitment to come through the message instead of a talk that sounds like it was hurriedly put together the day before.

How can we improve the quality of the sermons in our churches? I have three suggestions. First, we need to be more thoughtful and serious about supplementary material for the sermon. A small bulletin insert with three points is inadequate if, in fact, the sermon is a teaching vehicle. Instead, a detailed handout of two or three pages on regular-sized paper ought to be given to people. It should include detailed, structured notes following the sermon structure; a set of study exercises on the last page; recommendations for further reflection that week; and a bibliography. After a series is completed, these could be put together (with sermon tapes) to form a nice minicourse on the series topic for later study or distribution to those not attending the church.

Further, before a series begins, a book or commentary should be selected, order forms passed out, and copies sold the week before the series begins. Reading assignments could be given each week during the series. I once preached a series on 1 Peter, and seventy-five copies of a good commentary on the book were purchased by the congregation. I listed each week's text along with the relevant page numbers in the commentary on a sheet of paper the first week of the series. A number of people came to the sermon prepared to think about what I was teaching since they had read the commentary on the text prior to the message. Among other things, this forced me to work harder on my messages because people were not taking my word for it about the meaning of a passage! Can you imagine! They had their own ideas about the text!

Anything we can do with supplementary materials to get people reading and thinking about a series topic will enhance learning and growth.

Second, from time to time a minister should intentionally pitch a
message to the upper one-third of the congregation, intellectually speaking. This may leave some people feeling a bit left out and confused
during the sermon, which is unfortunate, but the alternative (which we
follow almost all the time) is to dumb down our sermons so often that
the upper one-third get bored and have to look elsewhere for spiritual
and intellectual food. The intellectual level of our messages ought to
be varied to provide more of a balance for all of the congregation.
Furthermore, such an approach may motivate those in the lower two-
thirds to work to catch up!

Finally, for two reasons I do not think a single individual ought to
preach more than half (twenty-six) the Sundays during the year. First,
no one person ought to have a disproportionate influence through the
pulpit because, inevitably, the church will take on that person's
strengths, weaknesses, and emphases. Now, who among us is adequate
for this? No one. By rotating speakers, the body gets exposure to God's
truth being poured through a number of different personalities, and that
is more healthy. If one person is a better speaker than the others, he
should train (equip) the rest over the years to be more adequate. As a
result, the local church will have a growing number of competent leaders able to preach and consequently not be so dependent on one person.

Here is an important question: Would it inordinately impact your
church's attendance and effectiveness if the main preacher went to
another church? If the answer is yes, your church is going about its
business in the wrong way. Leaders are not being developed in the body,
and the pulpit is not being adequately shared.

Second, no one who preaches week after week can do adequate study
for a message or deeply process and internalize the sermon topic spiritually. What inevitably happens is that a pastor will rely on his speaking
ability and skills at putting together a message. Unfortunately, I have
been in this situation myself, and my messages started sounding hollow
and packaged. After several weeks of preaching, I started giving talks
instead of preaching my passions and feeding others the fruits of my own
deep study. In one church where I was a pastor-teacher, we rotated preaching among four people and each of us knew that he would have a four- to
eight-week series coming up in, say, three months. That gave us the

chance to work on a subject for a long time. By the time our turn on the calendar arrived, we were well prepared intellectually and spiritually.

2. The church library: Those in charge of the church library should see their job to be one of enlisting a growing number of church members into an army of readers and learners who, over the years, are becoming spiritually mature, clearly thinking believers who know what and why they believe. The church library ought to be large, and it should contain intellectual resources and not just self-help books. I recognize that building the church library costs money, but our investment of funds should reflect our values and we should value intellectual resources enough to pay for them.

In one church where I was a pastor-teacher, we had a library of twelve thousand volumes. As with most church libraries, its location was off the beaten path. So every single Sunday different volunteers on a rotating basis set up tables in the foyer, placed five hundred books on those tables, and actually greeted people at the door and invited them to check out a book or purchase a minicourse from previous sermon series. Hundreds of books were regularly checked out and read that would have stayed on the shelf if we had simply left them in the out-of-sight-out-of-mind church library.

Church librarians should see to it that book reviews are regularly inserted into the bulletin and that each month several copies of a featured book are secured on consignment and sold in the lobby. For several years, the railroad industry all but died in this country because it wrongly defined its purpose. Railroad employees should have seen themselves in the transportation industry, not the railroad industry per se. Likewise, those who work in the church library must ask themselves what they are about. They do not serve to process books and keep the library open. They serve to enhance the development of a thinking, reading, literate congregation.

3. Sunday school and study centers: For many churches, the main purpose for a Sunday school class is to enfold, not to educate. A Sunday school class provides a place of contact with a mid-sized group numbering somewhere between the large congregational meeting and the small group. So understood, Sunday school classes require no preparation and little commitment to study on the part of their participants, and, if judged by their effects over several years, they accomplish little by way of actual education. Now it may surprise you to know that I do not think that this situation is bad in and of itself. More specifically, I think some vehicle for enfolding people and building group cohesion at a mid-sized-level church is appropriate, and Sunday school may well be that vehicle.

What we need, however, is to develop alternative, parallel classes that have a distinctively educational focus, so people can choose one or the other or alternate between the two. My friend Walt Russell and I co-labored at Grace Fellowship Church in Baltimore for three years in what we called the Grace Discovery Center. We developed a set of course offerings that changed each quarter of the year. A few weeks prior to a change in church quarter, we passed out a list of course offerings and signed people up for the study center classes.

Courses cost from $25 to $75 depending on the number of hours of classroom instruction required. We varied the times of meeting. Some Discovery Center classes met on Wednesday nights from 7:00 to 9:00 P.M., some met for three hours on four consecutive Saturday mornings, some lasted from 7:00 to 9:30 Friday evening and from 9:00 A.M. to 4:00 P.M. the following day with a lunch break, others ran parallel to the Sunday school hour. Each course had a syllabus, required texts, and assignments (papers, letters to the editor, etc.), and grades were given out. We had classes in Greek, counseling, systematic theology, church history, apologetics, the history of philosophy, various vocations (medical ethics, Christianity and science, education and childhood development), and other areas. We used books written by unbelievers as well as believers and published by companies ranging from Oxford University Press to standard evangelical houses. If your church doesn't have the teaching resources for such a study center, you should band together with two or three other churches and form a jointly sponsored study center.

The Discovery Center also sponsored very focused weekend retreats not of interest to everyone. For example, a group of around forty adults in the church had a special interest in Christianity and politics. So the Discovery Center responded to the need to equip these saints by hosting a weekend conference on the topic and flying in a Christian scholar who could address it competently, and we required that all attenders purchase and read a specific book on the topic (and state on a three-by-five-inch card they had done so) before they could attend.

The simple fact is that Sunday school as it's currently practiced is not doing the job of developing the Christian mind, and there may be more pressing, legitimate objectives (enfolding) for such classes. If this is so, we need to develop other ways of seeing to it that the local church develops Christian thinkers equipped to do the work of ministry. At the church in Baltimore, one group of twenty people studied psychology and pastoral counseling for a whole year under a local Christian psychologist. One Sunday morning, we called them all up to the front of the church and passed out a list of their names and phone numbers to the congregation, and the elders laid hands on them to dedicate this group to the body as those responsible for the counseling ministry in the church. None of us who were elders or paid staff members were especially gifted in this area, but we saw our biblical mandate to be that of ensuring the job was done by equipping others. Among other things, this freed us up to do more work in leadership development in the church while those with the training and desire to counsel fulfilled that role in the body.

Eighteen engineers and scientists in the body went through an eighteen-month study of science and Christianity. One Sunday morning we dedicated this group in front of the church just as we had the counseling group. These scientists and engineers were looked to by the body as people who could help families if issues in creation and evolution arose. For the first time in their lives, what these men and women had studied in college and chosen as a vocation became relevant to their discipleship unto Jesus and their ministry in the body! We need to offer more courses in church partitioned along vocational lines to tap into natural motivation, opportunity, and talent.

4. Deepening the value of the intellectual life and raising the visibility of Christian intellectuals and intellectual work: A group's values will largely determine the corporate and individual behavior of the group. And a group must find ways to foster, sustain, and propagate its values among its members. If the local church is to overcome its anti-intellectualism, it must find ways to raise conscious awareness of the value of the intellectual life among its members. Most believers know the names of leading Christian speakers and radio personalities. But how many of us know our Christian intellectuals, celebrate their accomplishments on our behalf, pray regularly for the intellectual war they wage, and hold them forth as heroes and vocational role models among our teenagers? If we do this for missionaries, why don't we do it for Christian intellectuals? We should, because we are in a struggle about ideas and need to raise up a new generation of Christian scholars. In our master of arts program in philosophy and ethics at Talbot School of Theology, one of our goals is to help raise up one hundred men and women in the next twenty-five years who will study under us, go on for their Ph.D., and become evangelical university professors at schools all across the country. The local church needs to be more intentional about fostering the intellectual life and mobilizing a new generation of Christian intellectuals. Here are some suggestions for doing this.

First, we should regularly incorporate vocational or apologetical testimonies and book reports on timely topics into our services. Selected worshipers should be given five minutes to share how they are growing to think more Christianly as a businessperson, a teacher, or whatever. They should share what they are reading, the issues with which they are grappling, and the progress they are making. People should share occasions where apologetics has aided their own ministry of evangelism and discipleship. Once a month we ought to entertain a brief book review of a key new book, some of which should be written by influential unbelievers. We can do a better job of encouraging a life of reading, apologetical argumentation, and vocational integration during our services.

Second, we ought to identify intellectual leaders who are associated with the evangelical community or historic Christianity more broadly conceived and find ways to hold forth their lifework as possible vocations for our young people. Further, Christian intellectuals, especially university professors, sometimes feel a bit estranged from the sociological ambience of their local churches and from the anti-Christian ideas of their colleagues. We need to do a better job of recognizing, celebrating, enfolding, and aiding these intellectuals in their work. An occasional bulletin announcement to pray for professor so-and-so who labors for Christ at a local college would be a wonderful thing. We get upset because we are underrepresented in the university. But how many churches have taken specific steps to encourage the university professors (and graduate students soon to be university professors) among their membership to be faithful to orthodoxy and to be bold in their vocation?

Third, we need to prepare teenagers for the intellectual world they will face in college. The summer after high school graduation, it would be a good idea to hold a summer institute in apologetics and try to offer some worldview instruction to prepare our young brothers and sisters to think more carefully about what they will study at the university. Such an institute could also be used to challenge teens with the ideal of vocation as the point of college in the first place. Having worked with college students for twenty-six years, I can testify that our churches are not preparing young people for what they will face intellectually in their college years, and we simply must be more intentional about this.

Fourth, we should be more proactive in supporting and enfolding members of the body who go to graduate school. Many churches have a number of people each year who engage in graduate studies. Often, these people begin to identify with their department of study in such a way that they are sociologized out of a vibrant evangelical commitment. Why should we abandon these students in this way? Graduate students do not simply need the same sort of fellowship as everyone else in the church. They need intellectual support as well. I think each August we should print a list of students heading off for graduate school that includes their names, universities, addresses, and majors. These students should be brought before the congregation, admonished to develop Christian minds in their graduate work, and dedicated to the Lord by the laying on of hands by the elders. If possible, they should be paired up with someone in the church who is engaged in the same vocation, and this person could be available for support through letters, phone conversations about issues in the discipline, and so forth. Can you imagine the extent to which the Christian mind would emerge in this culture if thousands of churches began to practice this?

Finally, we need to increase our individual and congregational giving to support Christian scholarship. When I speak in a church, I sometimes challenge people to ask themselves just how much of their individual giving or church budget goes to support the development of Christian scholarship? Most people have never even thought of such an idea. Evangelical colleges and seminaries are grossly underfunded. As a result, many such schools are tuition driven and their faculties are underpaid, strapped with inordinate teaching loads, and left with inadequate library resources and funds for professional conferences compared to their secular counterparts. And we expect those schools and their faculties to compete in the war of ideas!

Moreover, there is less scholarship money available to students who attend evangelical colleges and seminaries compared to those who attend secular institutions. When I did my doctorate at USC, I received $10,000 a year for three years. The university knew that if I (and other graduate students) had time to spend in the library and on academic work, this would increase my chances of getting a teaching job and making a contribution in the academic world, and eventually, would bode well for USC. Unfortunately, students at evangelical seminaries face high tuitions and, therefore, must work at part-time jobs when they could be in the library improving their educational experience and ministerial training. If we evangelicals are tired of being underrepresented in the media, the university, and the government, then we need to support evangelical scholarship, especially solid evangelical colleges and seminaries, because such institutions nurture the intellectual leaders of the future.

SUMMARY

The morning I began to write this chapter, I picked up the newspaper and read the editorial page. One of the featured editorials was a defense of Promise Keepers against feminist and liberal critiques of that movement.[6] The article was articulate, carefully written, overtly evangelical, and powerfully presented. And it was read by millions of people. What really stirred my heart, however, was not just the substance of the article but who wrote it—Brad Stetson. This may not mean much to you, but it was symbolic to me. I have met Dr. Stetson. He is a young, dedicated evangelical who did his Ph.D. in social ethics concurrently with two of my faculty colleagues and is symbolic of a new and, hopefully, growing breed of younger evangelical intellectuals. I was encouraged to see a faithful, well-trained evangelical scholar impact the public marketplace of ideas that is available to laypeople in the community.

What I am saying in this chapter is that we need one hundred thousand Brad Stetsons to write editorials, penetrate secular universities, write books, speak on talk shows, and much, much more. The local church needs to be more intentional in finding and developing the young Brad Stetsons now in her ranks. May almighty God help us to do just that.

Appendix 1
Intellectual Resources

Below is a list of intellectual resources for you or your church.

Organizations

The following organizations provide resources for the intellectual life—tapes, speakers for conferences or other events, or opportunities to interact about intellectual issues.

Answers in Action
PO Box 2067,
Costa Mesa, CA 92628
(714) 646-9042 / Web page: http:www.power.net/users/aia

Answers Information Ministry
921 S. Birch
Santa Ana, CA 92701
(714) 542-0784

Apologia
Web page: http:www.eskimo.com/~think/apologia/

Augustine Fellowship Study Center
PO Box 23
Hemet, CA 92543
(909) 654-1429

Centers for Christian Study, International
PO Box 1227
Monument, CO 80132
(719) 488-8720

Christian Answers Network
Web page: http:www.ChristianAnswers.Net/canhome.html

Christian Leadership Ministries
3440 Sojourn Dr., Suite 200
Carrollton, TX 75006-2354
(214) 713-7130

Christian Research Institute
PO Box 500-TC
San Juan Capistrano, CA 92693
(800) 443-9797
Web page: http://www.iclnet.org/pub/resources/text/cri/cri-home.html

The Francis Schaeffer Institute
12330 Conway Rd.
St. Louis, MO 63141
(314) 434-4044

Josh McDowell Ministries
PO Box 1000
Dallas, TX 75221
(800) 222-5674

J. P. Moreland Tape Ministry (tapes)
6332 Glendale Dr.
Yorba Linda, CA 92886

Ligonier Ministries
400 Technology Way, Suite 150
Lake Mary, FL 32746
(800) 435-4343
Web page: http://www.gospelcom.net/ligonier/ligcat/cattopics.html

Paul Cox Office
Perspective Ministries
PO Box 6424
San Bernardino, CA 92412
(800) 723-8442

Probe Ministries
1900 Firman Dr., Suite 100
Richardson, TX 75081
(800) 899-PROB
Web page: http://www.gocin.com/probe

Ravi Zacharias International Ministries
4725 Peachtree Corners Circle, Suite 250
Norcross, GA 30092-2553
(770) 449-6766
Web page: http://www.gocin.com/rzim/rzim.htm

Reasons to Believe (Hugh Ross)
Box 5978
Pasadena, CA 91107
(818) 335-1480
Web page: http://reasons.org/reasons/

Search Ministries
5038 Dorsey Hall Dr.
Ellicott City, MD 21042
(410) 960-9183

Stand to Reason
2420 Pacific Coast Hwy.
Hermosa Beach, CA 90254
(800) 2REASON
Web page: http://www.str.org

Summit Ministries (Director: Dr. David Noebel)
(focus on high school students)
PO Box 207
Manitou Springs, CO 80829
(719) 685-9103
Web page: http://www.ChristianAnswers.Net/summit/sumhome.html

Talbot Institute of Biblical Studies (Director: Frank Pastore)
Biola University
13800 Biola Ave.
La Mirada, CA 90639
(310) 944-0351 ext. 5558

The Trinity Institute
College at Main
Box 100
Tehuacana, TX 76686
(609) 497-1591
E-mail: 73741.1266@compuserve.com

Turner-Welninski Publishing (audio tapes) [They market some of
William Lane Craig's tapes]
PO Box 669
Elgin, IL 60120
(800) 474-2166

Veritas Forum
3939 International Gateway
Columbus, OH 43221
(614) 486-5437

Magazines and Journals

The following is a list of intellectually stimulating magazines and journals that provide good resources for developing a Christian mind.

Books and Culture
Subscription Services
PO Box 37011
Boone, IA 50037-2011

CBMW News
c/o Steve Henderson
229 Siloam Rd.
Easley, SC 29642
(864) 223-1158
E-mail: CBMWDeb@aol.com

Christian History
Subscription Services
PO Box 37055
Boone, IA 50037-2055

Christian Parenting Today
PO Box 545
Mt. Morris, IL 61054

Christian Scholar's Review
Circulation Department
Calvin College
Grand Rapids, MI 49546

Christian Research Journal
PO Box 500-TC
San Juan Capistrano, CA 92693
(800) 443-9797

Christianity Today
Subscription Services
PO Box 11617
Des Moines, IA 50340-1617

Clear Thinking
2420 Pacific Coast Hwy.
Hermosa Beach, CA 90254
(800) 2REASON

Faith & Facts
Box 5978
Pasasdena, CA 91107
(818) 335-1480

First Things
PO Box 3000, Dept. FT
Denville, NJ 07834-9848
(800) 783-4903

Journal of the Evangelical Theological Society
c/o James Borland
112 Russell Woods Dr.
Lynchburg, VA 24502-3530

Mars Hill Review
11757 W. Ken Caryl Ave., Suite F330
Littleton, CO 80127-3600
(800) 990-MARS
Origins & Design

Access Research Network
PO Box 38069
Colorado Springs, CO 80937-8069

Religious and Theological Students Fellowship
PO Box 100
Tehuacana, TX 76686
(817) 395-4444

Tabletalk
Ligonier Ministries
PO Box 54700
Orlando, FL 32854

Book Clubs and Publishers

Here is a list of book clubs and publishers that feature food for the mind.
You can call or write a publisher and request their academic catalog.

Baker Book House
PO Box 6287
Grand Rapids, MI 49516
(800) 877-2665

Broadman & Holman
127 Ninth Ave.
Nashville, TN 37234
(800) 251-3225

Christian Book Distributors
PO Box 7000
Peabody, MA 01961-7000
(508) 977-5000

Crossway Books
1300 Crescent St.
Wheaton, IL 60187
(800) 323-3890

Eerdmans Publishing Company
255 Jefferson Ave., SE
Grand Rapids, MI 49503
(800) 253-7521

Evangelical Book Club
1000 East Huron
Milford, MI 48381

(810) 685-8773

InterVarsity Press and IVP Book Club
430 E. Plaza Dr.
Westmont, IL 60559
(800) 887-2500

NavPress
PO Box 35001
Colorado Springs, CO 80935
(800) 366-7788

Zondervan Publishing Company
5300 Patterson Ave. SE
Grand Rapids, MI 49530
(800) 727-3480

Appendix 2
Sources for Integration

Here is a selected list of resources for building a personal library and for gathering sources that integrate Christian thought with different vocations/areas of university study. An important source for building a library is Cyril J. Barber, *The Minister's Library* (Chicago: Moody, 1985).

TOPICS OF GENERAL INTEREST TO CHRISTIANS

General Apologetics

Craig, William Lane. *Reasonable Faith*. Wheaton, Ill.: Crossway, 1994.

Geisler, Norman L., and Thomas Howe. *When Critics Ask*. Wheaton, Ill.: Victor, 1992.

Kreeft, Peter, and Ronald K. Tacelli. *Handbook of Christian Apologetics*. Downers Grove, Ill.: InterVarsity, 1994.

Lewis, C. S. *Mere Christianity*. New York: Macmillan, 1943. Rev. ed., 1952.

Moreland, J. P. *Scaling the Secular City*. Grand Rapids: Baker, 1986.

Moreland, J. P., and Kai Nielsen. *Does God Exist?* Buffalo: Prometheus, 1993.

Nash, Ronald. *Faith and Reason*. Grand Rapids: Zondervan, 1988.

Schaeffer, Francis. *The God Who Is There*. Chicago: InterVarsity, 1968.

Zacharias, Ravi. *A Shattered Visage*. Brentwood, Tenn.: Wolgemuth and Hyatt, 1990.

Biblical Studies

There is so much in this area, it is best to request academic catalogs from the publishers listed in Appendix 1. For a good book on how to approach a study of the Bible, see Gordon D. Fee and Douglas Stuart, *How to Read the Bible for All Its Worth* (Grand Rapids: Zondervan, 1981). Zondervan has the NIV Application Commentary Series (7 vols. at present), *The Expositor's Bible Commentary* (covers the entire Bible in 12 vols. at present), *The Zondervan NIV Bible Commentary* (2 vols.), and the following single-volume commentaries: *Asbury Bible Commentary* and *The NIV Compact Bible Commentary*. Baker has the *Evangelical Commentary on the Bible* (1 vol.) and the *Baker Exegetical Commentary on the New Testament* (Luke and Philippians currently available). Also useful is the two-volume set published by Victor Books: John F. Walvoord and Roy B. Zuck, eds., *The Bible Knowledge Commentary*, vol. 1: *Old Testament Edition* (1985), vol. 2: *New Testament Edition* (1983). InterVarsity produces the *Tyndale Old Testament Commentaries* (27 vols.), the *IVP New Testament Commentary* series (11 vols.), *The Bible Speaks Today* (32 vols.), *The New Bible Dictionary* (1 vol.), *Dictionary of Jesus and the Gospels*, and *Dictionary of Paul and His Letters*.
Important scholarly societies for biblical studies are:

American Academy of Religion
1703 Clifton Rd., NE, Suite G5
Atlanta, GA 30329-4075
Phone: (404) 727-7920; FAX: (404) 727-7959; Internet: aar@emory.edu

Society of Biblical Literature
1201 Clairmont Rd., Suite 300
Decatur, GA 30030
Phone: (404) 636-4744; FAX: (404) 248-0815; Internet: sblexec@emory.edu

AAR/SBL Membership Services
Phone: (404) 727-2345; Internet: scholars@emory.edu; World Wide
Web site for AAR/SBL is http://scholar.cc.emory.edu

Tyndale House
36 Selwyn Gardens
Cambridge, CB3 9BA, UK
Telephone from inside UK, prefix 01223. From outside UK, prefix 44
1223: Main Office: 566601; Administrator: 566602; Librarian:
566604; Residents/Readers: 566618, 566619; FAX: 566608. E-mail:
E-mail Librarian dib10@cam.ac.uk; E-mail Warden:
bw107@cam.ac.uk. Location: Tyndale House is on the western edge
of Cambridge, UK, within ten minutes' walk to the city center and
five minutes' walk to the university library.

Institute for Biblical Research
PO Box 275
Winona Lake, IN 46590-0275
For additional scholarly societies, see "Theology and Doctrine" below.

Church History/History of Doctrine
Christian History
Subscription Services
PO Box 37055
Boone, IA 50037-2055

Gonzalez, Justo. *A History of Christian Thought*. 3 vols. Nashville:
Abingdon, 1970.

Shelly, Bruce L. *Church History in Plain Language*. Waco, Tex.:
Word, 1982.

Walton, Robert. *Chronological and Background Charts of Church
History*. Grand Rapids: Zondervan, 1986.

Cults

Gomes, Alan, gen. ed. *Zondervan Guide to Cults and Religious
Movements*. 16 vols. Grand Rapids: Zondervan, 1995.

Cultural Analysis

Bellah, Robert N., William M. Sullivan, Ann Swidler, and Steven M. Tipton. *Habits of the Heart*. New York: Harper & Row, 1985.

Bloom, Allan. *The Closing of the American Mind*. New York: Simon & Schuster, 1987.

Chesterton, G. K. *Orthodoxy*. 1908. Reprint, San Francisco: Ignatius, 1995.

Johnson, Phillip E. *Reason in the Balance*. Downers Grove, Ill.: InterVarsity, 1995.

Hunter, James Davidson. *Culture Wars*. New York: HarperCollins, 1991.

Noll, Mark A. *The Scandal of the Evangelical Mind*. Grand Rapids: Eerdmans, 1994.

Postman, Neil. *Amusing Ourselves to Death*. New York: Penguin Books, 1985.

Schlossberg, Herbert. *Idols for Destruction*. Wheaton, Ill.: Crossway, 1990.

Ethics

Beckwith, Francis J. *Politically Correct Death*. Grand Rapids: Baker, 1992.

Beckwith, *Do the Right Thing*. Boston: Jones and Bartlett, 1996.

Fournier, Keith A., and William D. Watkins. *In Defense of Life*. Colorado Springs: NavPress, 1996.

Geisler, Norman L. *Christian Ethics: Options and Issues*. Grand Rapids: Baker, 1989.

Hauerwas, Stanley. *Suffering Presence*. Notre Dame, Ind.: University of Notre Dame Press, 1986.

Moreland, J. P., and Norman L. Geisler. *The Life and Death Debate*. Westport, Conn.: Praeger, 1990.

Pojman, Louis P. *Ethics: Discovering Right and Wrong*. Belmont, Calif.: Wadsworth, 1995.

Rae, Scott. *Moral Choices*. Grand Rapids: Zondervan, 1995.

Historical Apologetics

Bloomberg, Craig. *The Historical Reliability of the Gospels*. Downers Grove, Ill.: InterVarsity, 1987.

France, R. T. *The Evidence for Jesus*. Downers Grove, Ill.: InterVarsity, 1986.

Groothuis, Douglas. *Jesus in an Age of Controversy*. Eugene, Oreg.: Harvest House, 1996.

Habermas, Gary. *The Historical Jesus*. Joplin, Mo.: College Press, 1996.

McDowell, Josh. *He Walked Among Us*. San Bernardino, Calif.: Here's Life, 1988.

Wilkins, Michael J., and J. P. Moreland, eds. *Jesus Under Fire*. Grand Rapids: Zondervan, 1995.

Witherington, Ben III. *The Jesus Quest*. Downers Grove, Ill.: InterVarsity, 1995

Intellectual Life

Adler, Mortimer J., and Charles Van Doren. *How to Read a Book*. New York: Simon & Schuster, 1972.

Glaspey, Terry W. *Great Books of the Christian Tradition*. Eugene, Oreg.: Harvest House, 1996.

Sertillanges, A. G. *The Intellectual Life*. Washington, D.C.: Catholic University of America Press, 1946.

Sire, James W. *How to Read Slowly*. Wheaton, Ill.: Harold Shaw, 1978.

Sire, *Discipleship of the Mind*. Downers Grove, Ill.: InterVarsity, 1990.

Spiritual Formation and Discipleship

Augustine. *The Confessions*. Several editions.

Banks, Robert. *The Tyranny of Time*. Downers Grove, Ill.: InterVarsity, 1983.

Brother Lawrence. *The Practice of the Presence of God*. Several editions.

Foster, Richard J. *Celebration of Discipline*. Rev. ed. San Francisco: HarperSanFrancisco, 1994.

Foster, Richard J., and James Bryan Smith, eds. *Devotional Classics*. San Francisco: HarperSanFrancisco, 1994.

Kempis, Thomas à. *The Imitation of Christ*. Several editions.

Lewis, C. S. *The Screwtape Letters*. New York: Macmillan, 1961.

Nouwen, Henri M. *Reaching Out*. Garden City, N.Y.: Doubleday, 1966.

Wilkins, Michael J. *Following the Master: Discipleship in the Steps of Jesus*. Grand Rapids: Zondervan, 1992.

Willard, Dallas. *The Spirit of the Disciplines*. San Francisco: Harper and Row, 1988.

Willard, *In Search of Guidance*. San Francisco: Harper San Francisco, 1993.

Multnomah Press (in Portland, OR 97266) has a series entitled Classics of Faith and Devotion (gen. ed., James. M. Houston). Another outstanding series is The Classics of Western Spirituality (editor-in-chief, John Farina [New York: Paulist]; especially valuable is the volume entitled *Quaker Spirituality*, edited by Douglas V. Steere, 1984.

Theology and Doctrine

Elwell, Walter A., ed. *Evangelical Dictionary of Theology*. Grand Rapids: Baker, 1984.

Erickson, Millard J. *Christian Theology*. Baker, Grand Rapids, 1985.

Grudem. Wayne. *Systematic Theology*. Grand Rapids: Zondervan, 1994.

House, H. Wayne. *Charts of Christian Theology and Doctrine*. Grand Rapids: Zondervan, 1992.

Ryrie, Charles. *Basic Theology*. Wheaton, Ill.: Victor, 1986.

Wells, David. *No Place for Truth, or Whatever Happened to Evangelical Theology?* Grand Rapids: Eerdmans, 1993.

Evangelical theologians Donald G. Bloesch, Stanley J. Grenz, Alister McGrath, and Thomas C. Oden have written a number of books on themes in theology that ought to be consulted. Two important scholarly societies are the Evangelical Theological Society, which sponsors the *Journal of the Evangelical Theological Society* (membership inquiries and subscription requests may be addressed to the secretary, James Borland, 112 Russell Woods Drive, Lynchburg, VA 24502-3530), and the Religious and Theological Studies Fellowship, which sponsors the journal *Themelios* (address subscriptions requests to 38 De Montfort Street, Leicester, England LE1 7GP).

Three groups of interest within the American Academy of Religion are:

■ The Evangelical Theology Group within AAR. Proposals for papers are to be sent to Douglas Jacobsen, Messiah College, Grantham, PA 17027; office: 717/766-2511; FAX: (717) 691-6060. The cochair is Priscilla Pope-Levison, Duke University, Durham, NC 27708. Phone: (919) 660-3400; FAX: (919) 660-3473.

■ Systematic Theology Study Group. Philip Clayton, Department of Philosophy, California State University (Sonoma), Rohnert Park, CA 94928. Office: (707) 664-4042.

■ Christian Theological Research Fellowship. Alan G. Padgett, Department of Religion and Philosophy, Azusa Pacific

University, Azusa, CA 91700-7000; phone: (818) 815-6000
ext. 3232; FAX: (818) 815-3809; E-mail: padgett@apu.edu.

Worldview in General

Curtis, Edward M., and John Brugaletta. *Transformed Thinking:
Loving God with All Your Mind*. Franklin, Tenn.: JKO Press, 1996.

Geisler, Norman L., and William L. Watkins. *Worlds Apart*. Grand
Rapids: Baker, 1989.

Holmes, Arthur. *Contours of a World View*. Grand Rapids: Eerdmans,
1983.

Pepper, Stephen. *World Hypotheses*. Berkeley: University of
California Press, 1942.

Sire, James. *The Universe Next Door*. Downers Grove, Ill.:
InterVarsity, 1976.

Wainwright, William J. *Philosophy of Religion*. Belmont, Calif.:
Wadsworth, 1988, chap. 7.

SOURCES FOR INTEGRATION OF A CHRISTIAN WORLDVIEW AND DIFFERENT VOCATIONS

Anthropology and Missions

Heibert, Paul. *Anthropological Insights for Missionaries*. Grand
Rapids: Baker, 1985.

Lingenfelter, Sherwood. *Transforming Culture*. Grand Rapids: Baker,
1992.

Lingenfelter, "Mind, Emotion, Culture, and the Person." In *Christian
Perspectives on Being Human*, edited by J. P. Moreland and David M.
Ciocchi. Grand Rapids: Baker, 1993.

Lingenfelter, *Agents of Transformation*. Grand Rapids: Baker, 1996.

An important organization is the Network of Christian
Anthropologists. The address is Darrell Whiteman, Chair, Asbury
Theological Seminary, Wilmore, KY 40390; E-mail address:

Darrell_Whiteman@ATS.Wilmore.Ky.US. Phone: (606) 858-2215.
Journal: *Missiology*. In addition, there is an an excellent two-issue set
put out in Studies in Third World Societies, publications nos. 25 and
26 (which comes out of College of William and Mary), entitled
Missionaries and Anthropologists, parts 1 and 2.

Art and Aesthetics

Best, Harold. *Music Through the Eyes of Faith*. San Francisco:
Harper, 1993.

Dillenberger, John. *Style and Content in Christian Art*. Books on
Demand, London, 1986.

Halverson, William H. *A Concise Introduction to Philosophy*. New
York: Random House, 1967, chaps. 51–54.

Hospers, John. *Understanding the Arts*. Englewood Cliffs, N.J.:
Prentice-Hall, 1982.

Myers, Kenneth A. *All God's Children and Blue Suede Shoes*.
Wheaton, Ill.: Crossway, 1989.

Sayers, Dorothy. *The Mind of the Maker*. San Francisco: Harper &
Row, 1987.

Westcott, Brooke Foss. "The Relation of Art to Christianity." Pp. 319-
360 in *The Epistles of John*. London: 1883.

Wolterstorff, Nicholas. *Art in Action: Toward a Christian Aesthetic*.
Grand Rapids: Eerdmans, 1980.

Wolterstorff, *Works and Worlds of Art*. New York: Oxford University
Press, 1980.

Biology and Evolution

Coleman, William R. *Biology in the Nineteenth Century*. Cambridge:
Cambridge University Press, 1977.

Connell, Richard J. *Substance and Modern Science*. Notre Dame,
Ind.: University of Notre Dame Press, 1988.

Denton, Michael. *Evolution: A Theory in Crisis*. London: Burnett Books, 1985.

Johnson, Phillip. *Darwin on Trail*. Downers Grove, Ill.: InterVarsity, 1991.

Moreland, J. P., ed. *The Creation Hypothesis*. Downers Grove, Ill.: InterVarsity, 1993.

Morris, Henry. *Scientific Creationism*. El Cajon, Calif.: Master Books, 1985.

Ratzsch, Del. *The Battle of Beginnings*. Downers Grove, Ill.: InterVarsity, 1996.

Thaxton, Charles, and Walter Bradley. *The Mystery of Life's Origin*. New York: Philosophical Library, 1984.

Wright, Richard T. *Biology Through the Eyes of Faith*. San Francisco: Harper & Row, 1989.

Yockey, H. P. *Information Theory and Molecular Biology*. Cambridge: Cambridge University Press, 1992.

Biological Material on DNA

Barry, J. M. "Informational DNA: A Useful Concept?" *Trends in Biochemical Sciences* 11 (1986): 317-318.

Goodwin, B. C. "What Are the Causes of Morphology?" *BioEssays* 5 (1985): 32-36.

Goodwin, *How the Leopard Changed Its Spots*. New York: Simon & Schuster, 1994.

Locke, Michael. "Is There Somatic Inheritance of Intracellular Patterns?" *Journal of Cell Science* 96 (1990): 563-567.

Nijhout, H. F. "Metaphors and the Role of Genes in Development." *BioEssays* 12 (September 1990): 441-446.

Polanyi, Michael. "Life's Irreducible Structure." *Science* 160 (June 1968): 1308-1312.

Prehn, Richmond T. "Cancers Beget Mutations Versus Mutations Beget Cancers." *Cancer Research* 54 (October 1994): 5296-5300.

Wells, Jonathan. "The History and Limits of Genetic Engineering." *International Journal on the Unity of the Sciences* 5 (Summer 1992): 137-150.

Wells, "The Dogma of NDA." *Bible-Science News* 31, no. 8 (1993): 13-16.

Business

Beauchamp, Tom L., and Norman E. Bowie. *Ethical Theory in Business*. Englewood Cliffs, N.J.: Prentice-Hall, 1979.

Chewning, Richard, John W. Eby, and Shirley J. Roels. *Business Through the Eyes of Faith*. San Francisco: Harper & Row, 1990.

Houck, John, and Oliver Williams, eds. *The Judeo-Christian Vision and the Modern Corporation*. Notre Dame, Ind.: University of Notre Dame Press, 1982.

Rae, Scott, and Kenman Wong. *Beyond Integrity: A Judeo-Christian Approach to Business Ethics*. Grand Rapids: Zondervan, 1996.

Communication and the Media

Griffin, Emory A. *The Mind Changers: The Art of Christian Persuasion*. Wheaton, Ill.: Tyndale, 1976.

Lewis, Todd. *RT: A Reader's Theatre Ministry*. Lillenas Pub. Co., Kansas City, MO: 1988.

Lewis, *Communicating Literature: An Introduction to Oral Interpretation*. 2d ed. Kendall/Hunt, Dubuque, IA, 1995.

McComiskey, Thomas Edward. *Reading Scripture in Public: A Guide for Preachers and Lay Readers*. Grand Rapids: Baker, 1991.

Miller, Calvin. *The Empowered Communicator*. Nashville: Broadman and Holman, 1994.

Nash, Tom. *The Christian Communicator's Handbook*. Wheaton, Ill.: Victor, 1995.

Olasky, Marvin. *Prodigal Press: The Anti-Christian Bias of the American News Media*. Westchester, Ill.: Crossway, 1988.

Postman, Neil. *Amusing Ourselves to Death*. New York: Penguin Books, 1985.

The Religious Speech Communication Association (RSCA) is an incorporated interest group within the national Speech Communication Association (SCA) that addresses Christian concerns (Journal: *Journal of Religion and Communication*). The International Christian Visual Media Association is made up of Christians who make films and videos primarily for the church market. They are located at 4533 E. Peakview Avenue, Littleton, CO 80121-3231.

Economics

Brookes, Warren T. *The Economy in Mind*. New York: Universe Books, 1982.

Clouse, Robert, ed. *Wealth and Poverty: Four Christian Views of Economics*. Downers Grove, Ill.: InterVarsity, 1984.

Nash, Ronald H. *Social Justice and the Christian Church*. Milford, Mich.: Mott Media, 1983.

Olasky, Marvin N., ed. *Freedom, Justice, and Hope*. Westchester, Ill.: Crossway, 1988.

An important organization that promotes theological and political reflection on liberty and economics is the Acton Institute, 161 Ottawa NW, Suite 301, Grand Rapids, MI 49503 (phone: (616) 454-3080; E-mail: info@acton.org; World Wide Web page: http://www.acton.org/).

Education

Burgess, W. Harold. *Models of Religious Education*. Wheaton, Ill.: Victor, 1996.

Groome, Thomas. *Christian Religious Education*. New York: Harper & Row, 1980.

Habermas, Ronald, and Klaus Issler. *Teaching for Reconciliation: Foundations and Practice of Christian Educational Ministry*. Grand Rapids: Baker, 1992.

Issler, Klaus, and Ronald Habermas. *How We Learn: A Christian Teacher's Guide to Educational Psychology*. Grand Rapids: Baker, 1994.

Kilpatrick, William. *Why Johnny Can't Tell Right from Wrong: What We Can Do About It*. New York: Touchstone/Simon & Schuster, 1992.

Lickona, Thomas. *Educating for Character: How Our Schools Can Teach Respect and Responsibility*. New York: Bantam Books, 1991.

Marsden, George. *The Soul of the American University*. New York: Oxford, 1994.

Peterson, Michael L. *Philosophy of Education: Issues and Options*. Downers Grove, Ill.: InterVarsity, 1986.

Power, R. Clark, and Daniel Lapsley, eds. *The Challenge of Pluralism: Education, Politics, and Values*. Notre Dame, Ind.: University of Notre Dame Press, 1992.

Whitehead, John. *Rights of Religious Persons in Public Education*. Wheaton, Ill.: Crossway, 1991.

Wilson, Doug. *Recovering the Lost Tools of Learning: An Approach to Distinctly Christian Education*. Wheaton, Ill.: Crossway, 1991.

Key journal: *Christian Education Journal*, PO Box 650, Glen Ellyn, IL 60138. Professional association: Christian Educators Association International, PO Box 41300, Pasadena, CA 91114; phone: (818) 798-1124. Student memberships available for a nominal fee; some have regional chapters; receive a *Teachers in Focus* magazine copublished with Focus on the Family. A subdivision is the professional organization called TESOL, Teachers of English to Speakers of Other Languages. Within TESOL, there is a Christian "subgroup" known as CETESOL, Christian Educators in TESOL. They publish a newsletter three times a year available for a $3.00 donation from CETESOL, 126 N. Walnut Street, Yellow Springs, OH 45387 (phone: (513) 767-7099).

Environmental Studies

Bouma-Prediger, Steven. *The Greening of Theology: The Ecological Models of Rosemary Radford Ruether, Joseph Sittler, and Jürgen Moltmann.* Scholars Press, Atlanta, GA, 1995.

Cromartie, Michael. *Creation at Risk? Religion, Science, and the Environment.* Grand Rapids: Eerdmans, 1995.

Fowler, Robert Booth. *The Greening of Protestant Thought.* Chapel Hill: University of North Carolina Press, 1995.

Schaeffer, Francis. *Pollution and the Death of Man.* Wheaton, Ill.: Tyndale, 1970.

Wilkinson, L., ed. *Earthkeeping in the Nineties.* Grand Rapids: Eerdmans, 1991.

Young, R. A. *Healing the Earth.* Nashville: Broadman and Holman, 1994.

Important organizations are Christian Society of the Green Cross, 10 East Lancaster Avenue, Wynnewood, PA 19096, and Christian Environmental Association, 1650 Zanker Road, Suite 150, San Jose, CA 95112 (journal: *Green Cross: A Christian Environmental Quarterly*).

History

Butterfield, Herbert. *Christianity and History.* London: Bell, 1949.

Marsden, George, and Frank Roberts, eds. *A Christian View of History?* Grand Rapids: Eerdmans, 1975.

McIntire, C. T., ed. *God, History, and Historians: Modern Christian Views of History.* New York: Oxford University Press, 1977.

Montgomery, John Warwick. *Where Is History Going?.* Reprint, Minneapolis: Bethany, 1972.

Montgomery, *The Shape of the Past.* Minneapolis: Bethany, 1975.

Nash, Ronald H. *Christian Faith and Historical Understanding.* Grand Rapids: Zondervan, 1984.

Noll, Mark. "Traditional Christianity and Possibility of Historical Knowledge." *Christian Scholar's Review* 19 (June 1990): 388-406.

Wells, Ronald. *History Through the Eyes of Faith*. San Francisco: Harper & Row, 1989.

An important organization is the Conference on Faith and History (secretary-treasurer: Richard V. Pierard, Department of History, Indiana State University, Terre Haute, IN 47809; phone: (812) 877-2702; E-mail: hipier@ruby.indstate.edu; journal: *Fides Et Historia*, editor: Paul L. Gritz, Southwestern Baptist Theological Seminary, Fort Worth, Texas).

Journalism

Olasky, Marvin. *Prodigal Press: The Anti-Christian Bias of the American News Media*. Wheaton, Ill.: Crossway, 1988.

Olasky, *Telling the Truth: How to Revitalize Christian Journalism*. Wheaton, Ill.: Crossway, 1996.

Pippert, Wesley G. *An Ethics of News: A Reporter's Search for Truth*. Washington, D.C.: Georgetown University Press, 1989.

Law

Eidmore, John. *The Christian Legal Advisor*. Milford, Mich.: Mott Media, 1984.

Finnis, John. *Natural Law and Natural Rights*. Oxford: Clarendon, 1980.

Johnson, Alan J. "Is There Biblical Warrant for Natural-Law Theories?" *Journal of the Evangelical Theological Society* 25 (June 1982): 185-199.

Montgomery, John W. *Human Rights and Human Dignity*. Grand Rapids: Zondervan, 1986.

Montgomery, John W., ed. *Jurisprudence: A Book of Readings*. Strasbourg, France: International Scholarly Publisher, 1980 (available in the United States from Simon Greenleaf University, Anaheim, California).

Weinrib, Lloyd L. *Natural Law and Justice*. Cambridge, Mass.: Harvard University Press, 1987.

An important organization is Christian Legal Society, 4208 Evergreen Lane, Suite 222, Annandale, VA 22003-9926; phone: (703) 642-1070.

Linguistics

Pike, Kenneth L. *Linguistic Concepts*. Lincoln: University of Nebraska Press, 1982.

Silva, Moises. *God, Language, and Scripture: Reading the Bible in the Light of General Linguistics*. Grand Rapids: Zondervan, 1990.

Wilson, Clifford A., and Donald McKeon. *The Language Gap*. Grand Rapids: Zondervan, 1984.

For more information, contact the Summer Institute of Linguistics (7500 W. Camp Wisdom Rd., Dallas, TX 75236) and the Wycliffe Bible Translators (PO Box 2727, Huntington Beach, CA 92647). Both have Internet pages: WWW.SIL.ORG and WWW.WYCLIFFE.ORG. There is a professional organization for Christian professors of foreign language and literature called the North American Association of Christian Foreign Language and Literature Faculty (NACFLA). It meets each April at a Christian College Coalition campus. The president is Claude-Marie Baldwin of Calvin College (address: Calvin College, French Department, 3201 Burton Street, SE, Grand Rapids, MI 49546; FAX: (616) 957-8551; journal: *NACFLA Proceedings Journal*).

Literature

Barratt, David, Roger Pooley, and Leland Ryken, eds. *The Discerning Reader: Christian Perspectives on Literature and Theory*. Leicester: Apollos, 1995.

Buechner, Frederick. *The Clown in the Belfry: Writings on Faith and Fiction*. San Francisco: HarperSanFrancisco, 1992.

Corn, Alfred., ed. *Incarnation: Contemporary Writers on the New Testament*. New York: Viking/Penguin, 1990.

Gallager, Susan, and Roger Lundin. *Literature Through the Eyes of Faith*. San Francisco: Harper and Row, 1989.

Harris, James F. *Against Relativism*. LaSalle, Ill.: Open Court, 1992.

Hirsh, E. D. *Validity in Interpretation*. New Haven, Conn.: Yale University Press, 1967.

Leax, John. *Grace Is Where I Live: Writing as a Christian Vocation*. Grand Rapids: Baker, 1993.

Lewis, C. S. *Studies in Words*. Cambridge: Cambridge University Press, 1974.

Norris, Christopher. *The Truth About Postmodernism*. Oxford: Blackwell, 1993.

Sire, James W. *How to Read Slowly*. Wheaton, Ill.: Harold Shaw, 1989.

Walhout, Clarence, and Leland Ryken, eds. *Contemporary Literary Theory: A Christian Appraisal*. Grand Rapids: Eerdmans, 1991.

Image: A Journal of the Arts and Religion contains critical essays, fiction, and poetry by Christians. Published quarterly by the Hillsdale Review, PO Box 674, Kennett Square, PA 19348. To subscribe, send check or money order for $30 ($40 overseas) to: IMAGE, PO Box 3000, Denville, NJ 07834. The Conference on Christianity and Literature (associated with the Modern Language Association) focuses on the relationship between Christianity and literature. The president is Prof. Jewel Spears Brooker, Collegium of Letters, Eckerd College, St. Petersburg, FL 33711 (phone: (813) 867-6533); journal: *Christianity and Literature*; editor, Robert Snyder, Department of English, West Georgia College, Carrollton, GA 30118).

Mathematics

Barker, Stephen F. *Philosophy of Mathematics*. Englewood Cliffs, N.J.: Prentice-Hall, 1964.

Brabenac, R. L., et al. *A Christian Perspective on the Foundations of Mathematics*. Wheaton, Ill.: Wheaton College, 1977.

Cantor, George. *Contributions to the Founding of the Theory of Transfinite Numbers*. New York: Dover Publications, 1955.

Granville, H. Jr. *Logos: Mathematics and Christian Theology*. East Brunswick, N.J.: Bucknell University Press, 1976.

Medicine and Health Care

Ashley, Benedict M., and Kevin D. O'Rourke. *Health Care Ethics: A Theological Analysis*. St. Louis: Catholic Health Association of the United States, 1982.

Bouma, Hessel, et al. *Christian Faith, Health, and Medical Practice*. Grand Rapids: Eerdmans, 1989.

Kilner, John F., Nigel M. de S. Cameron, and David Schiedermayer, eds. *Bioethics and the Future of Medicine: A Christian Appraisal*. Grand Rapids: Eerdmans, 1995.

Pellegrino, Edmund D., and David C. Thomasma. *A Philosophical Basis of Medical Practice*. New York: Oxford University Press, 1981.

Pellegrino, and David C. Thomasma *For the Patient's Good*. New York: Oxford University Press, 1988.

> Important resources are:
> 1. Christian Medical and Dental Society (journal: *Christian Medical and Dental Society Journal*, 1616 Gateway Boulevard, Box 830689, Richardson, TX 75083-0689; phone: (214) 783-8384; Internet:http://199.227.115.30/cmds); and *Journal of Christian Nursing* (PO Box 7895, Madison, WI 53707-7895).
> 2. Christian Medical Ethics Page: CCME Home | Bioethics Links. Christian Medical Ethics Page.

3. Resources on Christianity, Medicine and Ethics: "Theological Ethics, Moral Philosophy; internet:http://ccmemac4.bsd.uchicago.edu/CCMEdocs/Christian - size 3K - 11 Jun 96.
4. Christian Medical Foundation International, Inc., 7522 North Himes Avenue, PO Box 152136, Tampa, Florida 33684-3126; phone: (813) 932-3688; E-mail:74435.52@compuserve.com.

Physical Science

Craig, William Lane, and Smith Quentin. *Theism, Atheism, and Big Bang Cosmology*. Oxford: Clarendon, 1993.

Harman, P. M. *Energy, Force, and Matter: A Historical Survey*. Cambridge: Cambridge University Press, 1982.

Leslie, John. *Universes*. London: Routledge, 1989.

Ross, Hugh. *The Fingerprint of God*. Orange, Calif: Promise Publishing, 1989.

Ross, *The Creator and the Cosmos*. Colorado Springs: NavPress, 1993.

Philosophy

Audi, Robert. *Belief, Justification, and Knowledge*. Belmont, Calif.: Wadsworth, 1988.

Chisholm, Roderick M. *Theory of Knowledge*. 2d. ed. Englewood Cliffs, N.J.: Prentice-Hall, 1977.

Chisholm, *On Metaphysics*. Minneapolis: University of Minnesota Press, 1989.

Clark, Kelly James, ed. *Philosophers Who Believe*. Downers Grove, Ill.: InterVarsity, 1993.

Geivett, R. Douglas, and Brendan Sweetman, eds. *Contemporary Perspectives on Religious Epistemology*. New York: Oxford, 1992.

Plantinga, Alvin. *The Nature of Necessity*. Oxford: Clarendon, 1974.

Swinburne, Richard. *The Existence of God*. Oxford: Clarendon, 1979.

Swinburne, *The Evolution of the Soul*. Oxford: Clarendon, 1986.

There are some very important resource tools in philosophy. Among the most important are: Robert Audi, ed., *The Cambridge Dictionary of Philosophy* (Cambridge: Cambridge University Press, 1995); Ted Honderich, ed., *The Oxford Companion to Philosophy* (Oxford: Oxford University Press, 1995); A. C. Grayling, ed., *Philosophy: A Guide Through the Subject* (Oxford: Oxford University Press, 1995); Thomas Mautner, ed., *A Dictionary of Philosophy* (Oxford: Blackwell, 1996); Simon Blackburn, *The Oxford Dictionary of Philosophy* (Oxford: Oxford University Press, 1996); A. W. Sparkes, *Talking Philosophy: A Wordbook* (London: Routledge, 1991); Hans Burkhardt and Barry Smith, eds., *Handbook of Metaphysics and Ontology*, 2 vols. (Munich: Philosophia Verlag, 1991); there is also an important series of volumes called the Blackwell Companions to Philosophy (Oxford: Blackwell). Three professional societies are: Evangelical Philosophical Society (EPS), c/o Dr. David K. Clark, secretary, Bethel Theological Seminary, 3049 Bethel Drive, St. Paul, MN 55112 (EPS produces the journal *Philosophia Christi*); Society of Christian Philosophers, c/o Kelley James Clark, secretary, Department of Philosophy, Calvin College, Grand Rapids, MI 49546-4388 (journal: *Faith and Philosophy*); American Catholic Philosophical Association, Room 403, Administration Building, the Catholic University of America, Washington, D.C. 20064 (journal: *American Catholic Philosophical Quarterly*).

Political Studies

Beckwith, Francis J., and Michael E. Bauman. *Are You Politically Correct?* Buffalo, N.Y.: Prometheus, 1993.

Callahan, Daniel. "Minimalistic Ethics." *Hastings Center Report* 11 (October 1981): 19-25.

Eidsmoe, John. *Christianity and the Constitution: The Faith of Our Founding Fathers*. Grand Rapids: Baker, 1987.

Gaede, S. D. *When Tolerance Is No Virtue*. Downers Grove, Ill.: InterVarsity, 1993.

Geisler, Norman L. "A Premillennial View of Law and Government." *Bibliotheca Sacra* 142 (July-September 1985): 250-266.

Hatch, Nathan. *The Democratization of American Christianity*. New Haven, Conn.: Yale University Press, 1991.

Linder, Robert D., and Richard V. Pierard. *Twilight of the Saints*. Downers Grove, Ill.: InterVarsity, 1978.

Maclear, J. F., ed. *Church and State in the Modern Age*. Oxford: Oxford University Press, 1995.

Marshall, Paul. *Thine Is the Kingdom: A Biblical Perspective on Government and Politics Today*. Grand Rapids: Eerdmans, 1984

Nash, Ronald H. *Freedom, Justice, and the State*. Washington, D.C.: University Press of America, 1980.

Neuhaus, Richard John. *The Naked Public Square: Religion and Democracy in America*. Grand Rapids: Eerdmans, 1984.

Satinover, Jeffrey. *Homosexuality and the Politics of Truth*. Grand Rapids: Baker, 1996.

Stone, Ronald H., ed. *Reformed Faith and Politics*. Washington, D.C.: University Press of America, 1983.

Weibe, Robert H. *Self-Rule: A Cultural History of American Democracy*. Chicago: University of Chicago Press, 1995.

Psychology

Boyd, Jeffery. *Reclaiming the Soul: The Search for Meaning in a Self-Centered Culture*. Cleveland: Pilgrim Press, 1996.

Carter, John D., and Bruce Narramore. *Integration of Psychology and Theology: An Introduction*. Grand Rapids: Zondervan, 1979.

Evans. C. Stephen. *Wisdom and Humaness in Psychology: Prospects for a Christian Approach*. Grand Rapids: Baker, 1989.

Jeeves, Malcom A., and David Myers. *Psychology Through the Eyes of Faith*. San Francisco: Harper & Row, 1989.

Moreland, J. P., and David M. Ciocchi, eds. *Christian Perspectives on Being Human*. Grand Rapids: Baker, 1993.

Myers, David. *Exploring Psychology*. 2d ed. New York: Worth Publishing, 1993.

Van Leeuwen, Mary Stewart. *The Sorcerer's Apprentice: A Christian Looks at the Changing Face of Psychology*. Downers Grove, Ill.: InterVarsity, 1983.

Vitz, Paul. *Psychology as Religion: The Cult of Self-Worship*. Grand Rapids: Eerdmans, 1994.

An important journal is the *Journal of Psychology and Theology* (Pacticia L. Pike, ed., Rosemead School of Theology, Biola University, 13800 Biola Avenue, La Mirada, CA 90639-4847; phone: (310) 903-4867). Key organizations are: Christian Association for Psychological Studies, PO Box 310400, New Braunfels, TX 78131; phone: (210) 629-2277; American Association of Christian Counselors (journal: *Christian Counseling Today*), 2421 W. Pratt, Suite 1398, Chicago, IL 60645; (804) 384-0564; American Psychological Association, Division 36, 1200 Seventeenth Street, NW, Washington, DC 20036.

Reductionism and the Soul/Mind-Body Problem

Connell, Richard. *Substance and Modern Science*. Notre Dame, Ind.: University of Notre Dame Press, 1988.

Cooper, John. *Body, Soul, and Life Everlasting*. Grand Rapids: Eerdmans, 1989.

Foster, John. *The Immaterial Self*. London: Routledge, 1991.

Habermas, Gary, and J. P. Moreland. *Immortality: The Other Side of Death*. Nashville: Nelson, 1992, chaps. 2–3.

Madell, Geoffrey. *Mind and Materialism*. Edinburgh: University Press, 1988.

Moreland, J. P., and David M. Ciocchi, eds. *Christian Perspectives on Being Human*. Grand Rapids: Baker, 1993.

Robinson, Howard. *Matter and Consciousness*. Cambridge: Cambridge University Press, 1982.

Robinson, Howard, ed. *Objections to Physicalism*. Oxford: Clarendon, 1993.

Swinburne, Richard. *The Evolution of the Soul*. Oxford: Clarendon, 1986.

Smythies, John R., and John Beloff, eds. *The Case for Dualism*. Charlottesville: University Press of Virginia, 1989.

Taliafero, Charles. *Consciousness and the Mind of God*. Cambridge: Cambridge University Press, 1994.

Science and Theology

Corey, M. A. *God and the New Cosmology: The Anthropic Design Argument*. Boston: Rowman and Littlefield, 1993.

Jaki, Stanley. *The Road of Science and the Ways to God*. Chicago: University of Chicago Press, 1978.

Montgomery, John Warwick. "The Theologian's Craft." In *Suicide of Christian Theology*, pp. 267-313. Minneapolis: Bethany, 1970.

Moreland, J. P., ed. *The Creation Hypothesis*. Downers Grove, Ill.: InterVarsity Press, 1994.

Pearcey, Nancy R., and Charles Thaxton. *The Soul of Science*. Wheaton, Ill.: Crossway, 1994.

Ratzsch, Del. *Philosophy of Science*. Downers Grove, Ill.: InterVarsity, 1986.

Two important associations and their journals are: Creation Research Society, 10946 Woodside Avenue North, Santee, CA 92071 (journal: *Creation Research Society Quarterly*; subscriptions: Glen W. Wolfrom, Creation Research Society Quarterly, PO Box 8263, St. Joseph, MO 64508-8263), and American Scientific Affiliation, PO Box 668, Ipswich, MA 01938 (journal: *Perspectives on Science and Christian Faith*; subscriptions: 55 Market Street, Ipswitch, MA 01938-0668). Another important journal is *Science and Christian Belief*, c/o

Paternoster Periodicals, PO Box 300, Carlisle, Cumbria, CA3 0QS, UK.

Sociology

Bellah, Robert, et al. *Habits of the Heart: Individualism and Commitment in American Life*. Berkeley: University of California Press, 1985.

Campolo, Tony, and David A. Fraser. *Sociology Through the Eyes of Faith*. San Francisco: Harper & Row, 1992.

Ellul, Jacques. *The Subversion of Christianity*. Grand Rapids: Eerdmans, 1986.

Ellul, *The Technological Society*. Grand Rapids: Eerdmans, 1990.

Hunter, James Davison. *Evangelicalism: The Coming Generation*. Chicago: University of Chicago Press, 1987.

Wuthnow, Robert. *God and Mammon in America*. New York: Free Press, 1994.

Wuthnow, Robert, ed. *Rethinking Materialism*. Grand Rapids: Eerdmans, 1995.

An important resource is Social Work & Christianity, Nacsw, PO Box 7090, St. Davids, PA 19087-7090. For a Christian professional association, contact the Christian Sociological Society (which publishes the *Christian Sociologist*, a newsletter that has a feature article and several book reviews), c/o Dale McConkey, Department of Sociology, 27 Berry College, Mt. Berry, GA 30109.

Women's Studies and Issues

Evans, Mary J. *Women in the Bible*. Downers Grove, Ill.: InterVarsity, 1983.

Kassian, Mary A. *The Feminist Gospel: The Movement to Unite Feminism with the Church*. Wheaton, Ill.: Crossway, 1992.

Kostenberger, Andreas, Thomas Schreiner, and H. Scott Baldwin. *Women in the Church*. Grand Rapids: Baker, 1995.

Piper, John, and Wayne Grudem, eds. *Recovering Biblical Manhood and Womanhood*. Wheaton, Ill.: Crossway, 1991.

Van Leeuwen, Mary Stewart. *Gender and Grace*. Downers Grove, Ill.: InterVarsity, 1990.

An important organization is the Council on Biblical Manhood and Womanhood (journal: *CBMW News*, c/o Steve Henderson, 229 Siloam Road, Easley, SC 29642; phone: (864) 269-7937; E-mail: CBMWDeb@aol.com).

Notes

Chapter One

1. R. C. Sproul, "Burning Hearts Are Not Nourished by Empty Heads," *Christianity Today* 26: (Sept 3, 1982), p. 100.
2. Neil Postman, *Amusing Ourselves to Death* (New York: Penguin Books, 1985), p. 9.
3. James Davison Hunter, *Culture Wars* (San Francisco: Basic Books, 1991).
4. Postman, p. 31.
5. For more on the Puritans, see Allen Carden, *Puritan Christianity in America* (Grand Rapids: Baker, 1990).
6. Cited in Carden, p. 186.
7. George Marsden, *Fundamentalism and American Culture* (New York: Oxford, 1980), p. 212.
8. For an accessible statement of Hume's and Kant's arguments, along with a Christian response and a development of theistic arguments, see Norman L. Geisler and Winfried Corduan, *Philosophy of Religion*, 2d ed. (Grand Rapids: Baker, 1988), chaps. 5–9.
9. For a critique of evolution, see Phillip E. Johnson, *Darwin on Trial*, 2d ed. (Downers Grove, Ill.: InterVarsity, 1993); also, J. P. Moreland, ed., *The Creation Hypothesis* (Downers Grove, Ill.: InterVarsity, 1994).
10. See Walt Russell, "What It Means to Me," *Christianity Today*, October 26, 1992, pp. 30-32.
11. Carl Henry, *The Christian Mindset in a Secular Culture* (Portland, Oreg.: Multnomah, 1984), pp. 145-146.

12. Charles Malik, "The Other Side of Evangelism," *Christianity Today*, November 7, 1980, p. 40.

13. See Marsden, pp. 184-188. As Marsden points out, after the Scopes trial, fundamentalism became associated with obscurantism partly because fundamentalists could not "raise the level of discourse to a plane where any of their arguments would be taken seriously" (p. 188).

14. R. C. Sproul, John Gerstner, and Arthur Lindsley, *Classical Apologetics* (Grand Rapids: Zondervan, 1984), p. 4.

15. For more on this, see J. P. Moreland, *Christianity and the Nature of Science* (Grand Rapids: Baker, 1989); Moreland, ed., *The Creation Hypothesis;* Nancy Pearcey and Charles Thaxton, *The Soul of Science* (Wheaton, Ill.: Crossway, 1994).

16. For more on this, see Phillip E. Johnson, *Reason in the Balance* (Downers Grove, Ill.: InterVarsity, 1995).

17. For a brief discussion of the classic understanding of happiness, see Louis P. Pojman, *Ethics: Discovering Right and Wrong*, 2d ed. (Belmont, Calif.: Wadsworth, 1995), pp. 160-185.

18. Ernst Mayr, *Populations, Species, and Evolution* (Cambridge, Mass.: Harvard University Press, 1970), p. 4.

19. David Hull, *The Metaphysics of Evolution* (Albany: State University of New York Press, 1989), pp. 74-75.

20. Daniel Callahan, "Minimalistic Ethics," *Hastings Center Report*, October 1983, pp. 19-25.

21. Carolyn Kane, "Thinking: A Neglected Art," *Newsweek*, December 14, 1981, p. 19.

Chapter Two

1. Mark A. Noll, *The Scandal of the Evangelical Mind* (Grand Rapids: Eerdmans, 1994), pp. 3, 4.

2. William Law, *A Serious Call to a Devout and Holy Life* (1728) (Grand Rapids: Eerdmans, 1966), p. 2.

3. These incidents are presented in Augustine's *The Confessions:* Faustus in bk. 5, chaps. 3, 6; Ambrose in bk. 5, chaps. 13 and 14, bk. 6, chaps. 1–4; Pontitianus, bk. 8, chap. 6.

4. Waltke states: "Since it (galah) is used of men as well as of God, it must not be thought of as a technical term for God's revelation. . . . Though not a technical term for divine revelation, the verb galah frequently conveys this meaning." See R. L. Harris, Gleason Archer, and Bruce Waltke, *Theological Wordbook of the Old Testament* (Chicago: Moody, 1988), p. 160.

5. John Wesley, "An Address to the Clergy," in *The Works of John Wesley*, 3d ed. (Grand Rapids: Baker, 1979; 1st ed., 1972), p. 481.

6. John Wesley, *A Plain Account of Christian Perfection* (London: Epworth Press, 1952; 1st Epworth ed.), p. 87.

7. Richard Baxter, *The Reasons of the Christian Religion* (London: Gildas Salvianus, 1656).

8. Augustine, *De genesi ad litteram* 1.21.

9. See Alan F. Johnson, "Is There a Biblical Warrant for Natural-Law Theories?" *Journal of the Evangelical Theological Society* 25 (June 1982): 185-199.

10. See Norman L. Geisler, "A Premillennial View of Law and Government," *Bibliotheca Sacra* 142 (July-September 1985): 250-266.

11. For an excellent discussion of the nature of faith, see R. C. Sproul, John Gerstner, and Arthur Lindsley, *Classical Apologetics* (Grand Rapids: Zondervan, 1984), pp. 21, 191-196.

12. "Candid Conversation with the Evangelist," *Christianity Today*, July 17, 1981, p. 24.

13. Billy Graham, "An Interview with the Rev. Billy Graham," *Parade*, October 20, 1996, p. 6.

14. Roy McCloughry, "Basic Stott," *Christianity Today*, January 8, 1996, p. 32.

Chapter Three

1. Address delivered on September 20, 1912, at the opening of the 101st session of Princeton Theological Seminary. Reprinted in J. Gresham Machen, *What is Christianity?*, Grand Rapids: Eerdmans, 1951. (The entire address is from pp 156-169. The quote is on p. 162.)

2. James L. Crenshaw, *Old Testament Wisdom: An Introduction* (Atlanta: John Knox, 1981), pp. 17, 18.

3. Technically, the problem is not that God is too big because God is not in space at all. Rather, God is too great to be the kind of being that could be spatial.

4. I cannot argue for this position here. I have done this elsewhere. See J. P. Moreland, *Scaling the Secular City* (Grand Rapids: Baker, 1986), chap. 3; Gary Habermas and J. P. Moreland, *Immortality: The Other Side of Death* (Nashville: Nelson, 1992), chaps. 1–3; J. P. Moreland, "A Defense of a Substance Dualist View of the Soul," in *Christian Perspectives on Being Human*, ed. J. P. Moreland and David M. Ciocchi (Grand Rapids: Baker, 1993), pp. 55-79.

5. For more details on biblical anthropology, see Robert Saucy, "Theology of Human Nature," in *Christian Perspectives on Being Human*, ed. J. P. Moreland and David M. Ciocchi (Grand Rapids: Baker, 1993), pp. 17-52.

6. The connection among anger, anxiety, depression, and brain chemistry is discussed repeatedly in Frank B. Minirth and Paul D. Meier, *Happiness Is a Choice* (Grand Rapids: Baker, 1978).

7. Biblical terms for different aspects of the human being ("heart," "soul," "spirit," "mind") have a wide range of meanings, and no specific use of a biblical term should be read into any occurrence. The context should be our guide. I am focusing here on a more narrow, specific use of the term "spirit."

8. The connection among anger, anxiety, depression and brain chemistry is discussed repeatedly in Minirth and Meier.

9. J. Gresham Machen, address delivered on September 20, 1912, at the opening of the 101st session of Princeton Theological Seminary.

10. George Marsden, *Fundamentalism and American Culture* (New York: Oxford, 1980), p. 188.

11. If someone else told me what a dog was supposed to be (for example, a brown, furry animal that barks), then I could recognize a dog the first time I saw one, provided I had already experienced the relevant parts of what it is to be a dog (brownness, furriness, the sound of a bark).

12. Richard Foster, *Celebration of Discipline* (New York: Harper and Row, 1978), p. 55. All of our mental states have intentionality and are about things. I am focusing on the mind because, often, the mind directs the other faculties as we saw in the case of seeing.

Chapter Four

1. Philip Cushman, "Why the Self Is Empty," *American Psychologist* 45 (May 1990): 600. Unfortunately, Cushman's own diagnosis and solution to the empty self are mired in a self-refuting form of postmodernism.
2. *Collected Works of C. G. Jung*, vol. 2, *Psychology and Religion: West and East*, trans. R. F. C. Hull, 2d ed., Bollingen Series, no. 20 (Princeton, N.J.: Princeton University Press, 1973), p. 75.
3. Herbert Schlossberg, *Idols for Destruction* (Nashville: Nelson, 1983), p. 322.
4. Stephen L. Darwall, introduction to *Joseph Butler: Five Sermons* (Indianapolis: Hackett Publishing, 1983), p. 1. Butler's series was entitled "Fifteen Sermons Preached at the Rolls Chapel" and was collected in 1726.
5. Though I disagree with much in the article, nevertheless, the following is helpful: Edward E. Sampson, "The Debate on Individualism," *American Psychologist* 43 (January 1988): 15-22.
6. Martin E. P. Seligman, "Boomer Blues," *Psychology Today*, October 1988, p. 55.
7. See Christopher Lasch, *The Culture of Narcissism* (New York: Warner Books, 1979), especially chap. 2.
8. Lasch, p. 262.
9. Jane M. Healy, *Endangered Minds: Why Children Don't Think and What We Can Do About It* (New York: Simon & Schuster, 1990), p. 196.
10. Healy, pp. 114-116, 195-217.
11. Lasch, p. 97. See also pp. 96-98.
12. Neil Postman, *Amusing Ourselves to Death* (New York: Penguin Books, 1984), p.7.
13. Pitirim A. Sorokin, *The Crisis of Our Age* (Oxford: One World, 1941).

14. Roy Baumeister, "How the Self Became a Problem: A Psychological Review of Historical Research," *Journal of Personality and Social Psychology* 52 (1987): 163-176.
15. Cushman, p. 600.
16. Robert Banks, *The Tyranny of Time* (Downers Grove, Ill.: InterVarsity, 1983), p. 59.
17. Os Guinness, *The Gravedigger File* (Downers Grove, Ill.: InterVarsity), p. 83.
18. For practical advice on several aspects of good health, see Richard Swenson, *Margin: Restoring Emotional, Physical, Financial, and Time Reserves to Overloaded Lives* (Colorado Springs: NavPress, 1992), chap. 8.
19. John G. Gager, *Kingdom and Community: The Social World of Early Christianity* (Englewood Cliffs, N.J.: Prentice-Hall, 1975), pp. 86-87.
20. Doubt is one form of the fear of losing control. For more on doubt itself, see William Lane Craig, *No Easy Answers* (Chicago: Moody, 1990); Os Guinness, *In Two Minds* (Downers Grove, Ill.: InterVarsity, 1976); Gary Habermas, *Dealing with Doubt* (Chicago: Moody, 1990).
21. Roger Trigg, *Reason and Commitment* (Cambridge, England: Cambridge University Press, 1973), p. 44.

Chapter Five

1. C. S. Lewis, *Mere Christianity* (New York: Macmillan, 1943; rev. ed., 1952), p. 75.
2. John Wesley, "An Address to the Clergy," in *The Works of John Wesley*, 3d ed. (Grand Rapids: Baker, 1979; 1st ed., 1972), p. 481.
3. Richard Foster, *Celebration of Discipline* (San Francisco: Harper & Row, 1978), p. 55.
4. For a more detailed treatment of these issues, see A. G. Sertillanges, *The Intellectual Life: Its Spirit, Conditions, and Methods* (Washington, D.C.: Catholic University of America Press, 1987), especially chap. 2. For an overview of different views about virtue in general, see John W. Crossin, *What Are They Saying About Virtue?* (New York: Paulist, 1985).
5. Joseph Pieper, *The Four Cardinal Virtues* (Notre Dame, Ind.: University of Notre Dame Press, 1954), pp. 117-133.

6. Dallas Willard, *The Spirit of the Disciplines* (San Francisco: Harper & Row, 1988), p. 156.
7. Jane M. Healy, *Endangered Minds: Why Children Don't Think and What We Can Do About It* (New York: Simon & Schuster, 1990), p. 105.
8. See Dallas Willard, "The Absurdity of Thinking in Language," *Southwestern Journal of Philosophy* 47 (1973): 125-132.
9. There are numerous good ones, but two books with which to start are Patrick J. Hurley, *A Concise Introduction to Logic* (Belmont, Calif.: Wadsworth, 1982), and Norman L. Geisler and Ronald M. Brooks, *Come Let Us Reason* (Grand Rapids: Baker, 1990).
10. Pair 1: P is sufficient, Q is necessary. Pair 2: P is necessary, Q is sufficient. Pair 3: P is sufficient, Q is necessary. Regarding pair 3, if something is a human, that is sufficient to guarantee that it is a person (there are no human nonpersons), but something could be a person and not a human (God and angels are persons, if God had created Martian or Vulcan persons, they would be persons but not humans).
11. Though false, the statement is not self-refuting because it is a philosophical statement about morality, not an absolute ethical rule of morality. Since the statement refers only to all moral rules (and claims that none of them is an absolute), and since the statement is not itself a moral rule, the statement does not refer to itself and, therefore, cannot be self-refuting. What makes the statement false is the existence of different sets of moral absolutes, not the self-refuting character of the statement itself.
12. These fallacies are called "informal" because they make it possible to reason from true premises to a false conclusion, but they can only be detected by examining the content of the argument and not simply by looking for defects in the argument's logical structure.
13. I have adopted this argument (and some others in this section) from Frank Beckwith, *Politically Correct Death* (Grand Rapids: Baker, 1993), pt. 2. Beckwith does a masterful job of cataloging the various informal fallacies used by pro-choice advocates. This book is must reading for anyone who desires to reason carefully about the abortion debate.

14. One can start by taking the Bible as merely a set of historical documents and not an inspired book, argue for its general historical trustworthiness, use its general trustworthiness to argue for both Christ's divinity (which would imply that as God, Christ would speak the truth since, for most forms of monotheistic belief, the Deity speaks all and only truths) and the fact that the New Testament contains enough history to know Christ's view of Scripture, and then show that Christ held to the full inerrancy of Holy Writ. Therefore, the Bible is inerrant.

Chapter Six

1. Peter Kreeft and Ron Tacelli, *Handbook of Christian Apologetics* (Downers Grove, Ill.: InterVarsity, 1994), pp. 23-24.
2. Thomas Sowell, "Playing with Fire on Church Burnings," *Orange County Register*, June 21, 1996, Metro section, p. 7.
3. Os Guinness, *The Gravedigger File* (Downers Grove, Ill.: InterVarsity, 1983).
4. William Wilberforce, *Real Christianity* (Portland, Oreg.: Multnomah, 1982; based on the American edition of 1829), pp. 1-2.

Chapter Seven

1. Dorothy Sayers, *The Mind of the Maker* (San Francisco; Harper & Row Publishers, 1941, 1968) p. xiii.
2. Sayers, p. 44.
3. Ronald H. Nash, *Faith and Reason: Searching for a Rational Faith* (Grand Rapids: Zondervan, 1988), p. 14.
4. E. Calvin Beisner, "A Reader's Guide to a Christian World View," *Discipleship Journal*, Issue 23, 1984, p. 37.
5. See Roderick Chisholm, *The Problem of the Criterion* (Milwaukee: Marquette University Press, 1973); Robert P. Amico, *The Problem of the Criterion* (Lanham, Md.: Rowman and Littlefield, 1993).
6. John Kekes, *The Nature of Philosophy* (Totowa, N.J.: Rowman and Littlefield, 1980), p. 158.
7. For more on this point, see John Searle, *The Rediscovery of the Mind* (Cambridge, Mass.: MIT Press, 1992).
8. John Stott, *Your Mind Matters* (London: InterVarsity Press, 1972), p. 12.

Chapter Eight

1. James Orr, *The Christian View of God and the World* (Grand Rapids: Eerdmans, 1954; 1st ed., 1893), pp. 20-21.
2. Cited in Mark Hartwig and Paul Nelson, *Invitation to Conflict* (Colorado Springs: Access Research Network, 1992), p. 6, emphasis added.
3. Rom Harre, *Varieties of Realism* (Oxford: Basil Blackwell, 1986), p. 1.
4. Martin Luther, *Table Talk*, cited in Richard Foster and James Smith, eds., *Devotional Classics* (San Francisco: Harper and Row, 1990), p. 132.
5. C. S. Lewis, *The Screwtape Letters* (New York: Macmillan, 1961), p. 20.
6. For a different but related discussion of devotional reading, see James M. Houston, "A Guide to Devotional Reading," in *The Love of God and Spiritual Friendship*, by Bernard of Clairvaux (Portland, Oreg.: Multnomah, 1983), pp. 253-260.
7. Aristotle's treatment of friendship is found in *Nichomachaen Ethics*, books 8 and 9. See also, Paul J. Wadell, *Friendship and the Moral Life* (Notre Dame, Ind.: University of Notre Dame Press, 1989), especially chaps. 2 and 3. See also, Gilbert Meilaender, *Friendship: A Study in Theological Ethics* (Notre Dame, Ind.: University of Notre Dame Press, 1981).

Chapter Nine

1. Harry Blamires, *The Christian Mind* (Ann Arbor, Michigan: Servant Books, 1978; first ed. London: SPCK, 1963), p. 20.
2. C. S. Lewis, *God in the Dock*, Walter Hooper, ed. (Grand Rapids: Wm. B. Eerdmans, 1970), p. 106.
3. Harry Blamires, *A God Who Acts* (Ann Arbor, Mich.: Servant, 1957), p. 67. Not everyone agrees that there is such a thing as a special vocation. While I am on the side of those who accept such a calling, my presentation does not require its acceptance. All my points require is that one agrees with the idea that a Christian should try to live and think Christianity in every aspect of life, including what he or she does forty or more hours a week.

Chapter Ten

1. Mark Noll, *The Scandal of the Evangelical Mind* (Grand Rapids: Eerdmans, 1994), p. 141.
2. Dallas Willard, *The Spirit of the Disciplines* (San Francisco: Harper & Row, 1988), p. 235.
3. G. K. Chesterton, *Orthodoxy* (San Francisco: Ignatius, 1995; 1st ed., 1908), p. 13.
4. Roger Trigg, *Reason and Commitment* (Cambridge, England: Cambridge University Press, 1973), p. 44.
5. I am indebted to my friend and colleague Walt Russell (professor of New Testament at Talbot School of Theology) for introducing me to this distinction. In this and many other ways, Dr. Russell has influenced my own understanding of new covenant ministry.
6. Brad Stetson, "The Promise of a Mature Masculinity," *Orange County Register*, July 3, 1996, Metro section, p. 8.

Author

J. P. MORELAND is professor of philosophy at Talbot School of Theology, Biola University in La Mirada, California. Dr. Moreland has four earned degrees: a B.S. in chemistry from the University of Missouri, a Th.M. in theology from Dallas Seminary, an M.A. in philosophy from the University of California-Riverside, and a Ph.D. in philosophy from the University of Southern California. He has planted three churches, spoken and debated on over 175 college campuses around the country, and served with Campus Crusade for Christ for ten years. Dr. Moreland has authored or co-authored twelve books, including *Scaling the Secular City*, *Does God Exist?*, *Immortality: The Other Side of Death*, and *The Creation Hypothesis*. He has also published over thirty articles in journals which include Philosophy and Phenomenological Research, American Philosophical Quarterly, Australasian Journal of Philosophy, and Faith and Philosophy. He and his wife, Hope, have two daughters, Ashley (seventeen years old) and Allison (fifteen years old). Dr. Moreland served for eight years as a bioethicist for PersonaCare Nursing Homes, Inc. headquartered in Baltimore, Maryland.

General Editor

DALLAS WILLARD is a professor in the school of philosophy at the University of Southern California in Los Angeles. He has been at USC since 1965, where he was director of the school of philosophy from 1982 to 1985. He has also taught at the University of Wisconsin (Madison), where he received his Ph.D. in 1964, and has held visiting appointments at UCLA (1969) and the University of Colorado (1984).

His philosophical publications are mainly in the areas of epistemology, the philosophy of mind and of logic, and on the philosophy of Edmund Husserl, including extensive translations of Husserl's early writings from German into English. His *Logic and the Objectivity of Knowledge*, a study on Husserl's early philosophy, appeared in 1984.

Dr. Willard also lectures and publishes in religion. *In Search of Guidance* was published in 1984 (second edition in 1993), and *The Spirit of the Disciplines* was released in 1988.

He is married to Jane Lakes Willard, a marriage and family counselor with offices in Van Nuys and Canoga Park, California. They have two children, John and Rebecca, and live in Chatsworth, California.

Senior Editor

STEVE WEBB is the founding editor of the Spiritual Formation Line for NavPress. He was instrumental in developing the line concept with General Editor Dallas Willard and Line Editor David Hazard along with the leadership team of NavPress—especially Steve Eames, Paul Santhouse, and Kent Wilson.

Steve is most recently president and C.E.O. of Centers for Christian Study, International, an organization that establishes and maintains centers for Christian study adjacent to strategic major college and university campuses that engage students, faculty, and the university community in serious thinking and discussion of the evangelical Christian worldview. In addition to leading CCSI, Steve continues his relationship with NavPress as an editor for the Spiritual Formation Line.

Steve has served in Christian publishing and ministry for over twenty years, serving as editorial director and senior editor at NavPress; vice president of publishing and development for Probe Ministries in Richardson, Texas; and chairman of the elder board at Tri-Lakes Chapel in Monument, Colorado, where he regularly teaches adult Sunday school. Steve's areas of specialized studies include the history of spirituality in the church, early American church history, and apologetics.

Steve holds his B.A. in journalism from West Texas State University, a Th.M. in historical theology from Dallas Theological Seminary, and has studied in the doctoral program at the University of Texas at Dallas. He and Shelley, his wife of twenty-three years, live in Monument, Colorado, with their three children, Amanda, Rusty, and Callie.

Follow the LEADER

Jesus asked us to follow Him. But to be good followers, we must have absolute trust in our leader. Unfortunately, many of us don't follow well because we are afraid to trust Christ completely.

Follow Me addresses the roadblocks that keep Christians from following Christ wholeheartedly. It examines our fear of giving God full control of our lives and our unwillingness to face our resistance to God. It encourages readers to examine their faith and make a new commitment to follow Christ more closely.

Follow Me (Jan David Hettinga)
A NAVPRESS SPIRITUAL FORMATION LINE BOOK
DALLAS WILLARD, GENERAL EDITOR
$14/Paperback

AVAILABLE FROM YOUR LOCAL BOOKSTORE, OR CALL (800) 366-7788 TO ORDER.